AF540703

ENCYCLOPAEDIA OF FORENSIC SCIENCE - 1

FORENSIC SCIENCE

By

Dr. Ashok Kumar

Deptt. of Zoology
Bundelkhand University
Campus Department
Jhansi (M.P.)
(India)

DPH

DISCOVERY PUBLISHING HOUSE PVT. LTD.
NEW DELHI-110 002

First Published - 2010

Reprinted - 2017

ISBN: 978-81-8356-422-9 (Set)

ISBN: 978-81-8356-564-6

Forensic Science

Published by:

DISCOVERY PUBLISHING HOUSE PVT. LTD.
4383/4B, Ansari Road Darya Ganj
New Delhi - 110 002 (India)
Phone: +91-11-23279245, 43596064-65
Fax: +91-11-23253475
E-mail: discoverypublishinghouse@gmail.com
sales@discoverypublishinggroup.com
web: www.discoverypublishinggroup.com

Printed at:
Infinity Imaging Systems
Delhi

Preface

The present title *"Encyclopaedia of Forensic Science"* has been written for undergraduate, post-graduate students and those engaged in pharmaceutical, pathological, and clinical research. Actually the explosion of new technologies with their vast potential has brought with it the need for forensic scientists to equip themselves and their laboratories with a whole array of new expertise. With the high discriminating power of the DNA systems has come high potential in evidentiary terms, high profile status for many investigations, and not least, a high degree of professional scruting of evidence produced by such technology. The present book provides protocols for the major methods of DNA analysis that have been introduced for identity testing in forensic laboratories. It also deals with the developments intersecting with the neighbouring fields of law inforcement and the justice system. This book will prove a useful guide for public awareness, health authorities, professional and industrial organizations. The aim of writing this book has .been to show how it is possible to enjoy the benefits of technology in detecting the criminals. The language used in it is simple and lucid, and illustrations are clear and labelled.

To make the work more comprehensive and informative, the author has consulted many authoritative books, research journals, abstracts, monographs etc., so there can be no claim to originality except in the .manner of treatment.

The author expresses his thanks to his friends and colleagues whose continue inspirations have initiated him to bring out this book.

The author expresses his gratitude to Mr. Wasan and staff of M/s Discovery Publishing House Pvt. Ltd. for their whole hearted co-operation in the publication of this book.

In the mean time, the author will remain sincerely responsible for any shortcomings of the book and be grateful to the readers for their suggestions and constructive criticism for the continuous betterment of the book. He takes this opportunity to appeal to the readers to send their suggestions straightaway to his Publisher.

Author

CONTENTS

1. Trends in Molecular Biology **1—42**

Developments Within the Field of Forensic Molecular Biology, Developments Influencing Law Enforcement- Operational Impacts, Developments Influencing the Justice System: Socio-legal Impacts, Electrophoresis in Forensic Science, Analytical Considerations, Method Preparation, Sample Preparation, Sample Injection, On-Line Sample Concentration, Capillary Surface Technology, CE-MS Compatible Buffers, CE-MS Interfaces for Peptide and Protein Analysis, CE-MS and Tendem MS: Biological Samples, Biologically Active Peptides, Biologically Active Proteins, On-Line Preconcentration-CE-MS of Peptides and Proteins, Operations in Capillary Electrophoresis, Cost, Speed, Potential for Automation, Accuracy, Sensitivity, and Precision, Modes of CE, Applications of Capillary Electrophoresis in Clinical Settings, Serum and Urinary Proteins, Lipoproteins, Analysis of Organ Function Tests, Serum and Urine Steroid Levels, Vitamins and Minerals, Serum Bilirubin, Cytokines, Hemoglobin and its Variants, Porphyrins, Inorganic Ions, Inborn Errors of Metabolism, Serum and Urine Analysis of Drugs, Urine Myoglobin, Cerebrospinal Fluid (CSF), Analysis of PCR Products.

2. DNA Structure and Genome **43—49**

DNA Structure, Organization of DNA into Chromosomes, Structure of the Human Genome, Coding and Regulatory Sequence, Extragenic DNA, Genetic Diversity of Modern Humans, Genome and Forensic Genetics, Tandem Repeats, Variable Number Tandem

Repeats – VNTRs, Short Tandem Repeats – STRs, Single Nucleotide Polymorphisms (SNPs).

3. **Age Detection** **50—58**

Fetal Body Measurements, Bone Formation and Growth, Growth: Infancy through Adolescence, Ossification Center Appearance and Epiphyseal Union, Bone Remodeling, Radiographic Approaches, Arthritic Changes, Chemical Changes.

4. **Extraction Techniques for Forensic Analysis** **59—84**

Principal Steps of DNA Extraction, Cell Lysis, DNA Extraction: Purification and Efficient Removal of PCR Inhibitors, DNA Extraction Techniques, Standard Phenol–Chloroform Extraction, Chelex 100 Extraction, Magnetic Affinity Solid-phase Extraction, Modified Techniques for DNA Extraction from Challenging Forensic Samples, Sperm Extraction – Differential Extraction, Extraction of DNA from Bone, Automation of DNA Extraction, BioMek 2000/ DNA IQ System, Qiagen BioRobot EZ1, Quiagen BioRobot M48, Recovery of High-Molecular-Weight DNA from Blood and Forensic Specimens, Automated DNA Extraction Techniques for Forensic Analysis, Quantification of DNA by Slot-Blot Analysis.

5. **Polymerase Chain Reaction** **85—105**

Evolution of PCR-based Profiling in Forensic Genetics, DNA Replication – Basis of the PCR, Components of PCR, PCR Process, PCR Inhibition, Sensitivity and Contamination, PCR Laboratory, Rapid Assessment of PCR Product Quality and Quantity by Capillary Electrophoresis, Materials, Methods, Kinship Testing, Paternity Testing.

6. **Role of 'X' and 'Y' Chromosomes** **106—136**

X Chromosome in Forensic Science, History of Forensic Utilization of the X Chromosome, Chromosome X Short Tandem Repeats, Power of ChrX Markers in Trace Analysis, Power of ChrX Markers in Kinship Testing, Chromosome X Marker Mapping and Haplotype Analysis, Chromosome X–chromosome Y Homologue Markers, Chromosome X STR Allele and Haplotype Distribution in Different Populations, Ethical Considerations in ChrX Marker Testing, Y-Chromosomal Markers in Forensic Genetics, Identification of the Male Sex, Identification of Male Lineages, Identification of a Male's Paternity, Identification of a Male's Geographical Origin, Future of Y-Chromosomal Markers in Forensics.

7. Single Nucleotide Polymorphism **137—143**

SNPs - Occurrence and Structure, Detection of SNPs, Sanger Sequencing, SNP Detection for Forensic Applications, Primer Extension, Allele Specific Hybridization, Forensic Applications of SNPs, Forensic Identification, Prediction of the Geographical Ancestry, SNPs Compared to SIR Loci.

8. Biological Acids and Steroid Analysis **144—182**

Amino Acid Analysis, Detection, Derivatization, Methods of Separation, Microchip Technology, Clinical and Biomedical Applications, Organic Acid Analysis, Flow Reversal, Detection Methods, Specimen Preparation, Application for the Clinical Laboratory, Steroid Analysis, Adrenal Glands, Physiological Effects of Glucocorticoids, Congenital Adrenal Hyperplasia, Use of Capillary Electrophoresis (CE) in the Separation and Detection of Steroids.

9. Data Presentation in Forensic Science **183—191**

Techniques, Differential Lysis, Autosomes (Nuclear DNA), Y Chromosome, Mitochondrial DNA (mtDNA), Messenger Ribonucleic Acid (RNA), Laboratory Issues, Statistical Analysis, Other Issues, 'Ceiling' Principle, Prosecutor's Fallacy and Defence Fallacy, Bayes' Theorem, Likelihood Ratio, Special Situations, DNA Mixtures, Complex Settings.

10. Single and Multilocus VNTR Analysis **192—208**

Single Locus VNTR Analysis, Materials, Method, Multilocus VNTR Analysis, Precautions, Labeling Nucleic Acids for Use as Probes, Theory of Nick-Translation, Theory of Radioactive Labeling of Oligonucleotide Probes by Means of T4 DNA Polymerase, Theory of Labeling DNA by Random Priming (Oligopriming), Theory of Filter Hybridization, Materials, Reagents Required for the "Standard" Nick-Translation, Reagents Required for Modified Nick-Translation, Reagents Required for Labeling with T4 DNA Polymerase, Required Reagents for Oligopriming, Reagents Required for the Prehybridization and Hybridization of Filters, Methods, "Standard" Nick-Translation, "Modified" Nick-Translation, Labeling with T4 DNA Polymerase, Oligopriming, Separation by Means of Column Chromatography, Control of Incorporation, Hybridization Procedures Using 32P-Labeled Single-Locus Probes, Autoradiography Procedure, Reprobing of Filters.

11. Analysis, Assessment and Interpretation of STR **209—227**
Analysis of STR, Structure of STR loci, Development of STR Multiplexes, Detection of STR Polymorphisms, Interpretation of STR Profiles, Assessment of STR Profiles, Stutter Peaks, Split Peaks (+/– A), Pull-up, Template DNA, Overloaded Profiles, Low Copy Number DNA, Peak Balance, Mixtures, Degraded DNA, Statistical Interpretation of STR Profiles, Population Genetics, Deviation from the Hardy–Weinberg Equilibrium, Statistical Tests to Determine Deviation from the Hardy–Weinberg Equilibrium, Estimating the Frequencies of SIR Profiles, Corrections to Allele Frequency Databases, Which Population Frequency Database should be Used?

12. Screening Significance **228—260**
Capillary Electrophoresis (CE) System, Sample Preparation, Sample Quality, Identity of Peaks, Use of the AmpliType PM + HLA DQA1 PCR Amplification and Typing Kits for Identity Testing. Materials, Method, Mitochondrial Analysis, Mitochondrial DNA (mtDNA) Biology, Identification of Individuals (mtDNA Typing), Topics of Forensic Interest.

Index **261—263**

1

Trends in Molecular Biology

Forensic science is part of a process beginning at a crime scene and concluding in a court room. This means that as one of the key forensic disciplines, the field of forensic molecular biology resides within the complex and adversarial context of the *criminal justice system* (CJS). The key areas of the CJS that are relevant to the use of forensic molecular biology are the domains of law enforcement and the justice system. Due to the intersection of these three domains, changes and developments in one can have a resultant impact on the other adjacent areas. Therefore, when considering the current and future trends in forensic molecular biology it is important to do so not only from the perspective of their effect within the forensic field itself, but also from the perspective of their interaction with neighbouring areas of the system. After all, it is in these neighbouring areas that forensic outcomes are eventually put to use.

Forensic molecular biology has developed rapidly into a comprehensive discipline in its own right and, perhaps more so than any scientific advance before it, has had a profound impact across the CJS. Within the forensic science discipline, as expected, development has been science and/or technology driven. It has followed a trend towards achieving greater sophistication, throughput and informativeness for the DNA-based outcomes of scientific analysis. Developments in forensic molecular biology that have influenced law enforcement could be thought of as operational developments as they predominantly apply to the manner or degree that forensic molecular biology is utilized.

As such, they typically have both a technical and policy-oriented basis. Progress in forensic biology has also influenced the justice sector. This is characterized, for example, by the iterative response of both the legislature and the courts to changes in the volume and nature of forensic DNA tests. Throughout the history of the field there has also been associated debate and controversy accompanying these legal developments. This reflects the array of socio-legal and ethical issues associated with more widespread use of forensic molecular biology.

This chapter chiefly describes the process of development within the forensic molecular biology field. It also touches briefly on the way such developments intersect with the neighbouring fields of law enforcement and the justice system. By considering developmental trends in this way the overall impact of changes in forensic molecular biology can be appropriately placed in context, allowing reflection on their effect to date and foreshadowing their potential effect in the future.

Developments Within the Field of Forensic Molecular Biology

From the time the field settled on a uniform technological platform, forensic molecular biologists have done a masterful job at extending the applicability of this testing regime as far as conceivably possible. The discriminating power of *short tandem repeat* (STR)-based tests has been increased by combining up to 16 STR loci into a single polymerase chain reaction (PCR). The sensitivity of the routine tests has also been driven downward so that successful analysis is now achieved from as little as 100 pg of starting template.

Advancing the capabilities of the DNA methodology has also expanded the range of criminal cases and sample types able to be successfully analysed. For many years forensic molecular biology was limited to testing templates such as blood, semen, hair and saliva. However, the increased efficiency of the STR-based methods now means that DNA can be successfully analysed from discarded clothing or personal effects, skin cell debris from touched or handled surfaces, dandruff, drinking containers, food and fingernail clippings and scrapings. Recent approaches such as reduced-amplicon STR analysis and *low copy number* (LCN) profiling have enhanced reaction sensitivity even further and improved the ability to analyse the most troublesome and highly degraded samples.

Many of the routine techniques have been adapted onto automated platforms so as to facilitate high-throughput analysis and reduce the amount of sample handling. Computer-assisted data analysis has also further streamlined the analytical process and reduced some areas of subjectivity, such as mixture interpretation. The next generation of laboratory instrumentation includes micro-scale electrophoresis devices that not only promise rapid analysis times but also allow for the possibility of remote or portable laboratory platforms.

The observable trend in the development areas mentioned above is that they are all directed towards improving the ability to undertake routine DNA-based identity testing. Whilst this refinement of routine typing technologies is of vital importance, it has meant that for the most part the field has sought only one dimension of information from biological evidence samples. Through recent research into the physical and genetic properties of human DNA this is now changing, allowing the forensic field to diversify its capabilities and begin to address questions beyond the identification of source.

There are already several examples of forensic molecular biology applications that either apply different forms of typing technologies or address a different line of genetic inquiry via new polymorphisms or loci. One such area is nonautosomal DNA profiling, particularly the analysis of mitochondrial DNA (mtDNA) and Y chromosome markers. Whilst mtDNA analysis has been widely used in human evolutionary biology for a number of years, its routine application to forensic work has been consistently evolving. In forensic science, mtDNA is most often analysed in circumstances where nuclear DNA fails to give a result, such as in the analysis of telogenic hairs, nail material and bone or when distant relatives must be used as reference. Analysis typically involves direct sequencing of the hypervariable regions 1 and 2 (HV1 and HV2, respectively) although SNP-based approaches offer the potential to complement or substitute the need for sequencing. Recent developmental progress in the forensic use of mtDNA has also been shaped by the context within which it has been required. In particular, the large-scale multi-national response to recent wars, refugee crises and mass fatalities has seen a rapid evolution of these and other specialist identification sciences so as to respond to the unprecedented logistical and technical challenges presented by these circumstances.

The analysis of polymorphisms on the non-recombining portion of the human Y chromosome (NRY) has also steadily developed into a valuable forensic technique. The male specificity of the Y chromosome makes it particularly suitable for the resolution of problematic situations such as complex mixtures. In a casework setting Y chromosome analysis is especially useful for typing mixed male–female stains that commonly occur as a result of sexual assaults. As with autosomal markers, microsatellites are favoured for forensic Y chromosome analysis and a number of suitable Y-STRs have been identified and validated for forensic use and a selection of them included into commercially available multiplexes.

Potentially the most valuable target markers for a diverse range of novel forensic molecular biology applications are *single nucleotide polymorphisms* (SNPs). These offer a range of forensic applications in traditional and novel areas and confer some particular advantages in comparison to STRs, including a low mutation rate (making SNPs highly suitable for kinship and/or pedigree analysis), amenability to high-throughput processing and automated data analysis, a shorter PCR amplicon size (assisting their ability to be multiplexed and making them good target loci for highly degraded samples), a vast abundance in the genome, and in some cases simplified interpretation (due to the absence of certain STR artifacts such as stutter). Single nucleotide polymorphisms are being investigated for use in forensics in both the identity testing and intelligence areas.

By virtue of the fact that there is greater allelic diversity at STR loci compared with SNPs, STRs have a profound advantage over SNPs in forensic identity testing. As a crude estimate, one would be required to type three to five SNP loci to discriminate between individuals at the same level as a single STR. This means that to approach the degree of certainty of the current STR kits up to 50 SNP loci would be needed, which presents a formidable technical challenge. In addition, changing routine target loci is undesirable, due largely to the significant investment in databases that has already occurred. In combination, these reasons make a universal change of DNA typing platform unlikely. Nonetheless, the recent development of more advanced SNP genotyping technologies, and the desirable properties of SNP loci, has seen a continued focus on developing highly informative SNP-based multiplexes for forensic identity testing.

Single nucleotide polymorphism markers in coding regions linked to physical or behavioural (personality-related) traits are also being researched for forensic purposes. This research aims to provide investigators with an inferred description of an offender, based on biological evidence recovered from a particular crime and subsequent DNA analysis. In one example researchers have described approaches for screening genetic mutations associated with the red-hair phenotype.

A comprehensive candidate gene study for variable eye colour has also been conducted by an American company DNA-Print Genomics. On the basis of this research DNA-Print Genomics have developed and validated RETINOME, a high-throughput genetic test for predicting human iris colour from DNA. A blind validation test of RETINOME on 65 individuals of greater than 80% European ancestry revealed that the test was 97% accurate in its predictions.

Other SNP-based techniques potentially enable the inference of biogeographical ancestry from a DNA sample. As SNPs can be found in areas of the genome subject to evolutionary-selective pressures, such as coding and regulatory regions of DNA, they can exhibit far greater allele and genotype frequency differences between different populations than other forensic loci. In 2003, Frudakis *et al.* developed a classifier for the SNP-based inference of ancestry. This research found that allele frequencies from 56 of the screened SNPs were notably different between groups of unrelated donors of Asian, African and European descent. Using this panel of 56 autosomal SNPs, Frudakis *et al.* report successful designation of the ancestral background of European, African and Asian donors with 99%, 98% and 100% accuracy, respectively. Applying a reduced panel of the 15 most informative SNPs the level of accuracy reduces to 98%, 91% and 97%, respectively. This work represents the most significant step towards the development of a DNA-based test for the inference of ancestry in a forensic setting and has led to the generation of a commercially available tool known as DNA Witness.

A significant amount of research effort has also been invested in the study of non-autosomal SNPs. This approach is commonplace in human migration studies, with a large body of work examining SNP haplotype diversity on the Y chromosome or mtDNA genome. In the forensic context Y- or mtDNA-SNPs are also potential markers of biogeographical ancestry. They have often been preferred in this capacity as they can be locally customized and applied also to understand local population substructure, which in turn can support statistical interpretation models. Large-scale non-autosomal SNP multiplexes already exist and population data and supporting information are readily available.

Commensurate with the advances in the molecular tools available to forensic scientists, the interpretation of DNA evidence has also had to develop considerably over recent years. Early in the history of forensic molecular biology this was an area of heated dispute requiring concerted efforts to address concerns of the scientific and legal community. Now there is a far greater depth of understanding and an important sub-discipline of the field has developed. Nonetheless, each new molecular adaptation brings an associated requirement to reassess the weight or meaning of the outcomes statistically. Approaches are continually being refined to deal with routine complexities such as mixed profiles, partial profiles and relatedness. In addition, novel theory has been needed to assess results obtained from LCN approaches, nonautosomal markers, DNA database searches, multi-trace cases, mass disasters and so on.

From this summary we can distil the following trends that appear set to characterize future years. The addition of more routine markers, and the wider use of known ones, appears likely to continue. Testing platforms will increase in their overall efficiency and move closer to the goal of rapid, portable micro-devices. Taking the DNA science out of the laboratory is a move that could bring considerable advantage to many investigations but is also one with associated challenges. Progress will continue towards answering more diverse questions than 'who is the source of this DNA sample?'. There is almost limitless potential as to where this approach may lead as we unravel the full potential of information accessible via genetic testing. Of course we must observe that with this increased capability comes an associated increase in complexity. Scientists have the potential to step beyond the routinely applied testing regimes, but to do so they must understand the strengths and weaknesses of new approaches and, importantly, be equipped to deal with associated complexities such as the statistical assessment of outcomes. The forensic community must take ownership of this challenge and continue to ensure that proper validation, training and independent research occur. This will at times be awkward given the growing demands for all forms of DNA analysis and an increasingly commercialized operational environment. It will also be important to ensure appropriate management of expectations regarding emerging capabilities on the part of police, legal professionals and the general public.

Developments Influencing Law Enforcement – Operational Impacts

The current environment where forensic molecular biology operates as a tool of the law enforcement community is starkly different to the mid-1980s, when its role in this context first began. This is unsurprising given the rapid evolution of the techniques, as described above. The most notable operational difference is the frequency of use of DNA evidence in criminal casework. Across the world the overall number of cases submitted annually for DNA analysis has increased by many fold. In the UK the average annual inclusion of crime samples onto the national DNA database (NDNAD) increased from 14,644 for the period 1995–2000 to 59,323 for the period 2000–2005. In Canada, 7052 crime samples were added to the national DNA databank in 2005 compared with 816 in 2000. In NSW (the most populous State of Australia) the annual DNA case submissions have risen from 1107 in 1998 to 10,146 in 2005.

The major driver of this change in case volume has been the global implementation of forensic DNA databases. Forensic DNA databases have altered the landscape of the criminal justice system and irrevocably re-shaped the field of forensic science. Their growth has been rapid with millions of STR profiles now held from convicted offenders, suspects and unsolved crimes. Links provided through DNA database searches have contributed valuable intelligence to hundreds of thousands of police investigations. Often links are provided for crimes that are notoriously difficult to resolve, such as burglary and vehicle theft.

Along with the increase in case volume that has been catalysed in part by the introduction of DNA databases, there has also been an alteration to the types of crimes and evidence submitted for biological analysis. In the 1980s and 1990s DNA profiling was primarily applied to serious crimes. Nowadays, however, forensic molecular biology contributes to the investigation of a broader spectrum of crimes. Data

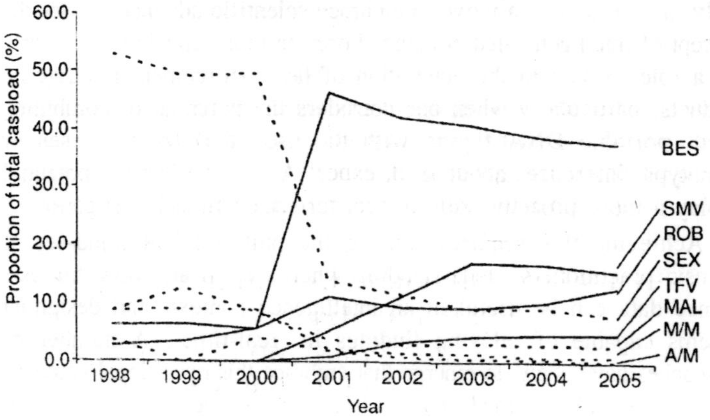

Fig. 1.1. Changing case submission trends of a state forensic DNA laboratory.

from the NSW State Forensic DNA Laboratory over the period 1998–2005 show a clear pattern of decrease in the proportion of cases from serious crime categories and an increase in the proportion of cases submitted from volume crime categories. The change in the case submission profile, that is, the proportions of different case types submitted for analysis, occurred from 2001 forward. This was the beginning of DNA database operations.

The changing nature of the case submission profile in forensic molecular biology laboratories has been accompanied by a changing evidence type away from traditional templates such as blood and semen to more discrete evidence types such as trace DNA and discarded items (including drinking containers and cigarette butts). This is again illustrated in data from the NSW State Forensic DNA Laboratory from between 2001 and 2005.

As well as having a profound effect on the number and types of cases submitted for DNA analysis, forensic DNA databases have also catalysed a re-think of the role that forensic evidence can play in the investigative process. Traditionally forensic DNA evidence has been thought of as information for the use of the court. This focus sees the scientist retrospectively attempting to obtain results for a given case to assist in the resolution of a single crime. The primary focus, therefore, is towards crime-solving rather than crime reduction or prevention. For some years now, policing strategy has evolved from a traditional focus on capturing or incarcerating offenders towards a more holistic understanding of crimes and criminals and a prevention-based approach to law enforcement. Forensic science has not contributed greatly to changes in policing and crime management strategies, although lately there has been a move to embrace scientific advances under the concept of intelligence-led policing. Forensic molecular biology clearly has a role to play in the generation of law enforcement intelligence products, particularly when one considers the potential of combining rapid, portable DNA typing with the use of DNA databases or phenotypic inferences about an offender. As such it has the potential to play a more proactive role in broader-scale crime investigation.

Achieving this requires shifting the philosophical mind-set of forensic practitioners, understanding where, when and how forensic science data can be useful in an intelligence context, and designing systems capable of relaying findings in 'real-time'. A number of approaches have begun to emerge that embrace this operational strategy. Some remain ill-informed and are based around centralized database creation. Other more successful examples create meaningful forensic intelligence and combine it with investigative and crime analysis tools.

In summary there has been a trend towards greater use of DNA, across a more diverse range of cases and in a more intelligence-based context or frame-work. It is important to note, however, that these developments (and the DNA databases that have predominantly catalysed them) remain at a preliminary stage. Standards and approaches still vary enormously between jurisdictions and in future there may be continued moves towards greater harmonization. Undoubtedly there will be progress towards greater cross-jurisdictional exchange of DNA information, possibly facilitated at the level of organizations such as Interpol. Managing this era of wider national and international use of forensic DNA profile information will be challenging as, through these developments, the science we apply moves increasingly into the public and political realm.

Developments Influencing the Justice System: Socio-legal Impacts

Practical and philosophical aspects of the legal system have been impacted by developments in the field of forensic molecular biology. Practical issues emanate from the construction of laws that regulate the collection of DNA material from persons associated with the justice system, and the subsequent use of any DNA-related evidence in our courts. These are flanked by important philosophical considerations in areas such as social justice, ethics and privacy.

From the time of its first introduction the courts have had mixed experiences with the presentation of forensic DNA evidence. Scientists, lawyers, judges and jurors have battled to come to terms with this new forensic application of a complex scientific technique. Initially complicating matters further was the public fanfare that accompanied early DNA successes, creating an aura of scientific certainty around the technology. Whilst forensic molecular biology is a powerful means of identification, this sort of misrepresentation in the public arena can create unrealistic perceptions of its capability. At a relatively early stage, the admissibility of DNA evidence in criminal trials was successfully challenged in the United States and elsewhere. Many of the issues upon which early challenges were mounted were the subject of conflict in the scientific community at the time. The scrutiny of the legal system in these instances must be seen to have been strongly positive as it brought about further refinement and validation of the forensic DNA methodology and the implementation of structures to regulate quality assurance. In recent times challenges to DNA admissibility are rarely successful, as, in general terms, the science has reached the important point of being accepted practice. This is not to say that legal scrutiny has abated entirely, rather, if anything, legal challenges have evolved in their complexity along with the evolution of the technology itself. Instead of focusing on general issues, it is now specialized components of the analytical or interpretative process that have become the subject of questioning.

ELECTROPHORESIS IN FORENSIC SCIENCE

Electrophoresis was first described by Arne Tiselius in 1930, for which he received a Nobel Prize in 1948. In this pioneering experiment, he used a U-shaped quartz tube to show the separation of different proteins in free solution as contiguous bands. His work was published in 1937 but received little notice until the late 1960s, when Hjerten described the first *capillary electrophoresis* (CE) apparatus. Hjerten's apparatus consisted of three units: (1) a high voltage power supply; (2) a detector; and (3) a unit holding a 1–3 mm ID quartz capillary tube, which was immersed in a cooling bath. He used this apparatus to prove numerous theoretical concepts in CE and was able to separate inorganic ions, proteins, nucleic acid, and microorganisms by *capillary zone electrophoresis* (CZE) or *capillary isoelectric focusing* (CIEF). In spite of the pioneering work by Hjerten, CE was still relatively unknown until Jorgenson and Lukacs published a series of papers in 1980. The availability of polyiimide-coated fused silica capillaries with a 75–100-μm internal diameter, in addition to sensitive absorbance detectors developed for micro-bore high-performance liquid chromatography (HPLC), were instrumental in the development of commercial CE applications. The smaller internal diameter eliminated band broadening caused by convection, whereas the plug flow characteristics of the *electroosmotic flow* (EOF) allowed efficiencies reaching hundreds of thousand of theoretical plates. Since the landmark publication in 1980 by Jorgenson and Lukacs research dealing with the applications of CE has grown exponentially.

Capillary electrophoresis (CE) is characterized by rapid analysis times and ultra-high resolution capabilities. Indeed, these characteristics, in conjunction with low sample consumption and improved analyte recovery, were expected to revolutionize the analysis of complex biological mixtures of peptides and proteins. Furthermore, the family of CE separation techniques affords numerous other separation mechanisms that differ from *high-performance liquid chromatography*

(HPLC) separation of peptides and proteins. In addition to free solution separations such as *capillary zone electrophoresis* (CZE), analyte separation of peptides and proteins can also be effected by *isoelectric focusing* (IEF), isotachophoresis, molecular weight sieving, and micellar electrokinetic chromatography (MEKC).

The use of *mass spectrometry* (MS) in conjunction with CE for the analyses of peptides and proteins has experienced explosive growth in recent years. In large part this can be attributed to the development of *electrospray ionization* (ESI) and its miniaturization, microspray ionization (μESI) and nanospray ionization (nano-ESI). These techniques enable rapid analysis of thermally labile, hydrophilic biopolymers, such as peptides and protein, in addition to being compatible with CE. The development of μESI and nano-ESI enabled the use of very low flow infusion rates (nanoliter/min) of analyte mixtures using only small amounts of precious peptide and protein sample mixutes.

As discussed previously, CE-MS was pioneered independently by Smith using a coaxial sheath liquid approach and by Henion who developed the liquid-junction interface. Since the first report of on-line CE-MS, it has undergone considerable developments in both instrumentation and applications, and has been the subject of a number of reviews. However, the development of on-line CE-MS has not been without significant challenges. First, optimal analyte resolution on CE and CE-MS is only achieved when the sample injection volume is <2% of the total capillary volume. Hence, sample injection volumes are usually in the range of tens of nanoliters for commonly used capillaries (e.g., 50 μm i.d.) to low picoliters for small internal diameter capillaries (<10 μm i.d.).

The concentration sensitivity of CE and CE-MS is, therefore, significantly inferior to HPLC, which can accommodate anywhere from 100 μL to >1 mL sample injection volumes. Thus, a high sample concentration is critical for CE and CE-MS analysis, which is not ideal for peptides or protein mixtures present in sample vials. At high analyte concentrations, these biopolymers often aggregate and then precipitate. In addition, at such high concentrations, peptides and proteins also readily adhere to pipet tips and sample vial surfaces, leading to significant sample losses. A variety of approaches have been developed to overcome this limitation for peptides and proteins and include analyte stacking, focusing, capillary isotachophoresis, and on-line analyte concentrators that include solid phase, and membrane preconcentration cartridges.

Another problem associated with CE and CE-MS analysis of peptides and proteins is that the bare silica of the capillary is not chemically inert. When filled with an aqueous solution, the silica surface takes on a charge that is pH-dependent. Although this is a primary factor in the development of *electro-osmotic flow* (EOF), it also provides an active surface for adsorption of peptides and proteins. Hence, the CE and CE-MS analysis of peptides and proteins often results in significant analyte loss and compromised resolution. Various approaches have been utilized, including pH extremes.

This chapter will focus on the use of CE-MS in the analysis of biologically active peptides and proteins. In particular, emphasis is placed on the robustness and sensitivity of the technology needed to analyze complex mixtures where the constituents are present at very low concentrations. Furthermore, strategies that facilitate on-line manipulation of samples to effect isolation, concentration, and analysis of compounds will also be described.

Analytical Considerations

Typically, the analysis of biologically active peptides and proteins requires minimal sample handling and maximum resolution and detection sensitivity of individual analytes. In this regard CE-MS appears to afford the "best of all worlds." However, it is important to realize that often times the biologically active or significant component in the complex mixture is present at very low concentrations and/or low absolute amounts. It is important to consider carefully the sample-handling strategy, as well as the intricacies of the method to be used in analysis of such compounds.

Method Preparation

Analysis of biologically active peptide and protein mixtures by CE and CE-MS requires attainment of reproducible migration times. In order to achieve this, it is necessary to prepare the CE capillary. The simplest approach is to use a hydroxide (or methoxide) solution to etch and clean the silica surface, followed by washing first with H_2O and, finally, with background electrolyte solution. For peptide analysis, it is usual to condition the capillary prior to CE separation. Typically, 2–5 analyses of a standard solution containing a peptide mixture is sufficient. In cases where a more rigorous cleaning regime is required, we have subsequently shown that a solution of 70% formic acid/30% n-propanol, followed by conditioning, will ensure migration time reproducibility.

It has been demonstrated that in free solution, peptide migration is proportional to $m^{2/3}/z$ (where m is mass and z is the charge of the peptide). A number of predictive programs now exist to correlate the pI of a peptide with the charge on the molecule at a specified pH. Thus, if the peptide composition of a mixture is known, the free solution conditions to effect CE separation can be predicted. In this instance the most important parameter to consider is the pH of the *background electrolyte* (BGE). Obviously, other important parameters to consider are the ionic strength of BGE, capillary dimensions, temperature and applied voltages. However, for peptides the most direct route to optimal separation conditions is to change the pH of the BGE. It is important that only volatile salts are used in the BGE for CE-MS. Hence, acidic BGEs are usually prepared with mixtures of NH_4OAc and CH_3COOH solutions. Basic pH conditions are usually achieved using mixtures of NH_4OAc, NH_4HCO_3, and NH_4OH. It is also important to note that these solutions do not have high buffering capacity and this can lead to irreproducible migration times as ions are depleted from the BGE. In order to overcome this limitation, frequent replenishment of BGE with fresh solution is necessary. We have found that in the analysis of peptides, a solution of 2 m*M* ammonium acetate in 1% acetic acid provides an excellent BGE for analysis by CE-MS. In addition, increasing the acetic acid to 5% (v/v) enhances peptide separation, which is attributed to increased BGE viscosity.

As noted earlier, the use of bare fused silica capillaries can lead to significant losses in peptide during analysis by CE and CE-MS. Thus, the use of polybrene-coated capillaries has found significant use in the CE-MS analysis of peptides. The polybrene coating reverses the charge on the capillary wall and under acidic BGE conditions prevents peptide adsorption to the wall. Typically, coating and conditioning the capillary allows optimal separation performance for 15–20 analyses. The capillary is then completely stripped and recoated to carry out further analyses. It should be noted that it is not possible to coat dynamically the CE capillary in the CE-MS analysis of peptides because this would adversely affect ESI-MS performance.

The development of CE-MS conditions for the separation of proteins is considerably more complex than for optimization of peptide separations. Protein denaturation, aggregation, precipitation, and solubility as well as severe adsorption to the capillary wall can all degrade CE and CE-MS performance. Therefore, for almost all CE and CE-MS protein analyses, a coated capillary is necessary. We recently evaluated the performance of a number of coated capillaries in the analysis of proteins derived from aqueous humor. We found that the salt matrix of this physiologically derived fluid interferred with the separation of the proteins that are present in this fluid. In most cases, only a single peak was detected. However, use of a polybrene capillary enabled good resolution of the components of this important physiological fluid. We have also found that a BGE composed of ammonium acetate and acetic acid to be very suitable for protein analysis by CE-MS, with increased acetic acid concentration often improving analyte resolution.

Sample Preparation

As noted above, extreme caution is required during preparation of dilute solutions of peptides and proteins. These analytes readily adhere to every surface that they contact. Therefore, manipulations need to be minimized. However, biologically relevant peptides and proteins are often most soluble in solutions of high ionic strength. Such solutions are usually not optimal for separation by CE. Typically, these solutions will reduce the effect of stacking mechanisms, or compress the pH gradient in cIEF separations. Clearly, the salt concentrations need to be reduced. This, however, should not be at the expense of analyte concentration. In this regard, use of an on-line sample preparation (e.g., *solid-phase extraction* (SPE)-CE-MS or *membrane pre-concentration* (mPC)-CE-MS) appears to be most appropriate. As described in detail later, these techniques enable analyte preconcentration and sample cleanup with minimal intervention by the operator with resulting improved analyte recovery. Furthermore, as we have found in our studies, the salt in the sample matrix may aid protein recovery from the solid phase or impregnated membrane. Also, traces of salt that remain after on-line cleanup may improve analyte stacking, provided a positively charged capillary is used for analyte separation. For peptides, the combination of reversed-phase HPLC (RP-HPLC) off-line with mPC-CE-MS has been proven to be a sensitive method of analysis, since subsequent sample preparation involves merely removing the organic solvent from fractions and diluting the residue in a suitable aqueous solvent. This method could be further improved by on-line coupling of these techniques, as has been demonstrated by Jorgenson's group. However, this tandem technique requires that the mass spectrometer be capable of high sensitivity at fast scan rates, since the CE separation is usually complete in just a few seconds. As such, the development of fast-scanning, highly-sensitive electrospray-time of flight mass spectrometers (ESI-TOF-MS) will make this technology more viable.

An area that has received only scant attention is that of on-line digestion CE-MS. Such methodology, demonstrated by Kuhr and his group, appears to be a useful way of generating peptide maps of small amounts of biologically relevant proteins. In conjunction with on-line SPE-CE-MS or mPC-CE-MS, digestion in an open tubular enzyme capillary, or an enzyme-modified solid support, would appear to be a powerful methodology for proteomic research. In addition, up-front separation by an appropriate chromatographic step (either HPLC or CE) could provide an attractive method for characterizing the protein composition of a biological system, that once optimized would need little operator intervention. Hence, analyte losses and sample contamination should be minimized. On-line, automated peptide/protein sequencing using tandem MS could also be achieved by this integrated approach.

Sample Injection

Typically three modes of sample injection into the CE capillary are used for analyte analysis with on-line MS detection. These include electrokinetic injecton, during which high voltage is applied to the sample solution. Analytes migrate into the capillary according to their electrophoretic mobility or may be transported by the migration of solvated ions. This mode of injection is affected by the salt concentration of the sample matrix. Thus the amount of analyte injected into the capillary can vary from sample to sample unless care is taken to ensure that each sample is isotonic. In addition, analytes of differing charge will migrate into the capillary at different rates introducings selectivity into the analysis. For these reasons, electrokinetic injection is not particularly useful for the analysis of biologically derived mixtures of peptides and proteins.

The two other sample injection modes for CE-MS are based on hydrodynamic flow. In one mode, the inlet of CE capillary is immersed in the sample vial and raised for a specific period to a predefined height above its outlet. The volume of sample injected is dependent on the back pressure of the capillary, the height differential between the capillary inlet and outlet, and the time of the injection. This technique is often used when a homemade CE system is connected to the mass spectrometer. For commercially available units, the CE capillary is inserted into a sealed sample vial to which a nitrogen head pressure is applied for a specific length of time. Sample is forced from the vial into the capillary. Since both of these techniques are based upon hydrodynamic flow, all components of a complex mixture are injected into the CE capillary, minimizing the selectivity observed with electrokinetic injections. However, salt from the matrix of biologically derived samples will be introduced along with analytes of interest into the capillary. This will significantly affect the performance characteristics of the separation.

On-Line Sample Concentration

A significant problem in the CE and CE-MS analysis of biologically active peptides and proteins is that the analytes are often present at very low concentration levels. In addition, the low internal volume of CE capillaries leads to a requirement of high analyte concentration for all CE and CE-MS studies. Analyte preconcentration can be achieved by off-line sample preparation, using lyophilization, or adsorption onto a solid phase to enable both sample cleanup and analyte concentration. However, manipulations of dilute solutions of peptides and proteins should be minimized since sample losses can be significant. Therefore, many investigators have attempted to improve the sample loading capacity of the CE capillary while maintaining optimal analyte resolution and separation efficiency.

Initially, a variety of electrophoretic concentration methods, including analyte stacking, field amplification, and transient *isotachophoresis* (tITP) were developed to preconcentrate analytes following injection of the sample into the capillary. All of these techniques occur as voltage is applied across the CE capillary causing analyte zones to concentrate due to different field strengths or chemical microenvironments that form within the CE capillary. Consequently, larger volumes can be analyzed with minimal loss of resolution and separation efficiency. In the most favorable cases, the sample can constitute up to approx 90% of the total CE capillary volume with minimal loss of CE performance. However, since the total capillary volume is small, maximum sample loading is usually limited to <1 μL. Also, as mentioned earlier, salts in the sample matrix can disrupt such analyte stacking and focusing processes. Such matrix components introduce zones of low electric field within the capillary upon application of high voltage. Analyte migration velocities are slower, and this can prevent the analytes from focusing into discrete zones. Therefore, preprocessing of biologically derived mixtures may be required to reduce their salt concentration prior to use of these stacking and focusing techniques. Nevertheless, use of CE-tITP-MS has provided a means for analyte preconcentration to a level sufficient to allow its use for the analysis of peptide and protein mixtures.

A technique that emerged from single-column tITP was the use of CE-cITP-MS. For this approach, cITP separations are performed in wide-bore (100–200 μm i.d.), larger volume capillaries. Following the cITP step, analytes are transferred into the CE capillary for further separation, and subsequent MS detection. This technique permits the analysis of sample volumes as large as 20 μL, and as such, it provides a practical means of enhancing the concentration sensitivity of CE-MS. However, this technique is significantly more complex than other strategies for concentration sensitivity enhancement, and is not well-suited to routine operation.

In another approach, capillary isoelectric focusing-mass spectrometry (cIEF-MS) enables the analysis of a full capillary volume of sample. This technique has proved to be particularly useful for the analysis of complex mixtures of proteins. Separations are usually performed in a coated capillary that exhibits negligible EOF. In a focusing step, ampholites, which are premixed with the sample, migrate through the capillary to form a pH gradient. Simultaneously, proteins migrate until they reach the pH zone that corresponds to their isoelectric point (pI), where they become neutral, hence no longer migrate. The proteins are focused into discrete zones and preconcentrated. Ultimately, a stationary state is achieved when all proteins have migrated into the pH zones that correspond to their pI. Mobilization of the proteins into the mass spectrometer is achieved using an electrophoretic approach, hydrodynamic flow or a combination of these techniques. While cIEF-MS has been shown to be useful for the analysis of proteins, the process of pH gradient formation and analyte focusing are severely compromised by the presence of salts. High salt concentrations lead to excessive currents during the focusing phase of the experiment, causing ampholyte zone broadening and a less well-defined pH gradient.

Recently, we have found that use of a 5–10 min gradient application of voltage facilitates on-line removal of salts. The current profiles observed in these experiments led us to conclude that the relatively slow application of the focusing voltage enables the ejection of highly mobile salts as the pH gradient is developed and proteins migrate to zones that correspond to their pl. Two protein solutions were analyzed using the same polyvinyl alcohol coated capillary. First, a solution containing lysozyme, cytochrome C, myoglobin, carbonic anhydrase, and trypsin inhibitor in water was analyzed using a standard cIEF approach. All five proteins were baseline resolved. Subsequently, the same proteins were dissolved in 200 m*M* sodium chloride. In this case analysis by a standard cIEF approach failed. As a voltage of 20 kV was applied to the capillary (over 30 s) to affect analyte focusing, the current rose to 45 μA and became unstable. It was impossible to obtain satisfactory results from this system without first removing the sodium chloride by means of a slow voltage ramp. This technique worked well and has been reproducible in our hands. As expected, a small shrinkage of the pH gradient was observed. This occurred during the desalting process when cations and anions are mobilized from the capillary and are replaced by counterions of the background electrolyte. While a UV detector was used to acquire the data described here, we subsequently demonstrated the efficacy of this approach for analysis of physiologically derived protein mixtures by cIEF-MS. It the latter study we demonstrated the detection of glycated hemoglobin chains in diabetic blood and the direct analysis of cerebral spinal fluid by cIEF-MS.

Analyte concentrators and membrane preconcentration devices have also been developed to overcome the relatively poor concentration limits of detection of CE and CE-MS. Briefly, such technology is based on the insertion of a small bed of adsorptive phase or impregnated membrane at the inlet of the capillary coupled to the MS. Analytes are adsorbed onto the absorptive phase to concentrate them. Injection volumes in excess of 200 μL are routine with this technology, which corresponds to an increase in concentration sensitivity of 100–1000 times that of a conventional CE injection method. In addition, since analytes are adsorbed onto a solid phase or impregnated membrane, on-line sample cleanup can be effected by washing with a suitable solvent. For biologically derived peptide and protein samples, this process enables the removal of salt and other hydrophilic contaminants that interfere with the electrophoretic separation. This eliminates the need for excessive off-line pretreatment, improving analyte recovery, which ultimately enhances concentration sensitivity.

Some of these techniques (e.g., membrane preconcentration) have also been shown to be compatible with contemporary CE stacking and focusing chemistries. Indeed, mPC-tITP-CE-MS has been shown to be an optimal technique for the separation and sequencing of low concentrations of peptides. A major consideration for optimal mPC-CE-MS performance is the use of a sufficient volume of an elution solvent (e.g., 80% methanol or acetonitrile in water) to ensure maximized peptide recovery. However, the use of an excessive volume

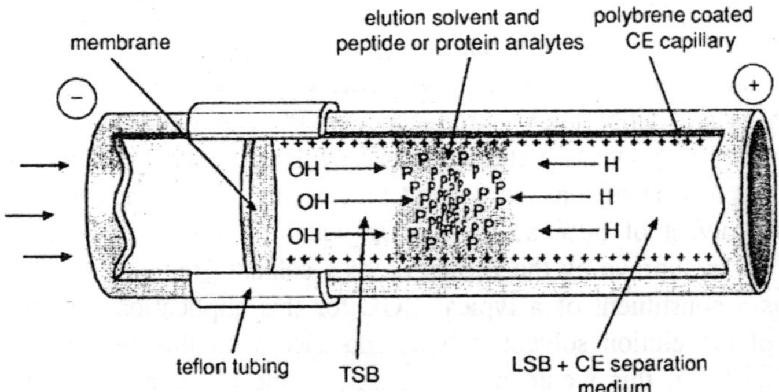

Fig. 1.2. Schematic of moving boundary ITP after peptide or protein analytes have been eluted from the adsorptive membrane.

of elution solvent severely degrades the performance of the analysis. Use of a tITP focusing strategy in conjunction with membrane preconcentration can overcome this problem, since analytes are focused into discrete zones as voltage is applied across the capillary. In a systematic study we have shown that this stacking/focusing regime is a complex combination of transient cIEF-tITP and analyte stacking, that needs to be fully optimized for each mPC-CE capillary used. However, once optimized, this system works extremely well.

Although peptide analysis by mPC-tITP-CE-MS can be achieved using an uncoated fused silica capillary and an acidic BGE, it is our experience that peptides and proteins are more optimally analyzed using a coated capillary. In our studies of MHC class I peptides, tear proteins, and the composition of aqueous humor, we have found a polybrene-coated capillary is most suitable. Again, the use of tITP in conjunction with mPC-CE-MS ensures that a larger volume of an elution solvent can be used with little degradation of performance. Indeed, unless a relatively large volume of elution solvent is used, proteins are not efficiently recovered from currently available impregnated membrane. In a systematic study, we found that the composition of the elution solvent was critical for elution of proteins from a C_2 impregnated membrane. Increasing acetonitrile concentration from 40 to 80% in water significantly improved protein recovery from the membrane, and overcame a selectivity problem at the lower acetonitrile concentrations. Furthermore, we demonstrated that there was no requirement for the addition of an acid to this elution solvent. Addition of 0.1% trifluoroacetic acid to the 80% acetonitrile elution solvent adversely affected protein separation. We attributed this result to localized interaction of the TFA, an efficient ion-pair reagent, with the positively charged polybrene-coated capillary. In addition, we found that use of a less efficient ion-pair reagent (such as acetic acid) did not influence protein recovery. We attributed this result to the fact that gaps are deliberately introduced in mPC cartridges as they are prepared. This prevents perturbation of EOF by the cartridge. However, turbulent mixing of injected solvent will occur. Thus, when using an elution solvent of 80% acetonitrile in water proteins will be eluted from the membrane by the formation of a solvent gradient. As acetic acid is a constituent of a typical BGE for this application, the front edge of the elution solvent will be modified with this reagent. We postulated that this would be beneficial for the recovery of analytes from the membrane.

From our studies it is clear that mPC-CE-MS analysis of protein mixtures is still in its infancy, being limited by the choice of impregnated membranes. This approach will undoubtedly be improved in the future as new impregnated membranes with more appropriate physico-chemical properties (e.g., wide-pore polymeric phases, such as PLRP-S 4000 Å) become available. In addition, further development of affinity capture analyte concentrators will prove to be very valuable for the isolation and analysis of target proteins.

Capillary Surface Technology

As noted earlier, CE was initially thought to be a new approach that would revolutionize the analysis of peptides and proteins. For some applications (e.g., the sequencing of MHC class I peptides) CE has been proved to be extremely valuable. However, capillary-surface technology has proved to be a major challenge for the analysis of these important biopolymers. The manufacture of fused silica capillaries that exhibit constant surface properties has been the subject of much industrial research by companies that supply this consumable to the users of CE. In our own hands, we have found that although a single CE capillary that is prepared from a bulk supply may provide high performance, the next length of fused silica may not condition at all. In addition, there is no way of predicting in advance which piece of fused silica will work. This can be both frustrating and time consuming. For peptides and proteins, capillary preparation is further complicated by potential analyte-wall interactions. As noted earlier, the internal surface of a fused silica capillary is ionized when filled with an aqueous BGE. While the degree of ionization is dependent upon the pH of the BGE, the ionized silanol groups of the CE capillary provide an active anionic surface to which peptides and proteins can adsorb. This problem is particularly evident for proteins. These analytes are amphiphilic, having a structure that allows the chemical environment to determine their characteristics (e.g., charge, polarity, and hydrophobicity).

The interactions of proteins at the liquid-solid boundary of fused silica CE capillaries have been thoroughly investigated. Forces that are invoked during these interactions include electrostatic, ion pairing, hydrophobic, and the formation of hydrogen bonds. In CE separations, adsorption equilibrium between proteins and the capillary wall cause severe zone broadening. Peaks also become asymmetric, which leads to decreased analyte resolution and separation efficiency. Furthermore, a changing capillary surface also affects the magnitude of the EOF causing analyte separations to become irreproducible.

To negate analyte-wall interactions, major efforts have been directed toward shielding or inverting the negative charge on the capillary wall. These include polymers, such as polyacrylamide (PAA), polyethylene glycol (PEG), polyethylene imine (PEI), polyvinyl alcohol (PVA), aminopropyltrimethoxysilane (APS), and C8 or C18 phases that contain siloxane bound anchor groups for covalent attachment to the capillary surface. Alternatively, static coatings, such as PEI and polybrene, have been adsorbed onto the capillary surface prior to the analysis of peptides or proteins. Similarly, dynamic coatings, such as PVA, can be added to the background electrolyte in an attempt to eliminate the interaction of analytes with the capillary wall. There have also been some investigations on the use of polymeric capillaries. However, these were difficult to make with a consistent small internal diameter and did not readily overcome the issue of protein interaction with the capillary wall since even polymers can take on a charge during electrophoresis.

By design, all capillary coatings change the chemistry of the silica surface. Characteristics of the polymer or chemical coating determine the nature of the capillary surface. For example, hydrophilic neutral coatings (such as PVA, PEG, and PAA) impart no charge to the capillary wall and effectively eliminate EOF. In these capillaries, analyte resolution is based solely on the differences of electrophoretic mobility of each analyte. Other coatings, such as PEI, APS, polybrene, or surfactants (such as cetyltrimethyl-ammonium bromide), reverse the charge on the capillary wall, and EOF flows from cathode to anode. CE capillaries coated with such positively charge materials have been shown to be especially advantageous for the analysis of basic proteins. More recently, we have reported that a polybrene-coated capillary is very useful for the analysis of the protein composition of physiologically derived fluids (such as aqueous humor). Indeed, separations in a polybrene-coated capillary were found to be less affected by the salty matrix of this fluid than other capillary coatings tested. In fact, in capillaries that were coated with a neutral polymer, we found that the high salt concentration of these samples prevented the separation of the proteins that were present in physiologically derived fluids. Often, only one peak was observed during separations under these conditions.

For CE-MS experiments, the use of a coated capillary further complicates this methodology. If the coating is not sufficiently anchored to the capillary wall, it can bleed into the MS. Here it may be ionized, thereby generating a large chemical background, or interfering with the electrospray processes to impair stability or reduce analyte sensitivity. Hence, in addition to preventing analyte adsorption, the coating has to be stable and remain in the capillary. Most of those described above, with the exception of the dynamic coating strategy, have been successfully used for protein analysis by CE-MS. In general, coatings that invert the charge on the capillary wall have been preferred for CE-MS analysis of proteins. This can be attributed to the stability of such coating in acidic background electrolytes, which is a regime that also promotes the formation of positively charged analytes, thereby enabling the use of positive ion MS conditions.

CE-MS Compatible Buffers

As mentioned earlier, the use of nonvolatile BGE in the CE capillary to separate analytes can be detrimental to electrospray MS performance. Buffers of relatively high ionic strength are often used for CE separations, since these help to prevent analyte–analyte and analyte–wall interactions. Involatile salts are also a favorite choice for CE separations when used in conjunction with detection devices other than MS. In contrast, volatile buffers (e.g., ammonium salts) of low concentration, ionic strength, and conductivity are typically used for most CE-MS experiments. This is to ensure stable electrospray conditions and help prevent MS contamination by salts and ultimately instrument breakdown. For peptides and proteins, Moseley et al. found that acidic buffers of low ionic strength provided best CE-MS sensitivity when using a sheath-liquid interface. Wahl and Smith compared the effect of BGE composition on CE-MS using both sheath-liquid and sheathless electrospray interfaces. The results of this study were in good agreement with theory and showed that CE-MS sensitivity was reduced with increasing buffer concentration and ionic strength. In addition, comparison of ammonium acetate/acetic acid and sodium phosphate buffer systems indicated that at a 1 m*M* concentration the latter buffer provided sevenfold less signal to background than the volatile acetate system. This was attributed to the difference in ionic strength and volatility of the BGEs examined. Other results of these studies demonstrated that the sheathless interface often provided better analyte detectability than a sheath-liquid interface for most buffer systems. Likewise, a smaller-bore capillary enabled improved tolerance of the buffer system, and this was attribute to the lower BGE flow rate. BGE flow rate in a 10 tm i.d. capillary is approx 0.8 nL/min for a 10 m*M* ammonium acetate/acetic acid BGE.

In other studies, organic modifiers have been added to the BGE to aid analyte solubility. Use of organic modifiers also changes the physical properties of the separation solution, which can lead to a reduced EOF. The organic solvent can alter the thickness of the electrical double-layer at the capillary wall, and/or change the viscosity of the BGE. As demonstrated, a nonaqueous BGE can also offer advantages for CE-MS analyses of hydrophobic peptides. Here, an ammonium acetate/formic acid BGE system dissolved in a mixture containing only acetonitrile and methanol (75:25 [v/v]) was used to separate two hydrophobic peptides, namely, Gramicidine S and Bacitracin. Both of these analytes are only sparingly soluble in aqueous solution, and poor analyte sensitivity was demonstrated using a conventional aqueous CE-MS BGE. However, a nonaqueous BGE enabled efficient analysis of these analytes by CE-MS when using a sheath-liquid interface (consisting of 5 m*M* ammonium acetate in 80:20 [v/v] isopropanol:water). Indeed, we were able to detect a number of minor contaminants in the samples of both peptides by CE-MS using the nonaqueous BGE system.

CE-MS Interfaces for Peptide and Protein Analysis

A number of elegant but different approaches have been reported in coupling off-line and interfacing on-line CE with MS. In this section we will briefly discuss coupling and interfacing strategies as they pertain to analysis of peptides and proteins. In particular the sheath-liquid interface has been one of the most widely used methods for connecting the CE capillary to the MS. Briefly, the CE capillary is extended through the ion source and is surrounded by a coaxial delivered sheath liquid used as a make-up flow and analyte entrainment process, as well as providing the electrical contact point for the ESI voltage. In their studies on protein mixtures, Karger et al. investigated ionic mobility in CE-MS using a sheath-liquid interface. Since ions migrate towards both anode and cathode, ionic components of the sheath liquid can migrate into the separation capillary. Both sharp and diffuse ionic boundaries were detected and resulted in migration delays, inversion of migration order, and often loss of analyte resolution. Here, while the BGE was the same in the two experiments, substitution of a sheath liquid containing 1% acetic acid in 50% methanol/water by 20 m*M* TFA in 50% methanol/water had a dramatic effect on the analysis of a mixture of these proteins. The time of the separation was compressed, and protein resolution was significantly different. Hence, the sheath liquid is a further parameter that requires close attention. In addition to avoiding the possible detrimental effects on analyte separation, careful selection of the sheath liquid can also lead to the use of background electrolytes that contain involatile buffers. Ions present in the sheath liquid can penetrate the CE capillary to prevent such involatile salts from entering the interface. Furthermore, this process can effectively remove adducts (e.g., phosphates) from proteins prior to entering the mass spectrometer. We have also noted on occasion that proteins may not be detected at the mass spectrometer (even though they have been seen to migrate past a UV windown that is close to the inlet of the CE capillary) when using a mostly organic sheath-liquid interface. In addition to the previous explanation, we have postulated that the mostly organic sheath liquid causes the proteins to precipitate as they elute from the CE capillary. As a result, proteins are neither ionized nor detected.

An alternative approach for coupling CE to MS is with the use of a liquid-junction reservoir. This approach was pioneered by Henion and consists of CE capillary placed in a buffer reservoir and analytes are transported into the MS via a transfer capillary that acts as an outlet from the buffer reservoir. One of the advantages of the liquid-junction interface in the analyses of peptides and proteins is its tolerance to involatile buffer agents. Such buffers are preferentially favored for optimal peptide and protein solubility. More recently the development of the sheathless interface has significantly reduced chemical background noise and enhanced MS sensitivity of analyte detection. A number of different designs have been described and have recently been compared and evaluated. Clearly, such miniaturized CE-MS interfaces will dominate the way analysis of peptides and proteins occurs in the future.

CE-MS and Tendem MS: Biological Samples

It is very clear that CE-MS and CE-tandem mass spectrometry (CE-MS/MS) can play a significant role in the analysis of biologically active peptides and proteins. However, to date, these techniques have been underutilized and underexploited. In particular it is interesting to note that in three very recent general reviews of pharmaceuticals and drugs, clinical chemistry and forensic science, no citation of CE-MS usage was noted in any of the reviews. We and others have utilized CE-MS and CE-MS/MS in the analysis of complex peptide and protein mixtures derived from physiological fluids and tissues. Although not all examples are specific to clinical chemistry, toxicology, or forensic science, it is hoped that the applications described highlight the usefulness and power of such an approach and will encourage greater use in the future.

Biologically Active Peptides

A significant and noteworthy use of CE-MS in the analysis of a complex peptide mixture from snake venom was carried out by Perkins and Tomer. They took lower molecular mass fractions (<8500 Daltons) from snake venom of the Jameson's Mamba (*Dendroaspis jamesoni kaimosae*) and the Eastern Coral Snake (*Mierurus fulvius*) and subjected them to CE-MS with single ion monitoring to enhance sensitivity detection limits. Using this approach, they were able to detect the presence of 83 peptides in the venom of the Jameson Mamba and 49 peptides from the coral snake, all in the molecular mass range of 6000–8500 Daltons. Their approaches readily demonstrate the excellent resolving capability of CE, coupled with the superb detection capability of on-line MS. Subsequently, Afifiyan et al. used a combination of RP-HPLC (and CE in conjunction with MS to isolate and identify four short chain neurotoxic peptides from the Malayan spitting cobra (*Naja naja sputatrix*). In this case, however, cDNA from the cobra were cloned and expressed in *Escherichia coli* and the peptides purified and identified using CE and MS.

More recently CE-MS has been utilized in the analysis of degradation products from neuropeptide Y. Optimal CE conditions were obtained with high formic acid concentrations (250 m*M*, pH 2.75) in conjunction with 25–50 m*M* triethylamine. The degradation products could be readily separated from the parent peptide. In addition, CE-MS analysis allowed the determination of which amino acids had been lost from the parent peptide.

Finally, Hennebicq et al. have used CE-MS in the analysis of different microsomal preparations obtained from gastric and colonic mucosa obtained from normal and tumor tissue. They analyzed the *O*-glycosylated products obtained from the selected-acceptor substrate peptide (TTSAPTTS) in the presence of *N*-acetylgalactosaminyl-transferases (GalNAc). Their analytical data was consistent with the existence of more than one form of GalnAc transferase, which were expressed differentially in the gastrointestinal tract (stomach or colon). They also showed that levels of enzyme activity were tissue-specific. Furthermore, they demonstrated using CE-MS that high dipeptidyl-aminotransferase activity was present in tumor gastric, as well as normal colonic tissue. This work indicates the strong potential of CE-MS in the detection and identification of new markers of disease, as well as affording a rapid screen for known markers of diseased tissue.

The use of CE-MS/MS in the analysis of biologically active peptides requires that an on-line preconcentration step of analytes occurs prior to sequence analysis. Almost all the work in this area has used mPC-CE-MS/MS and is described in more detail later.

Biologically Active Proteins

Most approaches for the analysis of proteins have utilized some type of on-line concentration step prior to CE separation and detection. One successful approach has been to use cIEF-MS. This has been demonstrated as a useful approach for the analysis of proteins by a number of groups including Lee, Smith, and Naylor. It has been useful in rapidly screening protein mixtures derived from whole blood, cerebrospinal fluid, and *E. coli* lysate from cultures. We have utilized this approach in the direct one-step analysis of human cerebrospinal fluid. By determining molecular weight of protein responses and interrogating the protein database, it is possible to readily identify proteins present in such a complex mixture. Obviously such an approach affords a very powerful tool in the clinical diagnosis of disease using protein markers.

On-Line Preconcentration-CE-MS of Peptides and Proteins

As noted earlier, most analyses of biologically active peptides and proteins have been carried out using on-line preconcentration-CE-MS. In particular, the group at Mayo has used on-line membrane preconcentration CE-MS (mPC-CE-MS) and CE-MS/MS (mPC-CE-MS/MS). Furthermore, in addition to analyte preconcentration, mPC-CE can also be used for efficient sample cleanup. Obviously, sample cleanup is particularly important for biologically active peptides and proteins derived from physiological fluids, such as blood, bile, and urine. The presence of high salt concentrations in such fluids can dramatically affect analyte separation efficiency in CE. Also, these biological matrix components can complicate and even degrade electrophoretic stacking

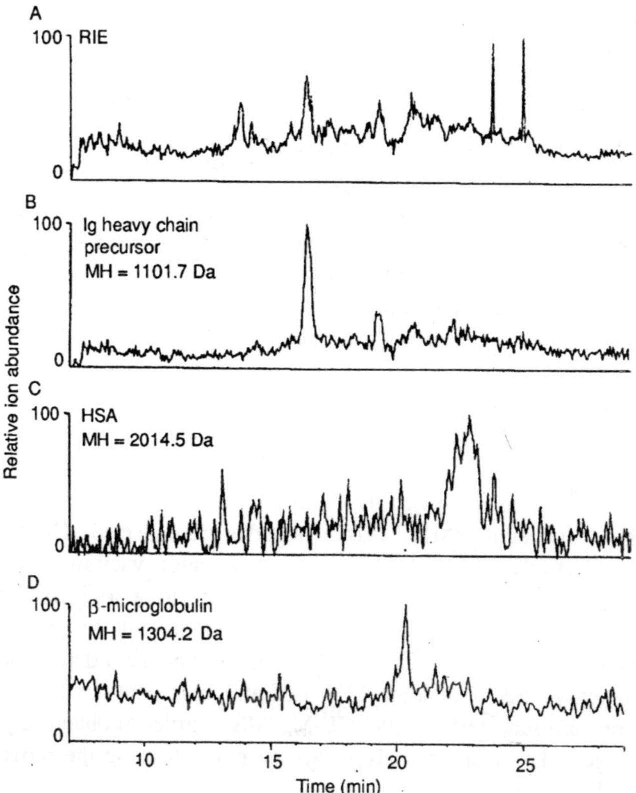

Fig. 1.3. cIEF-MS analysis of human cerebrospinal fluid (CSF). A–Reconstructed ion Electropherogram; B–Tentative identification of β_2-microglobulin with the CSF; C–Identification of human serum albumin (HSA); D–Identification of β_2-microglobulin within the CSF.

and focusing procedures. The mPC-CE-MS approach is relatively unaffected by such contaminants and the process actually removes them prior to CE electrophoretic separation.

Biologically active peptides

A number of studies have been undertaken in the use of mPC-CE-MS and tandem MS for the separation, detection, and sequencing of peptides. However, the ultimate goal was to develop a microanalytical technique for the analysis of peptides present in complex mixtures at low concentration levels (n*M*–p*M*), typically found in biological fluids, tissue, and cell cultures. In this regard, we have investigated the most suitable preconcentration membrane for use in such analyses, optimal peptide elution conditions, moving boundary tITP conditions, capillary coatings, and capillary internal diameter. Furthermore, we have demonstrated the use of an integrated approach of mPC-tITP-CE with microspray MS, as well as improved tandem MS sensitivity in conjunction with mPC-CE-MS.

Membrane PC-CE-MS has been used in the detection of growth factors IgF-I and IgF-II derived from cell media. However, the primary impetus for the development and optimization of mPC-CE-MS and tandem MS was in the analysis of MHC class I peptides. These 8–10 amino-acid peptides are important signals in mammalian immune systems. However, characterization and sequence determination of individual peptides presents a formidable analytical challenge. This because ~10,000–15,000 such peptides, each of unique sequence, can be presented at the cell surface. Also, many of these peptides are found at very low concentrations (10^{-12}– 10^{-18} *M*).

The strategy we have developed for sequencing MHC class I peptides has been described in detail, but, briefly, HPLC fractions (~100 μL) containing MHC class I peptides are collected. The organic solvent (CH_3OH or CH_3CN) is removed under vacuum and each fraction is diluted with CE separation buffer to a total volume of ~150 μL. Approximately 50 μL is loaded off-line via the pressurized bomb and subjected to mPC-CE-MS for molecular mass determination. Subsequently, precursor ions (MH^+) of antigenic peptides or peptides of interest are subjected to mPC-CE-MS/MS in order to obtain sequence information. These latter analyses are carried out using the remaining ~100 μL of sample.

In a specific instance, naturally processed MHC class I peptides were isolated from ~10^9 EG-7 mouse tumor cells. This cell line had been transvected with the ovalbumin gene, along with the actin promoter. The cells were harvested, lysed, and MHC class I peptides obtained as described previously. Subsequently, all HPLC fractions were subjected to a T-cell stimulation immunoassay. Once such fraction exhibited a positive T-cell stimulation response. This fraction (~50 μL) was then subjected to mPC-CE-MS analysis to ascertain the number and molecular weights of peptides present. A myriad of peptide responses were detected, indicating that in most cases such analyses should be carried out in conjunction with a targeted immunoassay or other bioassay approach. However, in this particular case, a peptide with migration time ~23 min afforded an ion MH_2^{2+} = 482.3. This corresponds to the molecular weight of an ovalbumin peptide, OVA, a known antigen of this particular mouse model system. Another EG-7

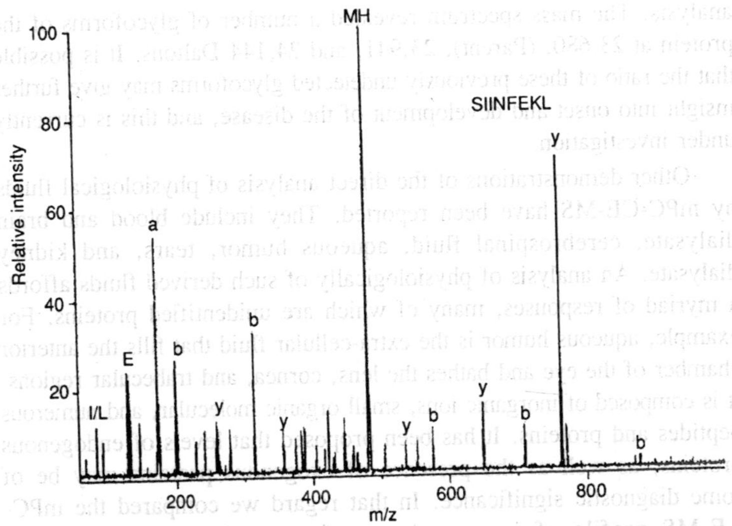

Fig. 1.4. Membrane PC-tITP-CE-microspray-MS/MS analysis of MH_2^{2+} =482.3.

tumor cell preparation was ultimately subjected to mPC-CE-MS/MS using a polybrene-coated capillary in conjunction with microspray-MS, in order to achieve maximum sensitivity and sequence data on the peptide. The ion at m/z 482.3 was subjected to collision induced dissociation conditions previously shown to afford significant fragmentation of the precursor ion. Based on both the clear 'y' and 'b' series of ions, as well as the returned SEAQUEST search, the sequence was determined to be SIINFEKL, confirming the presence of the OVA peptide in this fraction. This overall strategy has been used to successfully analyze and obtain other peptides sequence data from K^b EG-7, K^b EL-4, and PVG R1 rat spleen cell lines.

Proteins from physiological fluids

One-step, on-line analysis of physiological fluids (e.g., urine, bile, plasma, tears) by mPC-CE-MS has substantial potential in the development of suitable biomarkers for diagnosis of disease states. We have previously reported the utilization of this approach for the detection of Bence-Jones protein(s) in urine. This protein(s) is a known *biomarker* for patients suffering from multiple myeloma. Typically, a 24-h urine sample is collected followed by numerous sample handling and separation steps in order to detect the presence of the protein. This is in stark contrast to the ~30-min analysis time of the urine sample by mPC-CE-MS. Approximately 1.5 μL of urine obtained from a patient suffering from acute multiple myeloma was subjected to mPC-CE-MS analysis. The mass spectrum revealed a number of glycoforms of the protein at 23,680, (Parent), 23,941, and 24,144 Daltons. It is possible that the ratio of these previously undetected glycoforms may give further insight into onset and development of the disease, and this is currently under investigation.

Other demonstrations of the direct analysis of physiological fluids by mPC-CE-MS have been reported. They include blood and brain dialysate, cerebrospinal fluid, aqueous humor, tears, and kidney dialysate. An analysis of physiologically of such derived fluids affords a myriad of responses, many of which are unidentified proteins. For example, aqueous humor is the extra-cellular fluid that fills the anterior chamber of the eye and bathes the lens, cornea, and trabecular regions. It is composed of inorganic ions, small organic molecular, and numerous peptides and proteins. It has been proposed that levels of endogenous proteins, as well as the presence of exogenous proteins may be of some diagnostic significance. In that regard we compared the mPC-CE-MS profile of aqueous humor from patients with cataracts ("normal") to patients suffering from glaucoma. It is clear that the

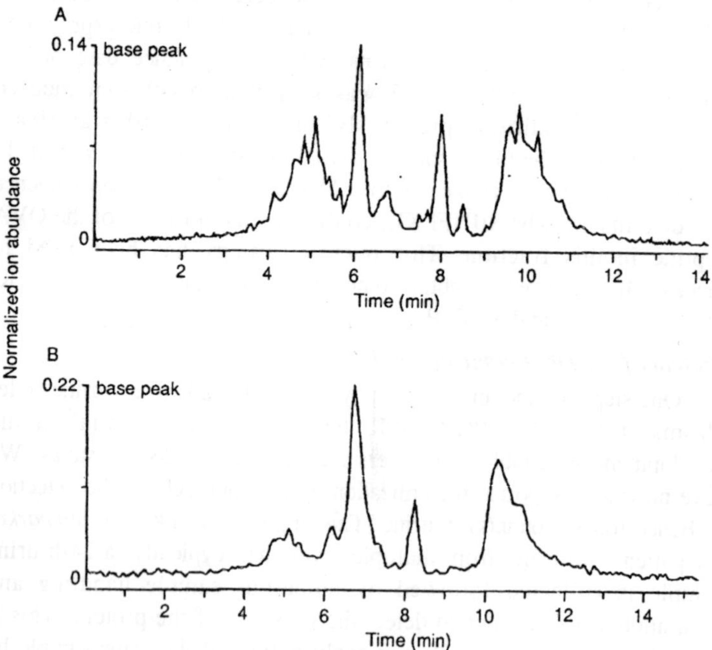

Fig. 1.5. Direct analysis by mPC-CE-MS of aqueous humor from a patient undergoing surgery for (A) cataracts, (B) glaucoma by mPC-CE-MS.

'normal' aqueous humor contains many more protein responses than that of the glaucoma aqueous humor, and we are in the process of attempting to identify individual protein constituents in order to understand the comparative differences. This may give more insight into the basic mechanisms involved in the onset of glaucoma.

It is clear from the mPC-CE-MS analysis of aqueous humor, described earlier, that ultimately rapid identification of proteins derived from physiological fluids is necessary. This has recently been described for the identification of a renal dialysate protein. A number of patients at Mayo had a rare renal tumor that was shown to inhibit renal epithelial phosphate transport. Approximately 200 L of renal dialysate was collected from these patients and ultimately reduced to ~6 mL.

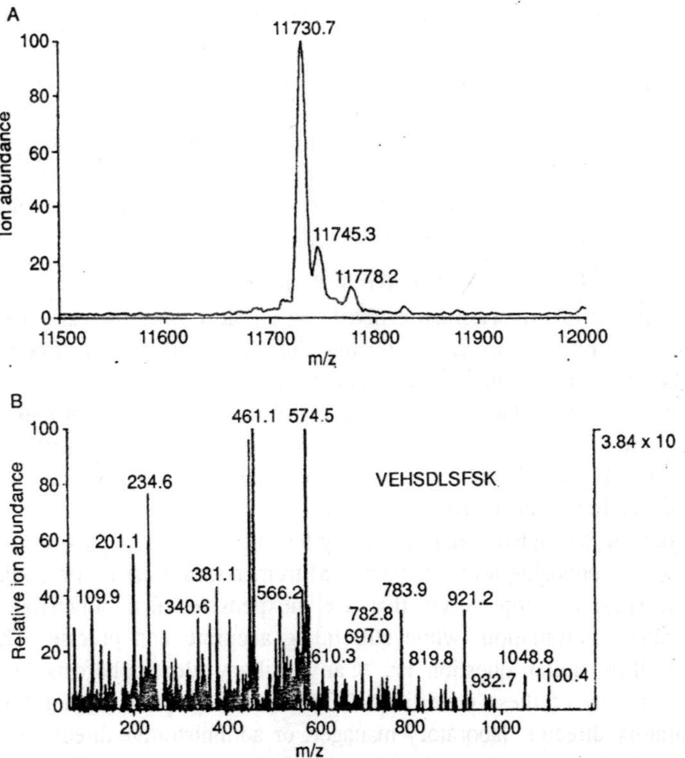

Fig. 1.6. Identification of human renal dialysate protein obtained from 200 L of dialysate by mPC-CE-MS and tandem MS. A–mPC-CE-MS analysis of active fraction shown to inhibit phosphate uptake in renal epithelial cells. B–mPC-CE-MS/MS of precursor ion $MH_2^{2+}=574.5$ derived from lysine-C proteolytic digestion of protein.

This was achieved through a series of dialysis and size-exclusion chromatography concentration steps. The active component(s) was tracked at each stage using an opossum kidney-cell phosphate (^{32}P-labeled) uptake assay. Approximately 100 μL of the dialysate active fraction was assigned for mPC-CE-MS and tandem MS analyses. Initially, 20 μL was subjected to mPC-CE-MS and one major ion response was detected at M_r = 11,729 Daltons. The remaining ~80 μL was then digested with lysine-C proteolytic enzyme and the resulting digest subjected to mPC-CE-MS and tandem MS analysis. A series of peptides were detected including an ion at m/z 574.5, corresponding to the MH_2^{2+} = 574.5. This spectrum was searched without prior interpretation using the SEAQUEST database. The resulting peptide sequence, VEHSDLSFSK was consistent with the peptide being derived from the protein β_2-microglobulin. Surprisingly, this is a common protein found in human dialysate. At present it is not clear if the elevated levels of β_2-microglobulin interfere with phosphate uptake in renal epithelial cells or perhaps another minor component co-migrates with it. This problem is still under active investigation. Nevertheless, it is clear that mPC-CE-MS and tandem MS can play a significant role in rapidly and unequivocally identifying proteins.

Operations in Capillary Electrophoresis

Clinical laboratories had evolved considerably since the early 1980s and will continue to do so during the next millennium. Reduced turnaround time, convenience, patient satisfaction (quick diagnosis), and physician satisfaction (improved real-time clinical decision-making) are some of the benefits gained from having more clinical testing to be done in the hospital laboratory. At the same time economies of scale, reduced cost, regionalization, and continuity of care are responsible for outsourcing laboratory testing to reference laboratories. These two opposing forces have placed tremendous pressure on clinical chemists to develop assays that are inexpensive, fast, amenable to laboratory automation, while still being accurate and precise. Thus the million dollar question is: "Can capillary electrophoresis fulfill some or any of these conditions?" This is a key question that every laboratory director, laboratory manager, or administrative director must answer before introducing a new technology for patient testing.

Cost

Because CE is a separation technique, it will compete with more traditional chromatographic techniques such as *gas chromatography* (GC) and HPLC. However, unlike the classical chromatographic techniques,

CE can also compete with classical electrophoresis, such as agarose gel and isoelectric focusing. The main cost savings comes from the use of fused silica capillaries, which are less expensive than HPLC or GC columns. For instance, the cost of an HPLC column used for clinical testing can range from $250 to 300, whereas a 10-m piece of CE fused silica capillary will cost about $80. Assuming that a CE method will use a 57-cm piece of fused silica capillary and that the capillary will last ~200 injections, a very conservative estimate, one can expect at least 1800 injections from 10 m of fused silica capillary instead of 800 injections for an HPLC column. Even neutral-coated capillaries, which are appreciably more expensive than uncoated, fused silica capillaries, are less expensive than *reverse-phase* (RP) or ion exchange HPLC columns. It should be noted that in this analysis we did not account for the labor component because in our experience, the hands-on labor for CE is comparable to traditional chromatographic and electrophoretic techniques.

Speed

It is well-established that capillary electrophoretic separations are much faster than routine gel electrophoresis. This is because of the high electric field (800 V/cm) that can be reached in CE, whereas in slab gel electrophoresis the electric fields are limited to 15–40 V/cm. The field strength that can be applied to slab gels is low owing to Joule heating, which is directly related to surface-to-volume ratio. Applying higher field strengths in slab-gel electrophoresis results in a significant increase in temperature, causing irreproducible separations. For example, a 14 × 11.5 × 0.15-cm slab gel will have a surface to volume ratio that is 40 times greater than that of a typical 57 cm × 75 μm ID fused silica capillary. This high surface-to-volume ratio in CE allows efficient dissipation of joule heat allowing the use of very high electrical fields. This is best illustrated by comparing the ability of CE to perform a serum protein electrophoretic separation in less than 1 min whereas a similar separation by agarose gel electrophoresis requires 20–25 min. The one advantage that gel electrophoresis holds over CE is the ability to analyze as many as 90 samples simultaneously, overcoming the limitation of slow separation speed. This is probably the main reason why CE has not been widely used for routine analysis of serum proteins in clinical laboratories.

Potential for Automation

Commercially available capillary electrophoresis systems are remarkably simple from an instrumentation point of view. The basic instrument consists of four parts: (1) a fused silica capillary holder, (2) a high voltage power supply, (3) a detector, and (4) a safety interlock. Most instruments also provide a mechanism to control the temperature in the capillary. This may be controlled either by air cooling, using a peltier device, or by enclosing the capillary in a cartridge, which is filled with a coolant that is maintained at a constant temperature. All components of the CE are monitored or controlled by computer software. This allows the end user to develop methods and then analyze the separated components, post-electrophoresis. In this respect current CE instruments compare favorably with automated HPLC systems used in the clinical laboratory. However, unlike the highly automated instruments found in a clinical laboratory, the operation of CE instruments requires an above average amount of technical expertise. In other words, these instruments are not black boxes that just require an operator to push a switch and then wait for a result to be generated. Most importantly, in order for CE to be used routinely in the highly automated clinical laboratory, primary sample tube sampling, the ability to read a bar code, and a bidirectional interface to Laboratory Information System are required. With the exception of Beckman Paragon CZE 2000, no other CE system has this capability.

Accuracy, Sensitivity, and Precision

In CE, accuracy has never been an issue because the analyte is usually separated from interfering substances. However, the *limit of detection* (LOD) has been and still is the main problem with CE. Various manufacturers of commercial CE units have tried to address this problem by using modified capillaries (i.e., bubble-cell or z- shaped cells) or by using *laser-induced fluorescence* (LIF). Typical detection limits range from 1×10^{-6} *M* for UV detection to 1×10^{-9} *M* for LIF. Alternatively, sensitivity can also be enhanced by sample stacking. Chien et al. has comprehensively reviewed sample stacking in capillary zone electrophoresis and its applications for routine analysis. Typically, sample stacking involves a movement of sample ions across a boundary, which divides regions into high (low-conductivity sample solution or water plug) and low (high-conductivity separation solution) electric fields inside the capillary. The sample is usually dissolved in a buffer having an ionic strength that is 1/10 that of the run buffer. As a result, the electric-field gradient across the sample zone is relatively high, causing the analyte ions to migrate rapidly until they reach the interface between the sample buffer and the run buffer. On reaching the interface, the ion mobility drops, causing stacking of sample at the boundary of two solutions giving a 5- to 10-fold increase in signal-to-noise ratio. Because sample stacking relies on the enhanced electrophoretic velocities of ionic species in the low-conductivity or high-electric field region, neutral analytes are not concentrated unless they are compartmentalized in an ionic micelle. Quirino et al. described an exceptional narrowing of neutral analytes zones in electrokinetic chromatography that allowed a 5000-fold concentration of neutral analytes, such as steroids, racemic herbicides, and other biologically important compounds. This special preconcentration phenomenon, dubbed as sweeping, works for all charged and neutral compounds. Detection limits ranging from 1.7 to 9.6 ng/mL have been reported by these authors for various clinically important steroids. Although very promising, the technique needs to be applied to real patient samples. It may also require a prior sample clean up in order prevent the interference of unwanted proteins and other analytes present in the sample that also under go preconcentration.

The ability to measure precisely (analytical imprecision) an analyte is very important in a clinical laboratory. Coefficients of variation (CV) <5% are routinely observed for various analytes, such as electrolytes, enzymes, proteins, and so forth, on automated analyzers. The various factors that can affect both with in- and between-run imprecision in CE are listed here:

Capillary surface

The inner surface of the capillary, which participates in the separation process, can be a major factor in the cause of imprecision in CE. Not only does the sample, and therefore the various analytes, come in contact with the surface, but the analytes can also bind to the surface, changing the properties of the capillary. For the most part, it is best to try and eliminate any interaction of the analyte with the surface of the capillary. This can be done by deliberately changing the surface by treating with polymers, various detergents, or simply by changing the buffer or buffer concentration.

Current

When a CE instrument is "turned on" a current is generated. It is extremely important to control this current, because a variation in the current can cause a change in the temperature. A change in the temperature can result in a change in pH, which can then lead to a change in the current, the original variable that was being controlled. With the power sources available today, controlling the current is not an issue.

Capillary conditioning

In order to ensure good reproducibility in bare and coated fused silica capillaries, daily conditioning with a series of buffers is required before a capillary is used. In our experience, a daily rinse of 30 min for serum protein electrophoresis, 30 min for hemoglobin variants using capillary isoelectric focusing, 15 min for steroids using coated capillary, and 45 min on a bare fused silica capillary are very typical. Furthermore, the rinsing time is very dependent on the capillary surface and can change from one lot of capillaries to another. Most of the buffers used for capillary conditioning are quite stable if protected from the atmosphere and stored at 4°C. Hence, buffer stability is not much of an issue. For IEF, preconditioning the capillary with a 0.04% methylcellulose and ampholine solution is extremely important to ensure reproducible migration times. In our hands, the CV for migration time increased from <5 to >20% when the pre-rinsing time is shortened from 30 min to 10 min for the analysis of hemoglobin variants using capillary isoelectric focusing on a bare fused silica capillary.

Buffer

Although the capillary wall can significantly affect the separation, the separation also takes place in the presence of a buffer. This buffer has multiple purposes, one of which is to control the pH. It is extremely important to control pH because analyte charge, EOF, and heat production all change with even small changes in pH. The actual buffer used can also have an affect on the separation process because of interaction between the buffer and the analyte. In addition some buffers, i.e., borate or zwitterionic buffers, carry less current than mono-functional buffers like phosphate. Buffer concentration is also important because higher buffer concentrations will lessen the interaction of the analyte with the capillary wall.

Temperature

Control of the temperature within the capillary is extremely important. However, temperature control is complicated by the generation of heat (Joule heating) when current passes through a buffered solution. As mentioned previously, multiple factors (temperature, pH, and current) are interrelated. In other words, what affects one will potentially affect the other. With current instruments, the temperature is controlled either by air cooling, a peltier device, or by enclosing the capillary in a cartridge, which is filled with a coolant maintained at a constant temperature. For most applications, the use of a coolant will control temperature better than air-cooling.

Sample injection

In the past, sample injection was a major source of error for traditional CE systems. However, with the use of high-precision pressure valves, this problem has been significantly reduced.

Modes of CE

CE is highly versatile, with numerous modes of operation, which are accessed, in many instances, by altering the buffer composition. The commonly used modes of CE include CZE, *capillary gel electrophoresis* (CGE), CIEF, and *capillary isotachophoresis* (CITP).

Capillary zone electrophoresis (CZE)

CZE, the simplest form of CE, requires filling the capillary with only running buffer. In this form of CE, the ionic solutes migrate with different velocities (as determined by their charge-to-mass ratio) forming discrete zones in the running buffer. By using the *electroosmotic flow* (EOF), separation of many of the cationic and anionic solutes is possible. Neutral solutes, which move with the EOF, are not separated. Applications of CZE include analysis of amino acids, peptides, protein analysis—including screening of proteins variants and evaluating protein purity—and forensic applications.

Micellar electrokinetic chromatography (MEKC or MECC)

MEKC is a combination of electrophoresis and chromatography in which both neutral and charged solutes can be separated. This form of CE takes advantage of a property that when the concentration of some surfactants reach the critical micelle concentration, aggregates (micelles) are formed that help separate neutral species. These spherical micelles contain the hydrophobic tails of the surfactant molecules directed towards the center and charged heads directed toward the outside buffer. The micelles are thus charged and migrate, depending on their charge, after application of a potential field across the capillary. Solutes are partitioned between the micelles and liquid phase leading to differential retention and separation of the solutes. The physical nature of the micelle can be changed using different types of surfactant thus altering the selectivity of the micelle. Some applications of MEKC include separation of amino acids, heavy metals, nucleotides, vitamins, drugs.

Capillary gel electrophoresis (CGE)

"Gels" used in CGE are a polymer network of compounds such as bispolyacrylamide, agarose, or methylcellulose, and separate high molecular weight compounds by the sieving effect of the polymer network. CGE can separate DNA and denatured proteins. CGE has been applied in the analysis of *polymerase chain reaction* (PCR) products, purity of oligonucleotides, sequencing of DNA, and so forth.

Capillary isoelectric focusing (CIEF)

CIEF is a technique that separates peptides and proteins on the basis of isoelectric point (pI) and can separate proteins with a pI difference of as little as 0.005 pI units. This technique is applied to the separation of hemoglobins and hemoglobin variants, protein isoforms, and immunoglobulins that are difficult to separate by other methods.

Capillary isotachophoresis (CITP)

CITP is a moving boundary electrophoretic technique that uses a combination of two buffer systems to create a state where the separated zones move at the same velocity. These zones are sandwiched between leading and terminating electrolytes, making it possible to separate either anions or cations, but not both, in a single experiment. CITP can be used to concentrate the solutes before CZE, MEKC, or CGE. When used in this manner it is known as transient CITP.

Applications of Capillary Electrophoresis in Clinical Settings

Serum and Urinary Proteins

Serum proteins that are routinely analyzed by thin-layer agarose gels can be separated and analyzed with greater precision by CZE. A combination of CZE and immunosubstraction has been shown to be well suited for routine serum protein analysis in the clinical laboratory. This system can detect different paraproteins at levels of 500 mg/L for IgG, 750 mg/L for IgA, and 750 mg/L for IgM. Using computer software available with current CE instrumentation, it is possible to magnify different regions of the electropherogram, improving the ability to distinguish abnormal peaks in the β-globulin region. One drawback of this system, however, is inability to detect β-lipoproteins and mini monoclonal bands that show up as faint bands on agarose gels. Ethanol precipitation for concentrating urine samples has been found to be an effective method to analyze urine proteins, including Bence-Jones proteins by CZE. It is also possible to detect Bence-Jones proteinuria (range 0.04–9.7 g/L), intact immunoglobulins, and Tamm Horsfall proteins in unconcentrated urine samples by CE.

Lipoproteins

CITP has been used to perform serum lipoprotein analysis. CITP can be used to directly identify apolipoprotein A-I (apoA-I) from serum, although identification of apolipoprotein A-II (apoA-II) requires some sample preparation because it migrates with the albumin. By plotting a graph of peak areas vs standard concentration it is possible to quantitate the two apolipoproteins. Thus, it is possible to predict the risk of development of premature atherosclerosis by determining the ratio of apoA-I and apoA-II. Although useful in research studies, the method lacks the simplicity offered by photometric or immunoassays available in the clinical laboratory.

Analysis of Organ Function Tests

MEKC has been used to determine antipyrine levels in saliva or plasma after oral administration to assess liver microsomal enzyme activity. CZE and MEKC methods have been developed to identify different phenotypes for hydroxylation and acetylation enzymes involved in metabolism of drugs by determining levels of different drug metabolites in urine.

Serum and Urine Steroid Levels

Determination of levels of different hormones in serum is important for diagnosing various endocrinological disorders. MEKC can effectively separate and quantify a variety of corticosteroids such as corticosterone, cortisone, cortisol, aldosterone, 21-deoxycortisol, 1-dehydroaldosterone, and 17-isoaldosterone. CE can also identify and separate estrogens such as urinary estrone and estriol, but not 17 β-estradiol, because its concentration is too low to be detected by this method. A competitive solution-phase immunoassay has been developed for separation and quantitation of serum cortisol by CE combined with laser-induced fluorescence. An assay for urinary free cortisol, unaffected by other urinary metabolites, has also been shown to detect cortisol concentrations as low as 10 μg/L.

Vitamins and Minerals

By using CZE, vitamin A and vitamin A binding protein can be detected from one or two drops of blood or from air-dried blood samples that have been collected on filter paper. This can be a useful tool for screening vitamin A levels in infants and young children. CE can detect vitamin C levels in urine, serum, and even fruit beverages. It is also possible to identify and quantitate trace amounts of iron in human serum by CE. This method, which is sensitive enough to detect iron in as little as a single drop (10 μL) of serum, could be suitable for diagnosing iron-deficiency anemia.

Serum Bilirubin

MECC in conjunction with LIF can separate and detect four bilirubin species, the unconjugated form, monoester and diester conjugates of bilirubin, and bilirubin covalently linked to albumin, directly from human serum. This method can also detect bilirubin at concentrations much lower than that detected by routine visible light absorption methods. Although it is possible to use CE to separate and detect various forms of bilirubin, it is unlikely that a CE assay will be used in the clinical laboratory. This is because at present, CE methods cost appreciably more than current automated methods.

Cytokines

Detection of cytokines involved in inflammation in pathological tissue samples can be a good indicator of persistence of disease in addition to help gauge its severity. Microdissection followed by CZE of frozen sections of renal biopsy material obtained from patients with *acquired immune deficiency syndrome* (AIDS) has been developed to identify tissue bound inflammatory cytokines, such as interleukin-1 (IL-1), interleukin-2 (IL-2), tumor necrosis factor-α (INF-α), and so on. This was done to study the pathobiology of renal disease in AIDS and showed higher levels of IL- 1, TNF-α and IL-6 in the glomerular and interstitial tissue of patients with HIV-associated glomerulonephritis as compared to non-HIV associated glomerulonephritis. Although useful in research, cytokine assays have not found a routine use in the clinical laboratory.

Hemoglobin and its Variants

Capillary isoelectric focusing (CIEF) has been helpful in making the differential diagnosis of S/beta thalassemia, G-Philadelphia trait, S/C-Harlem disease, and HbH disease. In addition, CIEF can identify hemoglobin-oxidation products, which can bias HbA1c results, produced by improper storage. Another important use of this method was in the detection of minor hemoglobin variants like HbA2', an indicator of an alpha globin mutation. CIEF has also been shown to be useful in the neonatal screening for hemoglobin variants using blood samples collected on filter paper.

Porphyrins

CZE or MECC with fluorescence detection can separate and quantitate porphyrin and its precursors in urine. Although cost-effective and potentially useful in the diagnosis of porphyria, CE has not yet found its way into laboratories involved in the study of porphyrin metabolism.

Inorganic Ions

CE can separate inorganic cations such as potassium, calcium, sodium, and magnesium in a single run from serum. It can also detect calcium, ammonia, sodium, magnesium, lithium, barium, and creatinine in urine. Biologically active ionized calcium and total calcium can also be identified and quantitated by CZE in human serum using indirect photometric detection in a single run. The ability to detect many components in one run can give CE an advantage over autoanalyzers. However, owing to the highly automated nature and speed of analyzers present in the clinical laboratory, it is highly unlikely that CE will be used as the method of choice for these analytes.

Nitrite and nitrate, oxidation products of nitric oxide, which is an important agent in shock and organ failure in critically ill patients, can be determined by CZE in plasma and urine samples without any pre-treatment of the samples. The clinical usefulness of such an assay is still to be determined.

Inborn Errors of Metabolism

CE allows easy, rapid identification and quantitation of organic acids such as methylmalonic, pyroglutamic, and glutaric acids in urine or serum. These organic acids can be increased owing to deficiency of enzymes in amino-acid metabolism. Methylmalonic acid can also be increased when there is a deficiency of folate or Vitamin B_{12}.

CZE can also effectively separate purine bases and nucleosides, such as adenine, guanine, hypoxanthine, and uric acid from neonatal plasma. Deficiency of adenylosuccinate lyase in the purine metabolism pathway leads to accumulation of succinyladenosine and succinyl-aminoimidazole carboxamide riboside in body fluids that can be identified by CE.

Serum and Urine Analysis of Drugs

MEKC has been applied to therapeutic drug monitoring. Using MEKC theophylline and its analogues have been separated in plasma. In addition, it has been used to detect and quantitate serum levels of digoxin. MEKC can also efficiently separate and quantitate antiepileptic drugs that are used in combination, especially ethosuxamide, phenobarbitol, phenytoin, and carbamazepine. CE has also been used in the clinical and forensic arena. In these cases, the use of urine to identify intoxication and/or drug abuse of opiates, barbiturates, benzodiazepines, stimulants, and doping screening is possible within a few minutes. It is also possible to use CE to screen post mortem fluids for illicit drugs or elevated levels of legal drugs. CE has also been applied to determine the tissue concentration of 5-Fluorouracil (5-Fl) in tumor and subcutaneous adipose tissue microdialysates from patients with primary breast cancer.

Urine Myoglobin

CE has been used separate myoglobin from hemoglobin, another pigmented protein in urine. It can detect and quantitate myoglobin in urine obtained from patients with muscular dystrophy, severe trauma, infections, and intoxication. This helps in monitoring muscle dystrophies, trauma, and acute myocardial infarction.

Cerebrospinal Fluid (CSF)

CZE can play an important role in the biochemical diagnosis of central nervous system (CNS) diseases identifying and quantitating lactate, pyruvate oxalate, fumarate, acetate, glutamate, and ascorbate in CSF. Increased ratios of lactate and pyruvate have been observed in cerebral infarction and bacterial meningitis. CZE can also identify ascorbic acid in CSF, which is decreased in inflammatory conditions of CNS. In addition, CZE has been shown to useful in detecting oligoclonal banding in unconcentrated CSF.

Analysis of PCR Products

Future trends are toward using combined PCR and CE for clinical analysis of PCR products. PCR can be used to amplify genomic material; however, it can not quantitate it. In conjunction with CE, reasonably rapid quantitation is possible. A good example of this is how CE has been used along with PCR to quantitate the viral load in HIV patients. CGE can also effectively separate DNA restriction fragments and specific amplified DNA sequences from HIV-1 virus in blood. Reverse transcription products generated from the RNA of poliovirus can be separated and quantitated by CGE. DNA sequencing by CGE is one of the fastest techniques in DNA analysis.

2

DNA Structure and Genome

Each person's genome contains a large amount of DNA that is a potential target for DNA profiling. The selection of the particular region of polymorphic DNA to analyse can change with the individual case and also the technology that is available. In this chapter a brief description of the primary structure of the DNA molecule is provided along with an overview of the different categories of DNA that make up the human genome. The criteria that the forensic geneticist uses to select which loci to analyse are also discussed.

DNA Structure

DNA has often been described as the '*blueprint of life*', containing all the information that an organism requires in order to function and reproduce. The DNA molecule that carries out such a fundamental biological role is relatively simple. The basic building block of the DNA molecule is the nucleotide triphosphate. This comprises a triphosphate group, a deoxyribose sugar and one of four bases.

The information within the DNA '*blueprint*' is coded by the sequence of the four different nitrogenous bases, adenine, guanine, thymine and cytosine, on the sugar-phosphate backbone.

DNA normally exists as a double stranded molecule which adopts a helical arrangement – first described by Watson and Crick in 1953. Each base is attracted to its complementary base: adenine always pairs with thymine and cytosine always pairs with guanine.

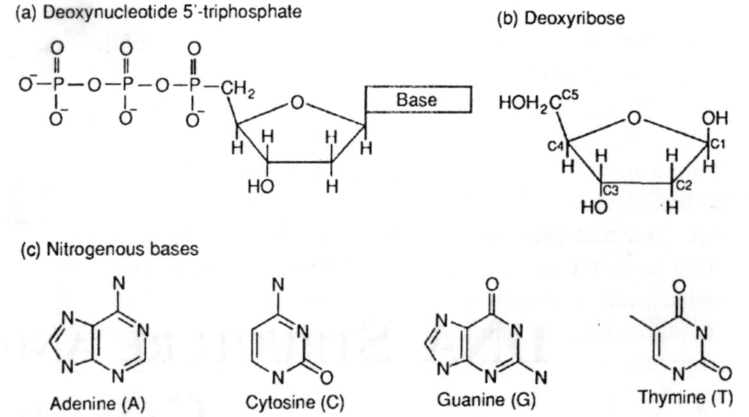

(a) Deoxynucleotide 5'-triphosphate

(b) Deoxyribose

(c) Nitrogenous bases

Adenine (A) Cytosine (C) Guanine (G) Thymine (T)

Fig. 2.1. The DNA molecule is built up of deoxynucleotide 5'-triphosphates. The sugar contains five carbon atoms (labelled C1 to C5); one of four different types of nitrogenous base is attached to the 1 prime carbon, a hydroxyl group to the 3' carbon and the phosphate group to the 5' carbon.

Organization of DNA into Chromosomes

Within each nucleated human cell there are two complete copies of the genome. The genome is 'the haploid genetic complement of a living organism' and in humans contains approximately 3200000000 base pairs (bp) of information, which is organized into 23 chromosomes. Humans contain two sets of chromosomes – one version of each chromosome inherited from each parent giving a total of 46 chromosomes. Each chromosome contains one continuous strand of DNA, the largest – chromosome 1 – is approximately 250 000 000 bp long while the smallest – chromosome 22 – is approximately 50000000 bp.

In physical terms the chromosomes range in length from 73 mm to 14 mm. The chromosomes are in the metaphase stage of the cell cycle and are highly condensed – when the cell is not undergoing division the chromosomes are less highly ordered and are more diffuse within the nucleus. To achieve the highly ordered chromosome structure, the DNA molecule is associated with histone proteins, which help the packaging and organization of the DNA into the ordered chromosome structure.

Structure of the Human Genome

Great advances have been made in our understanding of the human genome in recent years, in particular through the work of the Human Genome Project that was officially started in 1990 with the central

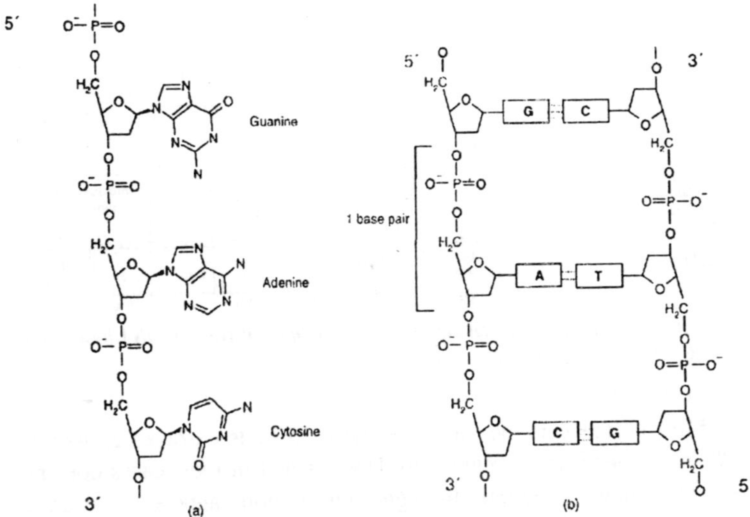

Fig. 2.2. In the DNA molecule the nucleotides are joined together by phosphodiester bonds to form a single stranded molecule (a). The DNA molecule in the cell is double stranded (b) with two complementary single stranded molecules held together by hydrogen bonds.

aim of decoding the entire genome. It involved a collaborative effort involving 20 centres in China, France, Germany, Great Britain, Japan and the United States. A draft sequence was produced in 2001 that covered 90 % of the euchromatic DNA, this was followed by later versions that described the sequence of 99% of the euchromatic DNA with an accuracy of 99.99%. The genome can be divided into different categories of DNA based on the structure and function of the sequence.

Coding and Regulatory Sequence

The regions of DNA that encode and regulate the synthesis of proteins are called genes; at the latest estimate the human genome contains only 20,000–25,000 genes and only around 1.5% of the genome is directly involved in encoding for proteins. Gene structure, sequence and activity are a focus of medical genetics due to the interest in genetic defects and the expression of genes within cells. Approximately 23.5% of the genome is classified as genic sequence, but does not encode proteins. The non-coding genic sequence contains several elements that are involved with the regulation of genes, including promoters, enhancers, repressors and polyadenylation signals; the majority of gene related DNA, around 23%, is made up of introns, pseudogenes and gene fragments.

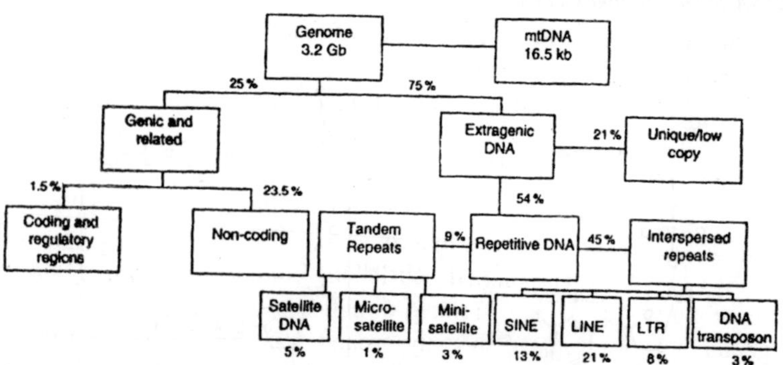

Fig. 2.3. The human genome can be classified into different types of DNA based on its structure and function.

Extragenic DNA

Most of the genome, approximately 75%, is extragenic. Around 20% of the genome is single copy DNA which in most cases does not have any known function although some regions appear to be under evolutionary pressure and presumably play an important, but as yet unknown, role.

The largest portion of the genome - over 50% - is composed of repetitive DNA; 45% of the repetitive DNA is interspersed, with the repeat elements dispersed throughout the genome. The four most common types of interspersed repetitive element - *short interspersed elements* (SINEs), *long interspersed elements* (LINEs), *long terminal repeats* (LTRs) and DNA transposons - account for 45% of the genome. These repeat sequences are all derived through transposition. The most common interspersed repeat element is the *Alu* SINE; with over 1 million copies, the repeat is approximately 300 bp long and comprises around 10% of the genome. There is a similar number of LINE elements within the genome, the most common is LINE1, which is between 6–8 kb long, and is represented in the genome around 900000 times; LINEs make up around 20% of the genome. The other class of repetitive element is tandemly repeated DNA. This can be separated into three different types: satellite DNA, minisatellites, and micro-satellites.

Genetic Diversity of Modern Humans

The aim of using genetic analysis for forensic casework is to produce a DNA profile that is highly discriminating - the ideal would be to generate a DNA profile that is unique to each individual. This allows biological evidence from the scene of a crime to be matched to an individual with a high level of confidence and can be very powerful forensic evidence.

The ability to produce highly discriminating profiles is dependent on individuals being different at the genetic level and, with the exception of identical twins, no two individuals have the same DNA. However, individuals, even ones that appear very different, are actually very similar at the genetic level. Indeed, if we compare the human genome to that of our closest animal cousin, the chimpanzee, with whom we share a common ancestor around 6 million years ago, we find that our genomes have diverged by only around 5%; the DNA sequence has diverged by only 1.2% and insertions and deletions in both human and chimpanzee genomes account for another 3.5% divergence. This means that we share 95% of our DNA with chimps! Modern humans have a much more recent common history, which has been dated using genetic and fossil data to around 150000 years ago. In this limited time, nucleotide substitutions have led to an average of one difference every 1000–2000 bases between every human chromosome, averaging one difference every 1250 bp – which means that we share around 99.9% of our genetic code with each other. Some additional variation is caused by insertions, deletions and length polymorphisms, and segmental duplications of the genome. There have been attempts to define populations genetically based on their racial identity or geographical location, and while it has been possible to classify individuals genetically into broad racial/geographic groupings, it has been shown that most genetic variation, around 85%, can be attributed to differences between individuals within a population. Differences between regions tend to be geographic gradients (clines), with gradual changes in allele frequencies.

From a forensic point there is very little point in analysing the 99.9% of human DNA that is common between individuals. Fortunately, there are well characterized regions within the genome that are variable between individuals and these have become the focus of forensic genetics.

Genome and Forensic Genetics

With advances in molecular biology techniques it is now possible to analyse any region within the 3.2 billion bases that make up the genome. DNA loci that are to be used for forensic genetics should have some key properties, they should ideally:

- be highly polymorphic (varying widely between individuals);
- be easy and cheap to characterize;

- give profiles that are simple to interpret and easy to compare between laboratories;
- not be under any selective pressure;
- have a low mutation rate.

Tandem Repeats

Two important categories of tandem repeat have been used widely in forensic genetics: minisatellites, also referred to as *variable number tandem repeats* (VNTRs); and microsatellites, also referred to as *short tandem repeats* (STRs). The general structure of VNTRs and STRs is the same. Variation between different alleles is caused by a difference in the number of repeat units that results in alleles that are of different lengths and it is for this reason that tandem repeat polymorphisms are known as length polymorphisms.

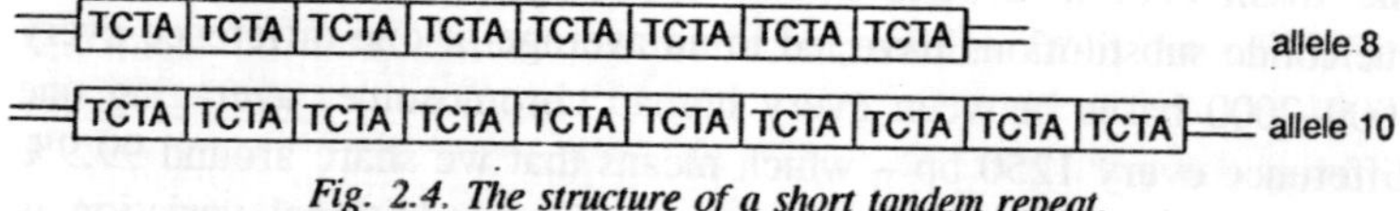

Fig. 2.4. The structure of a short tandem repeat.

Variable Number Tandem Repeats – VNTRs

VNTRs are located predominantly in the subtelomeric regions of chromosomes and have a core repeat sequence that ranges in size from 6 to 100 bp. The core repeats are represented in some alleles thousands of times; the variation in repeat number creates alleles that range in size from 500 bp to over 30 kb. The number of potential alleles can be very large: the MS 1 locus for example, has a relatively short and simple core repeat unit of 9 bp with alleles that range from approximately 1 kb to over 20 kb – which means that there are potentially over 2000 different alleles at this locus.

VNTRs were the first polymorphisms used in DNA profiling and they were successfully used in forensic casework for several years. The use of VNTRs was, however, limited by the type of sample that could be successfully analysed because a large amount of high molecular weight DNA was required. Interpreting VNTR profiles could also be problematic. Their use in forensic genetics has now been replaced by short tandem repeats (STRs).

Short Tandem Repeats – STRs

STRs are currently the most commonly analysed genetic polymorphism in forensic genetics. They were introduced into casework in the mid-1990s and are now the main tool for just about every forensic laboratory in the world – the vast majority of forensic genetic casework involves the analysis of STR polymorphisms. There are thousands of STRs that can potentially be used for forensic analysis. STR loci are spread throughout the genome including the 22 autosomal chromosomes and the X and Y sex chromosomes. They have a core unit of between 1 and 6 bp and the repeats typically range from 50 to 300 bp. The majority of the loci that are used in forensic genetics are tetranucleotide repeats, which have a four base pair repeat motif.

STRs satisfy all the requirements for a forensic marker: they are robust, leading to successful analysis of a wide range of biological material; the results generated in different laboratories are easily compared; they are highly discriminatory, especially when analysing a large number of loci simultaneously (multiplexing); they are very sensitive, requiring only a few cells for a successful analysis; it is relatively cheap and easy to generate STR profiles; and there is a large number of STRs throughout the genome that do not appear to be under any selective pressure.

Single Nucleotide Polymorphisms (SNPs)

The simplest type of polymorphism is the SNP; single base differences in the sequence of the DNA. SNPs are formed when errors (mutations) occur as the cell undergoes DNA replication during meiosis. Some regions of the genome are richer in SNPs than others, for example chromosome 1 contains a SNP on average every 1.45 kb compared with chromosome 19, where SNPs occur on average every 2.18 kb.

5'-GATGGCA-3' allele G

*

5'-GATAGCA-3' allele A

Fig. 2.5. A single nucleotide polymorphism (SNP).

SNPs normally have just two alleles, for example one allele with a guanine and one with an adenine, and therefore are not highly polymorphic and do not fit with the ideal properties of DNA polymorphisms for forensic analysis. However, SNPs are so abundant throughout the genome that it is theoretically possible to type hundreds of them. This will make the combined power of discrimination very high. It is estimated that to achieve the same discriminatory power that is achieved using 10 STRs, 50–80 SNPs would have to be analysed. With current technology, this is much more difficult than analysing 10 STR loci. With the exception of the analysis of mitochondrial DNA SNPs have not been used widely in forensic science to date, and the dominance of tandem repeated DNA will continue for the foreseeable future. SNPs are however finding a number of niche applications.

3

AGE DETECTION

The estimation of age at death based on anatomical information from the lower extremity involves an assessment of physiological age and an attempt to correlate it with chronological age. Specific techniques employed in this process vary with the sample available for analysis as well as the general age of the individual. Some techniques are specific to particular bones or even parts of bones. Techniques that would be ideal to use to estimate age at death in fetal remains are irrelevant in adults. Some consideration also must be given to sex and population differences and their impact on age indicators. In this chapter, the relevant literature will be reviewed and recommendations for appropriate procedures will be provided. In recognition of the focus of this volume, this discussion will be limited to the lower extremity, although workers should be aware that additional and perhaps more accurate techniques may be available when other anatomical areas are present.

The complex processes of growth, maturation, and subsequent degeneration associated with aging produce changes in the lower extremity that can prove useful in the estimation of age at death. Such changes include the increase in external dimensions, the appearance and union of epiphyses and other ossification centers, remodeling, bone loss, arthritic changes, and shifts in chemical composition. Information regarding growth, epiphyseal appearance, and union is most useful for immature individuals and has even been used to predict future growth in living individuals. The remaining processes provide information that is most useful for estimating age at death in adults.

FETAL BODY MEASUREMENTS

Fetal measurements provide useful information about changes with aging in forensic cases in which a sufficient amount of soft tissue is present.

According to pediatric literature the measurements most commonly used in the fetus are total body length and crown rump length; however, anthropometric information from the lower extremity is useful. Scammon describes methods of using data from the lower extremity, including leg length, thigh length (trochanter to knee), and foot length. Age is listed in terms of lunar months (i.e., calculated from the beginning of the last menstruation of the mother). De Vasconcellos et al. provide additional data on foot length.

Bone Formation and Growth

The formation and development of bone is a complex process. As noted by Gardner and Gray, prenatal development of the femur (as well as other long bones) involves the formation and subsequent erosion of a primary bone collar and calcification of cartilage with subsequent destruction of cartilage, endochondral ossification, periosteal bone formation, trabeculation of the bone collar, fusion of endochondral trabeculae with the inner aspect of the periosteal shell, and formation of a central medullary cavity free of trabeculae. Of course, variations of the normal ossification pattern may occur.

The increase in the dimensions of bones of the lower extremity provides a major source of information regarding age at death for immature individuals. With increasing age, differences between the sexes, among populations, and among individuals within populations lead to an increase in such variation, thereby limiting the accuracy of age estimation. The many factors that influence growth (genetics, nutrition, morbidity, etc.) also affect the correlation of bone size with chronological age. Accuracy diminishes with increasing age, even if these variables can be controlled (known sex, population, etc.). Such data are the most accurate and reliable sources of information in fetal remains.

Estimates of age at death can also be generated using measurements of skeletal remains. Scheuer et al. provide regression equations to estimate fetal age on the basis of limb bone length. Their study included measurements taken from radiographs of the femur and tibia from British fetuses aged 24 to 46 wk. Regressions are published separately for each sex as well as for both sexes combined.

Fazekas and Kosa provide a method for estimating chronological age at death from fetal remains through their analysis of a large Hungarian sample. They examined 138 fetuses (71 males and 67 females) with ages at death ranging from the third to the tenth lunar month and body lengths ranging from 9 to 55 cm. Measurements of bones in the lower extremity included femur length and width, tibia length, fibula length, and length of the first metatarsal. Regression equations for calculating body length from long bones in the lower extremity generated from this study consist of the following:

$$\text{femur length (cm)} \times 6.44 + 4.51$$

$$\text{femur width (cm)} \times 22.63 + 7.57$$

$$\text{tibia length (cm)} \times 7.24 + 4.90$$

$$\text{fibula length (cm)} \times 7.59 + 4.68$$

The formula for the maximum length of the first metatarsal is as follows:

$$\text{body length (cm)} = \text{length (cm)} \times 29.38 + 12.69$$

This approach differs from the method of Scheuer et al., in that it relies on body length, which must then be converted to chronological age.

One issue in assessing age at death based on fetal remains concerns differences in bone size as it appears in radiographs vs direct measurements of bone in a skeletonized condition. For example, the Scheuer et al. study, whose findings are summarized above, reported measurements from radiographs with soft tissue present.

The Fazekas and Kosa measurements were taken directly from the bones (no soft tissue). Similarly, the solution to forensic problems may involve measurements of recovered bones or radiographs of fetal remains with soft tissue present.

Growth: Infancy through Adolescence

After birth, the complex growth process causes the dimensions of bones in the lower limbs to continue to increase until maturity. The most accurate data correlating long bone length with chronological age at death originate from radiographic studies of the living.

These studies generally involve measurements of long bones and other skeletal data compared with estimates of age at death, usually derived from assessment of dental formation. Although age at death cannot be calculated as precisely after death as with tissue samples obtained from living individuals, these references provide valuable comparable data about long-bone growth in different populations.

Although bone size can provide important information regarding age at death, it is important to consider sex and population origin whenever possible. The comparative studies discussed above suggest considerable population variation, as well as considerable individual variation within populations. This variation increases with age. For example, given an individual of unknown sex, a maximum femur length of approx 310 mm would suggest an age at death of just under 8 yr if the individual was originally a member of an American population of European ancestry, but just under 12 yr if the individual was originally a member of an Eskimo population. These data reflect mean values; the actual variation among individuals could present even greater variation.

Humphrey demonstrated that the timing and expression of sexual dimorphism varies in different parts of the skeleton. Sex differences are apparent at birth in the maximum and minimum diameter of the diaphyseal femur. They are apparent at age 2.3 yr in the maximum diameter of the fibula diaphysis, 4.2 yr in the maximum diameter of the tibia diaphysis, 5.3 yr in the minimum diameter of the tibia diaphysis, 11.2 yr in the minimum diameter of the fibula diaphysis, and between 16.1 and 17.6 yr in the maximum lengths of the femur, tibia, and fibula.

If soft tissue is present, measurements can provide useful data on age. Several studies provide information on the growth of the foot. Correlations between age and calf circumference in different populations are available in Eveleth and Tanner.

Ossification Center Appearance and Epiphyseal Union

The appearance and union of the epiphyses associated with bones of the lower extremity can also provide useful information for estimating age at death, especially during adolescence. Epiphyses are the bony caps on the ends of long bones and on certain other bony structures. Their appearance and size in radiographic studies of bones with associated soft tissue are particularly useful in determining age at death.

In examinations of recovered skeletal remains, the small developing epiphyses can prove difficult to recognize and recover, and it can be difficult to identify their location within the skeleton.

This limitation also applies to newly formed ossification centers in general. Although formation data are available, they are most useful in radiographic studies when soft tissue is present, the anatomical location can be determined, and the sex is known.

Through their study of 136 human embryos, Noback and Robertson note the order of appearance of ossification centers in major bones of the lower extremity as follows: femur, tibia, fibula, metatarsals, distal phalanges, proximal phalanges, and middle phalanges. Kraus adds more detailed data on the sequence of 18 centers in the bones of the foot, beginning with the first distal phalanx and ending with the fourth intermediate phalanx. Additional supportive data are provided by O'Rahilly and Gardner, who note that ossification begins in the femur and tibia prior to the fibula.

Epiphyses are most useful in skeletal age estimation procedures when they are approximately fully formed and in the process of uniting with the associated diaphysis. The epiphyses of the lower extremity that are most useful in age estimation are those of the proximal femur, greater trochanter of the femur, distal femur, proximal tibia, distal tibia, proximal fibula, distal fibula, and the metatarsals and foot phalanges. Radiographically, ununited epiphyses can be recognized by a clear line of non-union between the epiphysis and the adjacent aspect of the bone. As the epiphyses unite, these lines diminish or disappear altogether. With bones devoid of soft tissue, evidence of non-articulation consists of an uneven and fracture-free articular surface (on the articular surfaces of both the epiphysis and the diaphysis or associated bone).

It is important to remember that a considerable length of time can elapse between the beginning and end of epiphyseal closure for each epiphysis. Thus, when using information from the literature to interpret observations on closure, attention must be paid to the definitions of closure that are used. Definitions of radiographic closure may differ slightly from those describing bones lacking soft tissue.

Since adolescent females mature earlier than males, sex should be considered in estimating age at death from epiphyseal union. Because many sources report data for the two sexes separately, sex-specific data should be consulted if the sex is known. If the sex is not known, the age range under consideration should be expanded to include the possibility of either sex. According to Lewis and Garn, many ossification centers occur approx 25% earlier in girls than in boys (e.g., approx 19% earlier in the knee area). Sex differences in the timing of union in epiphyses of the lower extremity can be in the magnitude of 1 to 2 yr.

Correlations between age at death and the timing of epiphyseal appearance and union is presented in many general references. Pyle and Hoerr provide a radiographic atlas for age progression in the knee region; a similar atlas is available for the foot and ankle. The Hoerr et al. radiographic atlas presents information and radiographic images of the foot and ankle of males and females between the ages of 38 fetal wk to adulthood.

McKern and Stewart present evidence for union in skeletal remains devoid of soft tissue, although for males of military age, only. Their study offers important data on the variation of epiphyseal union, rather than just the mean values. They found that among the epiphyses of the lower extremity, the head and distal end of the femur were especially useful.

Of course, the value of epiphyseal union for age estimation lies in the fact that all epiphyses do not unite simultaneously in any individual but vary considerably. Within the lower extremity, the epiphyses of the ankle and hip unite before those in the knee region. Note also that variations can occur, including "*pseudo-epiphyses*," which are diaphyseal extensions into the cartilaginous extremity of the bone. Individuals with a leg-length discrepancy show increased age-related variation.

Osborne et al. call attention to age changes in immature trabecular bone. Their radiological study of children aged newborn to 15 yr documents such changes in the proximal femur.

Bone Remodeling

The normal process of remodeling of compact bone in the long bones of the lower extremity provides histological information that can prove useful in estimating age at death, especially in adults. Bone remodeling involves the conversion of primary bone (i.e., that formed during the initial ossification of the bone) to secondary bone. Bone turnover is accomplished through the action of osteoclasts to create resorption spaces, which are subsequently filled in to form secondary osteons. This process begins early in life and continues until death. With increasing age, the original components of diaphyseal compact bone are gradually replaced by the new structures. Preexisting structures, such as lines of increased density, may be altered or removed. With advancing age, resorption spaces are created not only at the expense of the original circumferential lamellar bone and primary osteons but pre-existing secondary osteons as well, thereby forming secondary osteon fragments.

In 1965, Kerley introduced a histological technique based on the examination of thin cross-sections of undecalcified ground tissue removed from the mid shaft of the femur, tibia, and fibula. This technique calls for the examination of four circular fields, each measuring approximately 1.62 mm in diameter and located adjacent to the periosteal edge of the bone on its anterior, posterior, medial, and lateral surfaces. Within each of these fields, the numbers of primary osteons, secondary osteons, and osteon fragments must be counted, as well as the percentage remaining of the original circumferential lamellar bone. The technique recognizes that circumferential lamellar bone and primary osteons were formed during the original formation process. Secondary osteons and osteon fragments are created during the remodeling process. Thus with increasing age, the percentage of circumferential lamellar bone and the number of primary osteons decrease while the number of secondary osteons and osteon fragments increases. The Kerley system allows the age at death to be estimated through the use of a "*profile chart*" or regression equations. The profile chart is created by plotting age distribution data for each variable and then observing the age at which they overlap. The regression equations allow direct estimation of age for each variable.

The Kerley method is useful if complete cross-sections are available, but is limited if the external (periosteal) surface is damaged or otherwise missing. Error is introduced if visual fields are used other than those defined, because the histology of the bone cortex varies

Several modified or alternative methods have been introduced since Kerley introduced this technique. Ahlqvist and Damsten offered a modification of this technique in which the combined frequencies of secondary osteons and osteon fragments within fields located between those used by Kerley are examined. These field locations were chosen because they avoid Kerley's posterior field on the linea aspera, a site of muscle attachment and potential activity-induced change unrelated to age. However, their sample was more restricted than Kerley's, in terms of size and composition, and by combining two of Kerley's variables, they sacrificed some useful sources of information.

Another modification, suggested by Singh and Gunberg, examines the number of secondary osteons, the average number of lamellae per osteon, and the average shortest diameter between Haversian canals in two randomly selected fields within the periosteal third of the cortex. Regression equations are available from their study of 59 individuals aged 40 to 88 yr. These equations include those applicable to the femur and tibia.

In 1979, Thompson published a technique that utilizes only a small core of bone (4 mm in diameter) removed from the anterior mid shaft of the femur and the medial mid shaft of the tibia, as well as other bones. His complex method employing 19 variables was based on a sample of 116 adults. Although the method examines only one area of the bone cortex, it has the advantage of not requiring a cross section.

Watanabe et al. studied stained ground thin sections taken from the mid-shaft of the femur in 72 Japanese males aged 43 to 92 yr and 26 females aged 2 and 88 yr. They examined the area, maximum diameter, minimum diameter, and perimeter of intact osteons and Haversian canals, as well as type II osteons, fragments, and the triangular area of associated osteons. The osteon dimensions displayed a higher correlation with age than the Haversian canals.

Walker et al. reported that in individuals aged more than 50 yr, the density of osteons and osteon fragments correlated with cortical mass but not with age. These researchers urged caution in the use of these attributes to estimate histological age in individuals in this age bracket.

Of course, all of the histological methods are by nature destructive and require the necessary equipment. Experience with these techniques is also important to ensure correct identification of the structures involved.

Radiographic Approaches

A 1953 study by Hansen revealed that among adults, the medullary cavity increases in size with age. At the proximal end of the femur, the cavity advances (at the expense of trabecular bone) to the level of the surgical neck during the fourth decade and reaches the epiphyseal line between 61 and 74 yr. The medullary cavity also increases in width with aging, creating a loss of cortical bone and thickness in advanced years.

Walker and Lovejoy present radiographic data on age progression in the proximal femur and calcaneus in 130 individuals from the Hamann–Todd collection. For the femur, they present radiographic standards comprised of eight phases. Radiographic images of each phase are accompanied by descriptive narrative. The first of the eight phases has a suggested age range of 18 to 24 yr, and the final one is listed at 60 yr or more.

Ruff and Jones add that adult remodeling can alter asymmetry in cortical bone. With aging, patterns of adult cortical remodeling correlate with activity levels. Their study of mature tibiae indicates that the loss of cortical bone with remodelling likely produces shifts in asymmetry.

In older adults, bone density decreases with age. Note, however, that Atkinson and Weatherell found that within the femoral diaphysis, bone density varied at several locations in the diaphysis but was greatest at mid shaft. Density also varied at sites around the circumference of the diaphysis. The reader is encouraged to review the chapter entitled Radiology of the Lower Extremity for a comprehensive treatise on evaluating ossification centers from radiographs.

Arthritic Changes

General changes associated with arthritis provide an additional source of age information from bones in the lower extremity. Obviously, as adults age, the frequency and probability of arthritis-associated changes in the joints increases. Generalized changes provide clues to advancing age, but pathological conditions can produce such evidence prematurely or with varied expressions in different anatomical areas.

Chemical Changes

Ohtani et al. report that aspartic acid racemization ratios in the human femur may provide some information that is useful in age determination procedures. The normal L form of amino acids change to the D form with aging. Their study of femoral compact bone revealed that sex differences were apparent, with males demonstrating the greater increase in the D/L ratio with aging. They recommend using the total amino-acid fractions instead of the acid-insoluble collagen fraction.

4

EXTRACTION TECHNIQUES FOR FORENSIC ANALYSIS

Many different methods are used to extract DNA from the wide range of specimens commonly found at crime scenes. Techniques range from simple alkaline lysis followed by neutralization, to the well-known salting-out method that is used in cases of higher cell concentrations, to a simple closed-tube method utilizing a thermostable proteinase. Only a few of these methods are suitable for automation, and many of the steps involved are associated with a high risk of contamination.

PRINCIPAL STEPS OF DNA EXTRACTION

Cell Lysis

The first step in any DNA extraction method is to break the cells open in order to access the DNA within. Although DNA may be isolated by '*boiling*' cells, this rather crude means of disrupting the cell does not produce DNA that is always of sufficient quality and purity to be used in down-stream analytical techniques such as *polymerase chain reaction* (PCR) amplification. DNA isolated by simple boiling generally fails as a substrate for further analysis because it has not been sufficiently separated from structural elements and DNA-binding proteins, and these impurities compromise downstream procedures. In order for DNA to be released cleanly, the phospholipid cell membranes and nuclear membranes have to be disrupted in a process called *lysis*, which uses a detergent solution (lysis buffer), often containing the detergent *sodium dodecyl sulphate* (SDS), which disrupts lipids and thus disrupts membrane integrity. Lysis buffer also contains a pH-buffering agent to maintain the pH of the solution so that the DNA stays stable: DNA is negatively charged due to the phosphate groups on its structural backbone, and its solubility is charge-dependent and thus pH-dependent. Proteinases, which are enzymes that digest proteins, are generally added to lysis buffer in order to remove proteins bound to the DNA and to destroy cellular enzymes that would otherwise digest DNA upon cell lysis. The lysis procedure sometimes calls for the use of heat and agitation in order to speed up the enzymatic reactions and the lipid solubilization.

DNA Extraction: Purification and Efficient Removal of PCR Inhibitors

Cell or tissue samples may contain elements that inhibit the DNA extraction process at any of the various steps involved in DNA isolation. These inhibitors may interfere at any step of the process, but are generally problematic in three areas:

1. Interference with the cell lysis, the first step in DNA preparation.
2. Interference by degrading nucleic acids or by otherwise preventing their isolation after lysis is complete.
3. Inhibition of polymerase activity during the PCR amplification of target DNA after successful purification.

We focus here on the third type of inhibition: interference with PCR. After the initial isolation of DNA, it must be separated from the other cellular components that remain after the lysis procedure. This is often followed by further washing steps, which function to remove any remaining substances that could inhibit amplification of the DNA by PCR and its subsequent analysis. A wide range of PCR inhibitors have been reported. Common inhibitors include various body fluid components (e.g. haemoglobin, melanin, urea) as well as chemical reagents that are frequently used in clinical and forensic science laboratories (e.g. heparin, formalin, Ca^{2+}). Inhibitors also include microorganism populations, which are frequently an overrepresentation of bacterial cells or food constituents found at the scene. Similarly, environmental compounds at the crime scene or in the forensic laboratory can also act as PCR inhibitors. These include organic and phenolic compounds, glycogen, polysaccharides, humic acids, fats and laboratory items such as pollen, glove powder and plasticware residue. Carry-over of compounds such as those used in cell lysis (e.g. proteolytic enzymes or denaturants) and phenolic compounds from DNA purification procedures can also be problematic. Many of these PCR-inhibitory compounds, such as polysaccharides, urea, humic acids, haemoglobin, melanin in hair samples or indigo dyes from denim, exhibit a solubility similar to that of DNA, therefore they are not completely removed during classical extraction protocols such as detergent and phenol-chloroform extraction, and persist as contaminants in the final DNA preparation. Several methods have been developed to remove these contaminants, including glass bead extraction, size-exclusion chromatography, spin column separation, agarose-embedded DNA preparation or immunomagnetic separation.

DNA Extraction Techniques

There are, in general, three primary techniques used in forensic DNA laboratories: the phenol–chloroform extraction method, Chelex extraction and magnetic affinity solid-phase extraction.

Standard Phenol–Chloroform Extraction

The standard phenol–chloroform extraction protocol in use today is described in Sambrook *et al.* (1989). Samples are incubated with enzymatic lysis buffer (e.g. 10 mm Tris·HCl pH 7.4, 400 mm NaCl, 2 mm Na_2EDTA pH 8.1, 1% SDS and 667 μg/ml proteinase K) overnight at 37°C or for 2 hours at 56°C to partially digest cellular proteins. The resultant liquid-phase cell lysate is treated with equilibrated phenol, and the aqueous and organic phases are mixed thoroughly and then separated by centrifugation. The DNA remains in the aqueous phase while the cellular proteins are extracted into the organic phase and discarded. The aqueous supernatant is transferred to a new tube and an equilibrated mixture of phenol–chloroform–isoamyl alcohol in the ratio of 25 : 24 : 1 is added to ensure complete removal of the proteins. After agitation, the mixture is centrifuged and the resultant aqueous supernatant is transferred again to a new tube and a chloroform–isoamyl alcohol mixture in the ratio of 24 :1 is added and followed by further mixing and centrifugation in order to ensure the complete removal of phenol. The aqueous supernatant is collected, and an acetate salt and 2 volumes of 96% ice-cold ethanol are added to precipitate the DNA via shielding of the negative charges on DNA, allowing it to aggregate and precipitate. Samples are incubated at -20°C to increase the efficiency of precipitation, and are then centrifuged to collect the precipitated DNA. Ethanol is decanted and the DNA pellet is washed with 70% ethanol to remove the salt, then vacuum- or air-dried and resuspended in either sterile double-distilled water or low-salt buffer. Some protocols involve an additional purification and concentration step with spin columns, which remove inhibitors with solubility characteristics similar to DNA, such as heme or indigo dyes.

Phenol–chloroform extraction works very well for the recovery of double-stranded high-molecular-weight DNA. However, the method is time-consuming, involves the use of hazardous chemicals and requires multiple tube transfers as well as a final precipitation step, potentially increasing the risk of contamination and/or sample mix-ups. Nevertheless, the method works very well for extraction of DNA from nearly all of the common types of forensic samples, and is still used today as a last resort for DNA extraction from problematic samples because it produces relatively large yields of high-quality DNA, and the excellent DNA purity allows it to remain stable in long storage. In this respect, phenol–chloroform extraction remains the gold standard by which new methods are judged.

Chelex 100 Extraction

Chelex 100 is a medium used for the simple extraction of DNA for subsequent use in PCR-based typing. It is a styrene divinylbenzene copolymer containing paired iminodiacetate ions, which act as chelating groups in the binding of polyvalent metal ions such as magnesium or calcium. Chelex therefore binds bivalent ions such as Ca^{2+} and Mg^{2+} and deactivates unwanted enzymes such as DNases. Chelation of these cations may also result in the '*deactivation*', via structural changes, of proteins that make up the cellular architecture, leading to the destabilization of the whole cell and essentially resulting in cellular lysis. Addition of proteinase K, a Ca^{2+}-independent enzyme, breaks down the deactivated enzymes and proteins. Proteinase K is then itself deactivated by a subsequent boiling step. This method was introduced into forensic laboratories on the basis of a protocol by Walsh *et al.* (1991): biological samples are added to a 5% Chelex 100 resin, are boiled for several minutes and are then centrifuged to remove the Chelex resin, leaving the DNA in the supernatant. The single-stranded DNA can be used directly in PCR. Better results are often obtained if an initial incubation step is used in order to remove the '*forensic stain*' from the carrier. Besides, several protocols call for the additional incubation of 100 ng of proteinase K with the Chelex/stain mixture for two hours at 56°C or overnight at 37°C. The Chelex 100-based extraction has a definite advantage over other methods in that it is very fast and can also be carried out in a single tube without any transfer steps, which substantially reduces the possibility of contamination. However, DNA extracted by Chelex 100 requires further purification to reach the level of DNA quality obtained from a standard phenol–chloroform extraction.

Magnetic Affinity Solid-phase Extraction

Solid-phase DNA extractions have been in use for many years. In the advanced case of magnetic affinity solid-phase extraction, efficient DNA isolation relies on the binding of DNA to a silica surface on paramagnetic beads in the presence of chaotropic solutions. DNA isolation can therefore be performed in a single tube by adding and removing solutions such that contaminants are washed away while the DNA remains bound to the beads (until its eventual elution). Solid-phase extraction approaches are marketed by Qiagen GmbH, Hilden, Germany and Promega Corporation, Madison, USA. This extraction method is made possible by the tendency of DNA to bind to silica (glass) in the presence of chaotropic salts such as sodium iodide, *guanidinium thiocyanate* (GTC) or guanidinium hydrochloride. Cells are first lysed in a lysis and binding solution so that DNA is released. DNases are denatured and inactivated by the presence of the chaotropic salts, and magnetic beads are then mixed with the sample to allow DNA to bind. DNA requires high salt conditions to bind to the silica surface on the beads, but this DNA binding is reversible at pH <7.5, so when the washing steps are complete the DNA may be eluted by water or by a low-salt buffer. After binding, the magnetic beads containing the immobilized DNA are collected by simply applying a magnetic force. The soluble portion containing the unbound components (proteins, cell debris' etc.) is then removed and discarded. The magnetic particles with the attached DNA are then resuspended in a series of wash solutions in order to obtain highly purified DNA: a solution of chaotropic salts removes residual non-bound matter, ethanol removes residual chaotropic salts and a short rinse with water removes ethanol. The DNA is finally eluted from the magnetic beads by the addition of either water or low-salt buffer and is ready for use in downstream applications. Magnetic bead-based DNA isolation has several advantages over both the phenol–chloroform and Chelex 100 methods, including:

1. Elimination of traditional solvent extraction, thus avoiding the use of harmful organic solvents;
2. Elimination of precipitation, centrifugation and pellet-drying steps;
3. Rapid purification;
4. Removal of nearly all contaminants that could interfere with subsequent PCR;

5. Production of high-quality single-stranded DNA;
6. Scalable and reproducible extraction;
7. Suitability for adaptation for high-throughput extraction.

Modified Techniques for DNA Extraction from Challenging Forensic Samples

Magnetic bead-based purification is currently the technique best suited for DNA extraction from the majority of forensic samples. However, some sample types, such as sperm and skeletal remains, pose special challenges. For these more recalcitrant samples, extraction techniques must be modified in order to successfully extract usable DNA, as we discuss in the following sections.

Sperm Extraction – Differential Extraction

A special differential lysis treatment for forensic samples from sexual assault cases can separate epithelial cells from sperm cells; the most commonly used method was first described by Gill *et al.* (1985). Sperm nuclei are resistant to lysis by the usual SDS/proteinase K cell method, but can be lysed in a solution containing proteinase K plus the reductant dithiothreitol (DTT, e.g. 20 μl of 0.1 m DTT is added to 500 μl of lysis buffer), which breaks down the protein disulphide bridges present in sperm nuclear membranes. This method, known as differential lysis, is often used in forensic laboratories to separate sperm nuclei from vaginal cellular debris in samples obtained from semen-contaminated vaginal swabs, thus enabling the identification of cells specific to the male suspect in a sample of predominantly female cells. However, sperm cells would be absent in a number of situations: some perpetrators of sexual assaults could have a vasectomy or could be azoospermic (lacking any viable sperm), or may have a condition of either retrograde ejaculation (an emission of semen back into the bladder) or anejaculation (complete failure to emit semen). The code and spirit of criminal law states that a violation exists when a sexual act is enforced that highly humiliates the victim, especially when this act entails forced penetration into the body. In the special cases described above, a forensic examination would not reveal sperm cells but would reveal male-specific epithelial cells, providing evidence of a violation. Male DNA profiles can also be picked out of a background of predominantly female cells by analysing for the presence of Y chromosome-specific markers. This Y-specific *short tandem repeat* (STR) haplotype analysis, which is now as sensitive as the autosomal analysis, has superseded and replaced differential extraction in many forensic

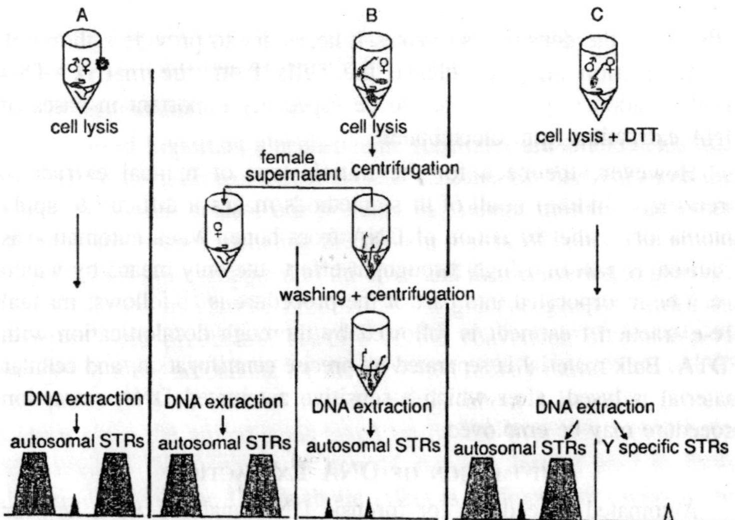

Fig. 4.1. Scheme of selective extraction versus Y-chromosomal analysis: (a) extraction of male and female epithelial cells; (b) differential extraction to separate male sperm cells from female epithelial cells; (c) extraction of male and female epithelial cells.

laboratories. As an indication for sperm cells, DTT is generally added to the cell lysis buffer.

Extraction of DNA from Bone

There are several protocols that describe different methods for the extraction of DNA from bones. All methods include freezing of the bone in liquid nitrogen and pulverization with a laboratory mill or a dentist's drill, often followed by decalcification to remove the bone matrix. Such methods were applied in the high-throughput bone-fragment-based DNA identification that was necessary after mass disasters such as the World Trade Center attack or the Southeastern Asia tsunami disaster. The methods differ from each other by what is used for the decalcification step. Prado *et al*. (1997) used only a short decalcification step that entailed overnight incubation of the bone with 0.5 m EDTA, while Holland *et al*. (1993) repeated this EDTA step three times. Hoss and Paabo (1993) extracted the DNA from bone meal without a decalcification step, and instead used guanidinium thiocyanate and the detergent Triton X-100 for cell lysis. However, in this case DNA could be extracted only from those cells that were exposed after bone pulverization. In a compact bone structure, the density of the surrounding cells provides protection against bacterial degradation for a time, but the density also makes it necessary to provide a thorough decalcification step to release the cells from the matrix. This decalcification step was noted to be especially important in cases of DNA extraction from older bones.

However, the need for the initial steps of manual extraction (freezing, grinding) in all of these methods makes it difficult to apply automation to the extraction of DNA from bone. When automation is required as part of a high-throughput effort, the only means by which it can be incorporated into part of the procedure is as follows: manual pre-extraction treatment is followed by thorough decalcification with EDTA. Bulk material is separated by precise centrifugation, and cellular material is lysed, after which a sensitive automated DNA extraction procedure may be employed.

Automation of DNA Extraction

Automated procedures for forensic DNA analyses are a key for high-throughput sample preparation as well as for avoidance of errors during routine sample preparation and for reproducible processing and improved sample tracking. The most important stage in PCR-based forensic analysis is DNA isolation, and both high yields and high purity are vital components of a successful analysis. A wide variety of high-quality automated instruments, each with its own unique benefits and features, are currently available. The National Genetics Reference Laboratory evaluated eight automated extraction systems covering both dedicated instruments with their associated chemistries (so-called '*integrated systems*') as well as kit-based chemistries that may be suitable for automation when adapted to standard liquid-handling robotic systems. These kits cover several different types of chemistry, including salt extraction, filter plate-based solid-phase extraction and extractions based on paramagnetic beads. The systems were tested for a number of output factors, including DNA yield, purity and integrity, and suitability of DNA for downstream applications such as PCR. Anonymized EDTA blood samples and mock samples (water blanks) were used in the testing, and the survey also provided specifications for each system, including throughput, sample volume capacity and costs. Most of the systems did not have a bar-code system included in their design, so samples had to be tracked manually by means of tube/sample location. A final analysis of the survey results concluded that the integrated systems, which combined dedicated instruments and extraction chemistry, gave significantly better results than those that adapted existing DNA extraction kits to an automated platform using standard liquid-handling robotics. The study further concluded that although these kit-based chemistries could be optimized to a level satisfactory for diagnostic use, such systems would most likely require an extended optimization time to ensure good results. In terms of the different extraction chemistries tested, the solid-phase extractions gave the best results in spite of issues involving blocked wells and insufficient vacuum power, problems that are particular to this methodology. Overall, the simplest and most versatile systems appeared to be those based on paramagnetic bead chemistries.

Adapting a robotic extraction system for forensic casework can be a formidable problem, since the system has to be flexible enough to function efficiently across the enormous range of variation in DNA content obtained from a wide variety of forensic samples, such as blood, saliva, hair, vaginal swabs and contact stains on various carrier materials. The number of cells present in a sample can vary broadly - from more than 1000 nucleated cells in half a micro-litre of blood to only a few cells in a sample obtained from a touch or a sneeze. Contact traces are becoming more and more prevalent in criminal cases, so the efficiency of extraction systems has to be rigorously successful down to picogram amounts of DNA while remaining exquisitely sensitive to the need to avoid potential contamination events.

Although there were early applications of automated extraction systems for clinical diagnostics, automated extraction systems for forensic evidentiary samples have only recently been reported with the application of the BioMek 2000 Workstation combined with the DNA IQ kit for forensic casework samples. Nagy *et al.* (2005) have validated the Qiagen BioRobot M48 workstation for nearly all types of forensic samples, and the smaller counterpart of this instrument, the Qiagen EZ1, was shown to be valid for forensics work by Anslinger *et al.* (2005) and Montpetit *et al.* (2005). The DNA IQ system has been automated for the initial testing of forensic samples on robotic platforms such as the Tecan Freedom EVO 100 as well as on the Maxwell 16 instrument. The Maxwell 16 instrument operates differently than many other automated DNA purification systems: rather than moving liquids from one well to another to carry out the various stages in DNA isolation and purification, the *paramagnetic particles* (PMPs) are moved from well to well during the purification process by individual magnets and disposable plungers.

Not surprisingly, all these described methods are based on the paramagnetic beads chemistry, which we and others have concluded is the simplest and most versatile system. However, the question of which automation system is best suited to forensic analysis remains open, and we now discuss three systems that are currently the most extensively validated robotic systems for forensics analysis: the Beckman BioMek 2000, the Qiagen M48 and the Qiagen EZ1. All three systems use an extraction method that comprises the following steps: cell lysis, binding of the DNA to the silica surface of paramagnetic particles in the presence of chaotropic reagents, washing steps to remove impurities and elution of the DNA.

BioMek 2000/DNA IQ System

This system uses the DNA IQ kit-based chemistry: cells are briefly lysed either in a proteinase K-containing buffer or in the DNA IQ lysis buffer at either 57°, 68° or 95°C, depending on the substrate composition. For semen stains differential extractions were performed. Lysates were then centrifuged prior to loading onto the robot. After initial contamination tests showed that a low level of contamination was introduced during the robotic extraction, the software method was modified to include automated resin addition, as well as the use of a 96-well deep-well plate and the replacement of the initial shaking step with a pipetting step. These changes are now included in the BioMek 3000 Workstation. Greenspoon *et al*. (2004) have validated the BioMek 2000/DNA IQ system by extensive contamination, efficiency and sensitivity tests described below. To detect contaminations a '*checkerboard*' test was used: samples containing a concentrated source of DNA were loaded into wells with DNA alternating with reagent blanks across the whole plate, forming a checkerboard pattern.

To assess a system's efficiency at extracting low levels of DNA, a sensitivity study utilizing different dilutions of triplicated bloodstain punches was carried out: one sample was extracted by the automated procedure, one by the manual DNA IQ process and one by phenol–chloroform extraction. At dilutions of 1 : 10 and 1 : 100, all three methods produced similar yields of DNA. However, at a dilution of 1 : 1000 there was clearly a better yield from the BioMek 2000/DNA IQ method than from manual extraction or from automated extraction using the PowerPlex 1.1 or 16 BIO systems. For sensitivity studies, blood from two different donors was deposited on various substrates (e.g. hand soap and lotion, carpet, black underwear, blue jeans, contraceptive foam, dirt, canvas). The aim of these different depositions was to study if inhibitory substances from the sample carrier might persist throughout DNA extraction and interfere with binding of DNA to the silica-coated paramagnetic resin. In this study, the STR profile was obtained for all of these depositions except for one donor's sample, which had been deposited on synthetic canvas. It seems likely that this failure resulted from the fact that the pre-heating step at 95°C can melt synthetic material and thus possibly destroyed the sample. However, STR profiles for synthetic canvas deposition were successfully obtained in the case of the second donor, indicating that these deposition conditions did not impose an absolute block to sample extraction; the exact reason for the failure in the first case is not known. DNA was successfully extracted from sexual assault samples, cigarette butts, blood stains, buccal swabs and various tissue samples, with no evidence of contamination throughout the extensive validation studies reported by Greenspoon *et al.* (2004). In addition, DNA extractions from manual pre-treated bone, hair and epithelial cells from touch evidence have been validated by Crouse *et al.* (2005).

Qiagen BioRobot EZ1

The Qiagen EZ1 is a compact benchtop instrument with its own integrated EZ1 DNA extraction chemistry designed to handle up to six samples in 15 minutes. The paramagnetic bead-based chemistry is conveniently packaged in a foil-sealed reagent cartridge (a robot-specific package), so the risk of contamination is extremely low. The instrument is controlled by a simple keypad and LCD screen, and different protocols are programmed by being loaded onto the instrument via cards that are plugged into a slot in the front of the instrument. The EZ1 was evaluated for DNA extraction from a variety of different evidence sample types, including blood, saliva and semen as well as cigarette butts, katagen and telogen hair roots, paraffin-embedded tissues and pulverized tooth. Forensic samples were pre-treated in a variety of ways – some were treated with lysis buffer from the extraction kit and proteinase K and were incubated at 56°C for various times, while vaginal swabs with sperm cells were extracted by a differential lysis protocol. Tooth and hair roots were lysed with a specific '*bone lysis buffer*'. For all extractions, the EZ1 DNA Tissue kit was used in combination with the 'Forensic' programming card with the exception of embedded tissues, which used the 'Tissue' card instead. DNA yields were comparable to those from phenol–chloroform extraction, and the EZ1 purification process effectively removed PCR inhibitors. Variation in purification efficiency of the EZ1 DNA tissue kit reported by Anslinger *et al.* (2005) is no longer an issue. QIAGEN implemented functional Quality Control Testing procedures in order to assure good lot–lot consistency of purification efficiency for the EZ1 DNA Tissue Mini kits.

Quiagen BioRobot M48

The Qiagen BioRobot M48 is a dedicated DNA extraction instrument that was designed with its own integrated MagAttract DNA extraction chemistry. This system can handle six samples in 15 minutes, and up to 48 samples in 2 hours. The workstation is equipped with special anti-contamination features, such as a completely enclosed robotic deck, a drop-catcher (as well as a control check for closing the door and cleaning the catcher), filter tips, a flat stainless-steel area and a UV sterilization system for decontamination between runs. After loading the instrument, there are no manual steps up until the point of collecting the pure DNA sample. The instrument is equipped with an interface that provides step-by-step instructions for the run set-up as well as options for sample data import and export. Nagy *et al.* (2005) have worked out a simple, manageable manual protocol for the pre-treatment of forensic samples combined with an extraction protocol that is suitable for the full range of forensic specimen (blood samples, buccal swabs, blood stains, vaginal swabs, hairs, cigarette butts, bone meal, etc.). In their recommended standard lysis protocol, the forensic specimen was completely covered with detergent lysis buffer (50 mm Tris·HCl pH 7.4, 100 mm NaCl, 100 mm Na_2EDTA pH 8.1, 1% SDS) and incubated for 15 minutes at 90°C with thorough mixing. The only specimens for which modifications were necessary were telogen hair, sperm and bone meal. For telogen hair (i.e. hair that is in the dormant part of its growth cycle), TN_{CA} buffer (10 mM Tris·HCl pH 8.0, 100 mM NaCl, 1 mM $CaCl_2$, 2% SDS, 39 mM DTT, 250 μg/ml proteinase K) was used instead of detergent lysis buffer. For sperm, differential extraction was not used: 20 μl of 0.1 M DTT was generally added to 500 μl of detergent lysis buffer in the presence of sperm cells. For bone meal, lysis was preceded by multiple decalcification steps with 0.5 M EDTA followed by a last precise centrifugation step. Using these sample-specific protocols, complete DNA profiles were even obtained from most different types of bones ranging from 2 to 16 years old (macerated and high-density bones included), as well as from 9-year-old teeth. The only sample for which a profile was not obtained was the macerated skeleton part, for which the analysis resulted only in a positive amplification of the amelogenin system. Results showed that PCR inhibitors were efficiently removed from all of the forensic samples, and the prepared DNA remained stable after 2 years of storage. The BioRobot M48 preparative technology system was evaluated by Nagy *et al.* (2005) on the basis of a defined cell number model so that the DNA recovery rates could be exactly determined. In a 'real-world' analysis using unknown samples, the M-48 BioRobot workstation has now been used in our laboratory for the extraction of DNA from more than 40,000 routine laboratory samples with a daily monitoring of the extraction efficiency. In addition, there has been no evidence of cross-contamination so far, as examined by PCR testing using 28–30 cycle reactions.

QIAGEN now offers automated DNA extraction kits specifically designed for both of their robotic systems. The company also offers protocols that enable processing of solid material directly in the sample tube with no need for centrifugation steps, so that high-quality DNA may be purified from a variety of forensic casework samples. Specific pre-treatment protocols for the DNA extraction from various forensic samples are included.

In conclusion, the precision, sensitivity and reliability of the extraction systems discussed here have been extensively validated for application to forensic casework, and results demonstrate that these systems can produce DNA of high quality such that potential PCR inhibitors are removed and there is no need for any further purification steps. Overall, the automated DNA extraction systems discussed here have been shown to carry out safe and successful extractions for practically all types of forensic sample evidence, and should considerably simplify the reproducible processing of large numbers of samples.

Recovery of High-Molecular-Weight DNA from Blood and Forensic Specimens

The isolation of genomic *deoxyribonucleic acid* (DNA) is a crucial step in the process of DNA profiling. The success of all subsequent genetic-typing procedures depends on the availability of sufficient amounts of highly purified DNA from biological crime stains as well as from reference blood samples. High-mol-wt DNA is usually only required for DNA-profiling protocols based on Southern blot analysis and hybridization with multi- and single-locus *variable number of tandem-repeat* (VNTR) probes in cases in which stain samples contain at least microgram amounts of DNA. The DNA extraction yield from biological stains is difficult to estimate in advance and depends on a number of unpredictable factors regarding the stain sample, e.g., storage conditions, exposure to heat, sunlight, moisture, or bacterial and fungal contamination, all of which influence the quality and final yield of the isolated DNA. However, the isolation of high-mol-wt DNA might also be appropriate for small stain samples that initially appear to be suitable only for *polymerase chain reaction* (PCR) typing. This allows a decision on the typing method after recovery of the stain DNA based on the amount and quality of the extracted DNA, thus providing more flexibility for the profiling procedure.

Materials

1. 50 m*M* KC1 (for hypotonic lysis of erythrocytes).
2. Lysis buffer: 25 m*M* ethylenediaminetetra-acetic acid (EDTA), 75 m*M* NaCl, 10 m*M* Tris-HCl pH 7.5. Add 200 mg/mL Proteinase K immediately before use.
3. 10% (w/v) sodium dodecyl sulfate (SDS).
4. ANE buffer: 10 m*M* sodium acetate, 100 m*M* NaCl, 1 m*M* EDTA.
5. Buffered phenol: Use only crystallized phenol, dissolve in a water bath at 65°C, and add approx 0.1–0.2 vol ANE buffer until an aqueous phase forms above the phenol; add 0.01% 8-hydroxyquinoline (w/v solid crystals).
6. Chloroform/isoamylalcohol: To 24 parts of chloroform, add one part of isoamylalcohol.
7. 6 *M* NaCl.
8. 3 *M* sodium acetate, pH 5.2: dissolve 40.8 g Na acetate in 80 mL distilled water, bring to pH 5.2 with concentrated acetic acid, and adjust final volume with water to 100 mL.
9. TE buffer: 10 m*M* Tris-HCl, 1 m*M* EDTA, pH 7.5.
10. 20X SSC: 175.3 g NaCl, 88.2 g Na citrate/L, adjust to pH 7.0 with NaOH.
11. 0.2 *M* sodium acetate, pH 7.0.
12. 10 mg/mL Proteinase K stock solution: dissolve 10 mg proteinase K in 1 mL of 10 m*M* Tris-HCl, pH 8.0, and store frozen in small aliquots.
13. Phosphate-buffered saline (PBS): 50 m*M* phosphate buffer, pH 7.4, 0.9% NaCl.
14. PBS/S: PBS + 2% sarcosyl.
15. PBS/PKS: PBS + 100 μg/mL proteinase K + 1% SDS (= 10 μL PK stock solution + 100 μL 10% SDS/mL PBS).
16. PBS/Lys: PBS + 100 μg/mL Proteinase K + 2% sarcosyl + 10 m*M* DTT + 25 m*M* EDTA (= 10 μL PK stock + 10 μL 1 *M* DTT stock 50 μL + 0.5 *M* EDTA stock/ mL PBS/S).

Methods

DNA extraction from fresh blood samples

Purification of white blood cells

1. Place 10–15 mL EDTA blood into 50-mL polypropylene tube. In addition, transfer two 0.5-mL aliquots of blood into 1.5-mL microfuge tubes as reference samples and store them frozen at –20°C.
2. Add 50 m*M* KCl up to 50 mL, mix well, and incubate in water bath at 37°C for 10 min.
3. Spin for 10 min at 500g in a clinical centrifuge at room temperature.
4. Remove the supernatant with a Pasteur pipet connected to a water jet or vacuum pump; leave the pellet intact (hold the tube in front of a light source to see the white-cell pellet).
5. Repeat steps 2–4 once or twice, until the pellet is free from red cells.
6. Add 15 mL lysis buffer and shake vigorously to resuspend the cell pellet.
7. Add 1.5 mL 10% SDS and mix carefully. The sample should now become very viscous because of cell lysis.
8. Incubate overnight at 37°C or at 55°C for 4–5 h.

Organic extraction of DNA

1. Add 1 vol buffered phenol to the proteinase K-digested cell extract and mix the aqueous and organic phases carefully to achieve a homogeneous suspension; avoid vigorous shaking.
2. Spin for 10 min at 1500g in clinical centrifuge at room temperature.
3. The aqueous phase containing the DNA is on top, and the phenolic phase is below. Transfer the aqueous phase to a fresh 50-mL polypropylene tube using a widebore glass pipet. The interphase containing proteins and protein-DNA complexes may also be transferred at this step.
4. Add 1 vol of a 1:1 mixture of phenol and chloroform/isoamyl alcohol (24:1) and extract as described in steps 1–3.
5. Add 1 vol of chloroform/isoamylalcohol and repeat the extraction as described in steps 1–3. At this step, avoid transferring any residual protein debris from the interphase.

Inorganic extraction of DNA

1. Add 5 mL of 6 *M*NaCl (one-third of the original volume) to the proteinase K-digested cell extract and shake vigorously for 10–15 s.

2. Spin for 10 min at 1500g in a clinical centrifuge at room temperature to separate the salt-precipitated proteins.
3. Pour the supernatant into a fresh 50-mL tube.

DNA precipitation

1. After organic extraction, add 0.1 vol of 3 M sodium acetate (i.e., 1.5 mL for the procedure described here) and 2 vol of ice-cold absolute ethanol. After salt precipitation with 6 M NaCI, add only the ethanol.
2. Mix carefully without vigorous shaking. The DNA should precipitate by forming viscous strings first and finally a compact pellet, which may float on top of the solution.
3. Melt the tip of a Pasteur pipet on a Bunsen burner to form a hook. Use this tool to recover the floating DNA pellet from the solution.
4. Rinse the DNA pellet attached to the glass hook twice in 70% ethanol to remove excess salt.
5. Dry the pellet briefly in the air and resuspend the DNA in an appropriate volume (300–500 μL depending on the size) of 0.IX TE.
6. Incubate the sample for 1 h at 65°C or overnight at 37°C in a water bath to dissolve the DNA. If the sample is still very viscous, add more 0.IX TE and incubate again at 65°C until a homogeneous solution is obtained.

Rapid DNA extraction from small aliquots of frozen blood samples

1. To a 0.5-mL blood aliquot in a 1 5-mL microcentrifuge tube add 1 mL IX SSC, mix gently, and spin for 1 min in microfuge. The blood sample must have been frozen previously to achieve complete red-cell lysis.
2. Remove 1.2 mL of supernatant without disturbing the pellet, add 1.2 mL IX SSC, mix gently, and spin for 1 min.
3. Remove 1.4 mL of supernatant, add 375 μL of 0.2 M sodium acetate, and resuspend the pellet by vortexing.
4. Add 25 μL of 10% SDS + 10 μL of 10 /mL proteinase K stock solution, vortex for 1 s, and incubate for 1 h at 56°C.
5. Spin tube for 1 s, add 120 μL of a 1:1 mixture of phenol and chloroform/isoamylalcohol (24:1), vortex for 10 s, and spin for 2 min.
6. Transfer the aqueous upper phase (approx 400 μL) to fresh tube, add 1 mL of absolute ethanol, and mix by inverting the tube until DNA precipitate forms.

7. Spin for 15 s, remove the supernatant and add 200 μL of 0.2 *M* sodium acetate, leave the tube for 2 min at room temperature, and redissolve the pellet by vortexing for 10 s.
8. Add 500 μL ethanol, precipitate the DNA again, spin for 15 s, and remove the supernatant.
9. Add 1 mL of 70% EtOH, mix, and spin again for 30 s. When removing the supernatant, watch the pellet, since it may not stick to the tube wall.
10. Dry the pellet briefly by keeping the tube inverted for 15 min, and add 50 μL 0.1X TE. Incubate for 15–30 min at 65°C to dissolve the DNA.

DNA extraction from dried blood stains

1. Cut the fabric with the blood stain into small pieces. Depending on the size of the stain, transfer the fabric pieces into a 1.5-mL microcentrifuge or a 15-mL polypropylene tube and add 0.5-5 mL PBS/Lys. Incubate overnight at 37°C with mild agitation.
2. Add an equal volume of buffered phenol and mix the aqueous and organic phases carefully to achieve a homogeneous suspension.
3. Spin for 10 min at 1500g in clinical centrifuge (15-mL tubes) or at maximum speed in a microcentrifuge (1.5-mL tubes) at room temperature. The fabric pieces remain in the phenolic phase and will thus be separated from the DNA in the aqueous phase. Transfer the upper phase into a fresh tube.
4. Add 1 vol of a 1:1 mixture of phenol and chloroform/isoamylalcohol (24:1) and extract as described in steps 2 and 3.
5. Add 1 vol of chloroform/isoamyl alcohol and repeat the extraction as described in steps 2 and 3. At this step, avoid transferring any residual protein debris from the interphase.
6. Transfer the final supernatant to a Centricon-30 microconcentrator tube and purify DNA from salt, SDS, and contaminants with three washes with 2 mL distilled water each. Concentrate the sample to a final volume of 100–150 μL.

DNA extraction from vaginal swabs and from semen stains

Differential lysis procedure for vaginal swabs

1. Soak swab or fabric with stain containing mixed male/female secretion in PBS/S (2–5 mL depending on size) in an appropriate tube and incubate overnight with mild agitation at 4°C.
2. Vortex briefly, remove the swab or fabric, and spin down cells at 2500g for 10 min at 4°C. Save supernatant in a separate tube.

3. Wash the swab or fabric in 1.5 mL PBS/S in a microcentrifuge tube. Punch a small hole in the bottom of the closed tube, insert this tube into an open second tube, and punch another hole in the lid of the tube containing the sample. Spin both tubes for 10 min at 1500g in a microcentrifuge. After centrifugation, the upper tube should contain the dry swab or fabric (do not discard) and the lower tube the buffer and cell pellet. Save the supernatant and combine the cell pellet with the pellet from step 2 in 1.5 mL PBS/S.
4. Wash the pellet twice in 1.5 mL PBS/S in a microfuge tube and spin it down for 10 min at 1500g. Resuspend the pellet in 50 μL PBS and remove 3–5 μL for microscopic analysis.
5. Add 500 μL PBS/PKS and incubate for 2 h at 50°C with mild agitation for lysis of vaginal epithelial cells. Recover sperm heads by centrifugation at 1500g for 10 min at 4°C.
6. Save the supernatant (= female fraction) for further analysis of female DNA. Resuspend the pellet (containing the sperm heads) in 30 μL PBS and remove 2–3 μL for microscopic analysis.
7. Lyse the sperm heads by adding 500 μL PBS/Lys and incubate for 3 h at 50°C with mild agitation (= male fraction).
8. Separately purify DNA from female and male fractions by three subsequent extractions with an equal volume of phenol, phenol/chloroform/isoamylalcohol (25:24:1), and chloroform/isoamylalcohol (24:1), as described for blood stains.
9. Transfer both supernatants to two separate Centricon-30 microconcentrator tubes, and purify DNA from salt, SDS, and contaminants with three washes with 2 mL distilled water each. Concentrate samples to a final volume of 100–1 50 μL.

DNA extraction from dried semen stains

1. Wash fabric with sperm stain as described previously.
2. Resuspend combined pellets in 500 tL PBS/Lys and incubate for 3 h at 50°C with mild agitation.
3. Purify sperm DNA as described previously.

Notes

1. After this step, the cell pellet can be stored frozen without buffer at –20 or –70°C. The pellets may also be shipped on dry ice for extraction by the receiving laboratory.
2. The organic-extraction protocol is designed to obtain very high-mol-wt DNA >50 kb. Therefore, vigorous shaking of the sample has to be avoided after adding SDS. To avoid shearing of high-

mol-wt DNA during pipetting, a pipetman equipped with a disposable blue tip where the narrow end has been cut off may be used to transfer the aqueous phase. Alternatively, the phenolic phase may also be removed by piercing a hole into the bottom of the 50-mL tube and holding it over a glass beaker. When the phenolic phase has been drained, the aqueous phase has to be poured immediately into a fresh tube. Wear protective gloves and goggles to avoid skin or eye contact with the caustic phenol.

3. The "salting out"-method is routinely used in our laboratory, because it generates high-mol-wt DNA of sufficient quality both for *restriction-fragment-length polymorphism* (RFLP) and PCR applications without the use of hazardous organic chemicals.
4. If no DNA precipitate forms for any reason, incubate the tube at –20°C overnight and recover the DNA by centrifugation for 15 min in a clinical centrifuge at 4000g and 4°C. Remove the supernatant, rinse the pellet carefully in 70°C ethanol, and dry it briefly by keeping the tube inverted for 15 min on a paper towel. Dissolve the pellet in 100–200 μL 0.1X TE.
5. When small amounts of DNA are precipitated, the pellets may be very small or almost invisible. It is easier to locate them after centrifugation if the tubes are inserted into the microfuge rotor with the fixtures of the tube caps pointing outward.
6. If possible, remove dried-blood particles from the carrier surface (e.g., leather, wood, or plastic material) to avoid transfer of inhibitory substances interfering with restriction enzyme or *Taq* polymerase activity. The dried-blood particles can be added directly to the PBS/Lys solution for Proteinase K digestion. Alternatively, you may also wash the stain carrier first in an appropriate volume of PBS at 4°C, with occasional shaking to remove the blood cells. After this step, remove the stain carrier, spin down the cells, and add the PBS/Lys solution for Proteinase K digestion.
7. The volume reduction by spin dialysis instead of ethanol precipitation generates a higher yield of extracted DNA. Ethanol precipitation is not very efficient in solutions with a low DNA concentration and might result in poor recovery. Using spin dialysis with microconcentrator tubes, the sample should be washed very carefully to remove all residual salts and SDS, which might inhibit restriction enzyme or *Taq* polymerase activity.
8. Before beginning with the extraction procedure, it is absolutely necessary to prepare a stained smear from the swab on a

microscope slide for visual analysis to check for the presence of spermatozoa and to determine the relative amount of sperm heads compared to female epithelial cells. If only a very small number of spermatozoa is present in the sample, it might be advisable to extract the sample as a whole without differential lysis and to interpret the mixed sample based on the VNTR genotype combinations. In addition, a protocol has been described for a mild differential lysis enriching the relative amount of sperm cells compared to epithelial cells.

9. All supernatants from intermediate steps should be saved until completion of the procedure, when the presence of sufficient amounts of DNA from the swab material has been demonstrated. Thus, the supernatants can be reprocessed in case of unexpected low yields of DNA. It cannot be excluded that spontaneous lysis occurs with some cells earlier than expected because of mechanical disruption of their membranes.

Automated DNA Extraction Techniques for Forensic Analysis

Many methods also require centrifugation and solvent extraction steps and thus are also not easily adapted for automation. Most of the methods used for DNA extraction can meet only one of the several standards for an optimal DNA extraction process: high DNA yield, rapidity of the method, high throughput and high DNA quality. Thus, for a long time the method of choice for many forensic samples was the traditional but hazardous use of phenol–chloroform extraction, which had to be performed under stringent safety measures. The end-product of the extraction sometimes was not sufficiently pure and still needed to undergo further purification steps using membranes or columns, so this method is not ideal in several respects. In order to assess the utility of other methodologies for DNA extraction, we first examine the principal steps in isolating DNA from biological material.

Quantification of DNA by Slot-Blot Analysis

Quantification of template DNA is an essential step in the analysis of samples using *polymerase chain reaction* (PCR). Once a PCR reaction has been optimized, the amplification of too little genomic DNA may yield only partial results, and the addition of too much template may increase the tendency for amplification of artifact products.

Extracts obtained from items submitted for forensic analysis often only contain a low concentration of DNA, which may be degraded.

Extraction with Chelex resin renders DNA partially single-stranded. Any method used for quantifying the amount of DNA present in such extracts must be designed to detect subnanogram quantities of denatured and possibly degraded DNA. In addition, preparations from samples other than fresh blood will probably contain components from bacteria and yeasts as well as human genomic DNA. A reliable assay of template DNA for PCR therefore needs to detect human genomic DNA specifically, rather than the total DNA present.

These requirements are met by using a slot-blot (or dot-blot) hybridization procedure, as described by Walsh et al. This method involves the hybridization of a biotinylated oligonucleotide probe to DNA samples immobilized on a nylon membrane and subsequent binding of streptavidin-horseradish peroxidase conjugate to the captured biotin molecules. With the addition of chemiluminescent detection reagents, hydrogen peroxide is reduced by the peroxidase bound indirectly to the DNA samples. This reaction is coupled to the oxidation of luminol, and the photons emitted are detected using autoradiography film. The size and density of the dots or slots produced on the film are related to the amount of DNA immobilized on the membrane in each position. Therefore, it is possible to estimate the quantity of DNA present in the sample extract slots or dots by comparison with the dots produced from a dilution series of a standard DNA sample.

This methodology can be used with Chelex-extracted DNA, because the denaturation of samples is central to the procedure. The sequence of the oligonucleotide probe is complementary to any satellite repeat region, D17Z1, found only in higher primates, so the assay is "human" DNA-specific. Degraded DNA can be detected using this method because the probe is a 40-mer and will therefore hybridize to small fragments of DNA. In addition, this method of quantification is sensitive to 0.1 ng of DNA. It is simple and relatively quick to perform and only requires a minimum of laboratory equipment.

Materials

1. Biodyne B membrane.
2. 5 *N* NaOH (store at room temperature for up to 3 mo). *Caution:* 5 *N* NaOH is highly caustic.
3. 0.5 *M* EDTA, pH 8.0 solution.
4. 1 *M* Tris-HCl, pH 8.0.
5. TE buffer: 10 m*M* Tris-HCl, 0.1 m*M* EDTA, pH 8.0. Mix 1 mL 1 *M* Tris-HCl, pH 8.0, 20 µL 0.5 *M* EDTA, pH 8.0; make up to 100 mL with distilled water (autoclave in 10-mL aliquots and

store at room temperature for up to 3 mo; discard remnants of an aliquot once opened).

6. Prewetting solution: 0.4 *N* NaOH, 25 m*M* EDTA. Mix 80 mL 5 *N* NaOH, 50 mL 0.5 *M* EDTA, pH 8.0/L (autoclave and store at room temperature for up to 4 wk).
7. Hybridization tray and lid.
8. 0.04% (w/v) bromothymol blue (prepare using sterile distilled water, aliquot, and store at 4°C for up to 3 mo).
9. Spotting buffer: 0.4 *N* NaOH, 25 m*M* EDTA, 0.00008% (w/v) bromothymol blue. Mix 6 mL 5 *N* NaOH and 3.75 mL 0.5 *M* EDTA, made up to 75 mL with sterile distilled water and autoclaved before adding 150 μL 0.04% (w/v) bromothymol blue (store at 4°C for up to 1 wk).
10. Standard DNA solution: 0.2 μg/uL K562 DNA solution, diluted to 100 pg/μL (store at 4°C for up to 3 mo).
11. Slot-blot/dot-blot apparatus: the Convertible Filtration system.
12. Vacuum source with a pressure of at least 8 0 in. Hg.
13. 20X SSPE solution: 3 *M* NaCl, 200 m*M* NaH_2PO_4, 20 m*M* EDTA, pH 7.4.
14. 10% (w/v) SDS solution (Ultrapure reagent, available from BDH).
15. Hybridization solution: 5X SSPE, 0.5% (w/v) SDS. Mix 250 mL 20X SSPE, 50 mL 10% (w/v) sodium dodecyl sulfate (SDS)/L (autoclave and store at room temperature for up to 4 wk).
16. 5' Biotinylated oligonucleotide probe: Dilute to 15 pmol/μL and store at 0°C in aliquots. Once an aliquot is opened, store at 4°C and discard after 2 wk. The oligonucleotide can be ordered from Oswel, sequence (5' '): TAG AAG CAT TCT CAG AAA CTA CTT TGT GAT GAT TGC ATT C.
17. 30% hydrogen peroxide (store at 4°C).
18. Shaking water bath, adjustable to 50°C.
19. Wash solution: 1.5X SSPE, 0.5% (w/v) SDS. Mix 75 mL 20X SSPE, 50 mL 10% (w/v) SDS/L (autoclave and store at room temperature for up to 4 wk).
20. Streptavidin-horseradish peroxidase conjugate (store at 4°C).
21. Orbital shaker.
22. Citrate buffer: 0.1 *M* sodium citrate, pH 5.0. Adjust pH to 5.0 with 20% HCl (autoclave and store at room temperature for up to 4 wk).
23. ECL Detection solutions (store at 4°C).

24. Antistatic acetate sheets (18 24 cm).
25. 95% ethanol.
26. Autoradiography cassette.
27. Hyperfilm autoradiography film.

Method

1. Wearing clean gloves, cut a piece of Biodyne B membrane to fit the slot-blot apparatus and place in 50 mL of prewetting solution in a hybridization tray. Allow to equilibrate for up to 30 min while preparing the samples.
2. Prepare samples for assay by adding an aliquot of each to 150 μL of spotting buffer.
3. Prepare standard DNA samples by adding the following volumes of standard DNA solution to 150 μL of spotting buffer: 1 μL (0.1 ng), 2.5 μL (0.25 ng), 5 μL (0.5 ng), 10 μL (1 ng), 20 μL (2 ng), 30 μL (3 ng), 40 μL (4 ng), 50 μL (5 ng), 70 μL (7 ng), 100 μL (10 ng). Also prepare a negative control sample by adding 100 μL of TE, used to prepare the standard DNA solution, to 150 μL of spotting buffer.
4. Vortex all tubes briefly and then spin for 50 s.
5. Using clean forceps, place the wetted membrane on the gasket of the slot-blot apparatus and turn on the vacuum source. On the manifold, turn the clamp vacuum on and the sample vacuum off, then press down on the top plate to ensure that a seal is formed.
6. Pipet each sample into a different well of the slot-blot apparatus, taking care not to introduce air bubbles or to touch the surface of the membrane with the pipet tip.
7. When all samples and standards have been pipeted, turn the manifold sample vacuum on slowly and leave on until all samples have been drawn through onto the membrane (30 s-1 min), giving a uniform blue slot or dot.
8. On the manifold, turn the clamp vacuum off, while leaving the sample vacuum on, and remove the top plate.
9. Without allowing the membrane to dry out, make an orientation mark on the DNA side of the blot in pencil, then remove from the apparatus.
10. Immediately transfer the membrane to 100 mL of prewarmed hybridization solution in a hybridization tray. Add 5 mL of 30% H_2O_2, place the lid on the tray, and incubate at 50°C in a shaking water bath for 15 min.

11. Pour off the solution and add 30 mL of prewarmed hybridization solution to the tray. Tilt the liquid in the tray to one side and add 1 μL of probe solution to it. Replace the lid and incubate at 50°C in a shaking water bath for 20 min.
12. Pour off the liquid and rinse the blot briefly in 100 mL of prewarmed wash solution by rocking the tray for 50 s. Pour off the solution.
13. Add 30 mL of prewarmed wash solution to the tray. Tilt the liquid in the tray to one side and add 90 μL of streptavidin-horseradish peroxidase conjugate to it. Replace the lid and incubate at 50°C in a shaking water bath for 10 min.
14. Pour off the solution and rinse the membrane in 100 mL of prewarmed wash solution by rotating the tray on an orbital shaker for 1 min at room temperature. Repeat this rinse step.
15. Pour off the solution and add a further 100 mL of prewarmed wash solution to the tray. Replace the lid and rotate the tray on an orbital shaker for 15 min at room temperature.
16. Pour off the solution and rinse the membrane briefly in 100 mL of citrate buffer by rocking the tray.
17. Pour off the solution and prepare the ECL-detection solution by adding 5 mL of ECL reagent 1 to 5 mL of ECL reagent 2.
18. Add the 10 mL of ECL-detection solution to the tray and shake for exactly 1 min at room temperature.
19. Using forceps, remove the membrane from the tray and place between two sheets of acetate. Smooth over the surface of the acetate with a ruler to remove any air bubbles and excess ECL-detection reagent from the blot and then clean the outside of the acetate sheets with 95% ethanol.
20. Secure the blot in an autoradiograph cassette, DNA-side uppermost.
21. Under safe red-light illumination, place a piece of Hyperfilm in the cassette, on top of the blot, taking care not to move the film once in contact with the blot. Close the cassette.
22. Expose the film to the blot for approx 45 min at room temperature.
23. Develop the film either manually or by using an automatic film processor.
24. Check that the negative control sample did not give a detectable slot or dot.
25. Estimate the quantity of DNA present in the sample aliquots by comparing the intensity and size of the slots or dots produced with those produced from the DNA standards.

Notes

1. We prepare the DNA standard solution by diluting the stock solution purchased to 1 ng/μL in TE buffer. This solution is then diluted further to the working concentration of 100 pg/μL. Mix the solutions well at each stage, but avoid excessive use of the vortex mixer. Refer to the specification sheet sent out with the stock solution for the accurate starting concentration of the product. Having prepared a new batch of DNA standard solution, we check its performance against the batch in use by loading both onto one blot and assessing the compatibility of results obtained.
2. This apparatus allows for a number of alternative blot formats, depending on the choice of top plate. We use the top plate that gives 96X 3-mm dots, which, in our experience, are easier to "read" than slots.
3. We use a diaphragm vacuum pump.
4. We assay samples in duplicate and 2 μL aliquots of extracts from fresh blood or hair roots, 4 and 7 μL aliquots of extracts from all other types of stain.
5. We load two sets of standards onto each membrane and check for the compatibility of results. Alternative concentrations of standard DNA samples may be prepared, depending on the test samples to be assayed.
6. If using a 128 array of sample wells with the manifold, it is useful to place the tubes in a 128 rack at this stage in the same positions as the samples are to be pipeted onto the membrane.
7. If the sample is not pulled onto the membrane, it may be gently pipeted back into a clean tip and repipeted onto the membrane.
8. Soak the dot-blot apparatus in 0.1% (w/v) SDS solution after each use. Pay special attention to cleaning the gasket and plate that come into contact with the membrane. Rinse well and allow to air-dry.
9. Do not allow the membrane to dry out at any stage in the procedure.
10. Solutions may be prewarmed by placing in a 50°C water bath or incubator and should be at 37°C before use.
11. The temperature of the water in the water bath should be 50°C.
12. The water-bath platform should be set to shake at 19000 strokes/min.
13. The orbital shaker should be set at 500 rpm.

14. Do not prepare the ECL-detection solution more than 5 min before use.
15. Immediately after each use, wash the hybridization tray and lid in water and rinse with distilled water, then air-dry.
16. We use an X-OGRAPH Compact X2.
17. If a detectable dot is produced from the negative control sample, this would suggest that either a solution used was contaminated or that the manifold was not clean before use.
18. It may be necessary to reassay a sample using a larger or more dilute aliquot so that the result obtained is within the range of the DNA standards. To allow easy visualization of very weak slots or dots, the autoradiography film may be exposed overnight to the blot.
19. The (Quantiblot Human DNA Quantitation kit) (ABD, Perkin-Elmer) contains enough streptavidin-horseradish peroxidase and Quantiblot D17Z1 probe for 10 blots. The protocol provided with the kit is similar to that described here, except that the autoradiography film requires only a 15 min exposure, because of the design of the Quantiblot probe.
19. It is possible to automate the "reading" of quantification blots using a flatbed scanner and image-processing software. However, we have not found a flatbed scanner capable of resolving the OD range (typically 0 OD units) developed on the autoradiography film when using the DNA standards described here.

5

Polymerase Chain Reaction

In 1985, the year of the first DNA '*fingerprint*', a new method – the polymerase chain reaction (PCR) was reported. The PCR can amplify a specific region of DNA and it has revolutionized all areas of molecular biology, including forensic genetics. The technique allows extremely small quantities of DNA to be amplified. Under optimal conditions, DNA can be amplified from a single cell. The increased sensitivity of DNA profiling using PCR has had a dramatic effect on the types of forensic sample that can be used and it is now possible to analyse trace evidence and highly degraded samples successfully – albeit with less than 100 % success.

Evolution of PCR-based Profiling in Forensic Genetics

PCR technology was rapidly incorporated into forensic analysis. The first PCR based tool for forensic casework amplified the polymorphic HLA DQα locus (the α subunit of the DQ protein is part of the major histocompatibility complex). It was used for the first time in casework in 1988 to analyse the skeletal remains of a 3-year-old girl. The DQα system's major drawback was that it had a limited power of discrimination.

VNTRs were widely used in casework but required a relatively large amount of DNA. In an attempt to overcome this limitation, PCR technology was applied to the analysis of VNTR loci, and alleles between 5–10 kb could be faithfully amplified from fresh biological material. However, it was of limited value for many forensic samples, which often contained small amounts of DNA that could be highly degraded. To overcome the problems caused by degradation, tandem repeats, called AMP-FLPs (*amplified fragment length polymorphisms*), that were smaller than 1 kb were selected for PCR based analysis. However, as with VNTRs, their use was limited in forensic contexts because of the size of the larger alleles, which were difficult to analyse in degraded samples. By the early 1990s, a large number of *short tandem repeats* (STRs) had been characterized. The STR loci were simpler and shorter than VNTRs and AMP-FLPs, and were more suitable for the analysis of biological samples recovered from crime scenes. The STR markers were not individually as discriminating as the VNTR and AMP-FLPs but had a major advantage that several of them could be analysed together in a multiplex reaction. The short tandem repeat markers have become the genetic polymorphism of choice in forensic genetics and the PCR is a vital part of the analytical process.

DNA Replication – Basis of the PCR

The PCR takes advantage of the enzymatic processes of DNA replication. During every cell cycle the entire DNA content of a cell is duplicated. This copying of DNA can be replicated outside of the cell *in vitro* to amplify specific regions of DNA.

Components of PCR

A PCR has the following components: template DNA, at least two primers, a thermostable DNA polymerase such as *Taq* polymerase, magnesium chloride, deoxynucleotide triphosphates and a buffer.

Template DNA

The amount of DNA added to a PCR depends on the sensitivity of the reaction: for most forensic purposes the PCR is highly optimized so that it will work with low levels of template. Most commercial kits require between 0.5 and 2.5 ng of extracted DNA for optimum results. This represents between 166 and 833 copies of the haploid human genome – one copy of the human genome contains approximately 3 pg of DNA. Most forensic profiling can be carried out successfully with fewer templates – even below 100 pg or 33 copies of the genome; however, the interpretation of profiles can become more complex as the amount of template DNA is reduced.

Taq DNA polymerase

The first PCRs were carried out using a DNA polymerase that was isolated from *E. coli*; in each cycle of the PCR the enzyme was inactivated by the high temperatures in the denaturation phase and fresh enzyme had to be added. Fortunately this is no longer necessary.

Scientists were able to isolate the DNA polymerases from the thermophilic bacteria, *Thermus aquaticus*, which was discovered in the 1960s in the hot springs of Yellowstone National Park, USA. The *Taq* polymerase enzyme can tolerate the high temperatures that are involved in the PCR and works optimally at 72–80°C . Using the thermostable enzyme greatly simplifies the PCR procedure and also increases the specificity, sensitivity and yield of the reaction. The *Taq* polymerase enzyme exhibits significant activity at room temperature that can lead to the creation of non-specific PCR products; adding the enzyme to a pre-heated '*hot start*' reaction reduces the non-specific binding and again improves the specificity and yield of a PCR. Modifications to the commonly used *Taq* polymerase led to the development of the AmpliTaq Gold polymerase. The enzyme is inactive when it is first added to the PCR – it only becomes active after incubation at 95°C for approximately 10 minutes. This 'hot start' enzyme allows the PCR to start at an elevated temperature and minimizes the non-specific binding that can occur at lower temperatures.

Primers

The primers used in PCR define the region of the genome that will be analysed. Primers are short synthetic pieces of DNA that anneal to the template molecule either side of the target region. The primer sequences are therefore limited to some degree by the DNA sequence that flanks the target sequence.

When designing primers for forensic analysis it is important that they will bind to conserved regions of DNA and therefore effectively amplify human DNA from all populations while at the same time not binding to the DNA of other species. When designing a multiplex PCR, the allelic size ranges are also important considerations for the

```
01  ggagctgggg ggtctaagag cttgtaaaaa gtgtacaagt gccagatgct cgttgtgcac
61  aaatctaaat gcagaaaagc actgaaagaa gaatcccgaa aaccacagtt cccattttta
121 tatgggagca aacaaagcag atcccaagct cttcctcttc cctagatcaa tacagacaga
181 cagacaggtg GATAGATAGA TAGATAGATA GATAGATAGA TAGATAGATA GATAtcattg
241 aaagacaaa  cagagatagga cagagatagga atgcttacag atgcacacac aaacgctaaa
```

Forward Primer: 5'-GGG GGT CTA AGA GCT TGT AAA AAG-3'
Reverse Primer: 5'-GTT TGT GTG TGC ATC TGT AAG CAT -3'

Fig. 5.1. The forward and reverse primers that are used to amplify the STR locus D16S539 in the Promega Powerplex 1.2 kit are shown and the position that they bind to within the sequence is indicated by the arrows.

position of the primer binding sites. There are a number of basic guidelines for primer design. Primers are normally between 18 and 30 nucleotides long, and have a balanced number of G/C and A/T nucleotides. A primer should not be self complementary or be complementary to any of the other primers that are in the reaction. Self complementary regions will result in the primer pairing with itself to form a loop, whereas primers that are complementary will bind to each other to form primer dimers.

The temperature at which primers anneal to the template DNA depends upon their length and sequence – most primers are designed to anneal between 50 and 65°C. A basic rule of thumb can be used when designing primers to estimate the melting temperature: for each A or T in the primer 2°C is added to the melting temperature and for each C or G 4°C is added – Cs and Gs will bind to the complementary nucleotide with three hydrogen bonds and are therefore more thermodynamically stable. To estimate the annealing temperature 5°C is subtracted from the melting temperature. PCR primers can be designed manually or with help using software such as Oligo and Primer 3.

Magnesium chloride, nucleotide triphosphates and reaction buffer

Magnesium chloride is a critical component of the PCR. The primers bind to the template DNA to form a primer–template duplex: magnesium chloride stabilizes the interaction. The concentration of $MgCl_2$ is typically between 1.5 mM and 2.5 mM; the template–primer stability increases with higher concentrations of $MgCl_2$. The *Taq* polymerase also requires magnesium to be present in order to function.

The building blocks for the PCR are deoxynucleotide triphosphates, which are incorporated into the nascent DNA strand during replication. The four nucleotides are in the PCR in equal concentration, normally 200 μM. The reaction buffer maintains optimal pH and salt conditions for the reaction.

PCR Process

The PCR amplifies specific regions of template DNA. In theory, a single molecule can be amplified one billion-fold by 30 cycles of amplification; in practice the PCR is not 100% efficient but does still produce tens of millions of copies of the target sequence.

The amplification of DNA occurs in the cycling phase of PCR, which consists of three stages: denaturation, annealing and extension. In the denaturation stage the reaction is heated to 94°C; this causes the double stranded DNA molecule to 'melt' forming two single stranded

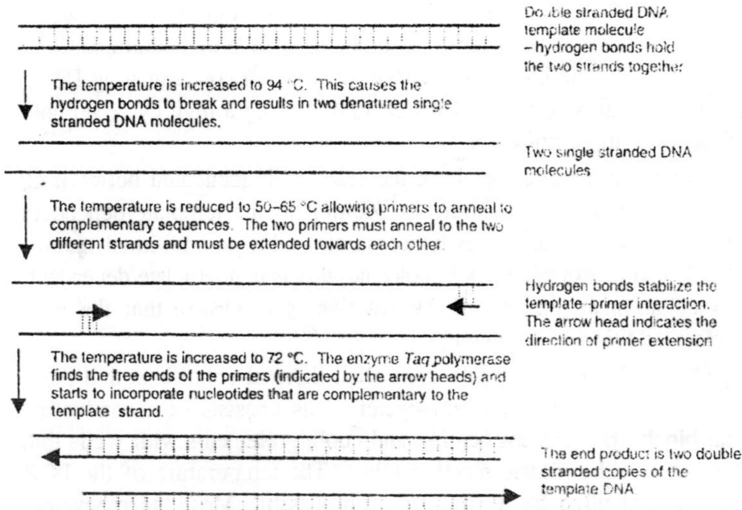

Fig. 5.2. The PCR process - each PCR cycle consists of three phases: denaturing, annealing and extension.

molecules. DNA melts at this temperature because the hydrogen bonds that hold the two strands of the DNA molecule together are relatively weak. As the temperature is lowered, typically to between 50 and 65°C, the oligonucleotide primers anneal to the template. The primers are in molar excess to the template strands and bind to the complementary sequences before the template DNA reassociates to form double stranded DNA. After the primers have annealed the temperature is increased to 72°C, which is in the optimum temperature range for the *Taq* polymerase. Nucleotides are added to the nascent DNA strand at the rate of approximately 40–60 per second. The enzyme catalyses the addition of nucleotides to the 3' ends of the primers using the original DNA strand as a template; it has a high processivity, catalysing the addition of approximately 50 nucleotides to the nascent DNA strand before the enzyme dissociates – several *Taq* polymerase enzymes will associate and disassociate during the extension phase of longer PCR products.

The normal range of cycles for a PCR is between 28 and 32. In extreme cases, where the amount of target DNA is very low the cycle number can be increased to up to 34 cycles. It has been demonstrated that going above this cycle number does not increase the likelihood of obtaining a profile but does increase the probability of artefacts forming during the PCR. Using 34 cycles is known as *low copy number* (LCN) PCR and it is sparingly employed as extreme precautions have to be taken to reduce the chance of contamination – the more cycles the higher the chance of detecting contaminating DNA. The interpretation of the profiles generated using a high cycle number also become more complex.

Following the cycling phase the reaction is incubated between 60 and 72°C for up to one hour. In addition to the template-dependent synthesis of DNA the *Taq* polymerase also adds an additional residue to the 3' end of extended DNA molecule, this is non-template dependent; the incubation at the end of the reaction is to ensure that the non-template addition is complete.

The PCR requires tightly controlled thermal conditions and these are achieved by using a thermocycler. This consists of a conducting metal block that contains heating and cooling elements with wells that accommodate the plastic reaction tubes. The temperature of the PCR block is controlled by a small microprocessor. Most thermocyclers also contain a lid that is heated to over 100°C; this prevents the reaction evaporating and condensing on the cooler lid and thereby maintains the reaction volume, thus keeping the concentration of the reaction components stable throughout the PCR. After amplification the results of a PCR can be visualized on an agarose gel.

PCR Inhibition

When analysing forensic samples a problem that can be encountered is inhibition of the PCR. DNA extraction methods do not produce pure DNA, some chemicals will co-purify and in some cases inhibit the *Taq* polymerase. Potent inhibitors include haem compounds from blood, bile salts and complex polysaccharides from faeces, humic substances from soil and urea from urine. High concentrations of ions, in particular calcium and magnesium, can also act as potent inhibitors of the *Taq* polymerase. EDTA is used in high concentrations for the isolation of DNA from bone and will inhibit PCR unless removed as it binds ions such as magnesium ions that are essential for PCR. In a forensic science context, the blue dye in clothing such as denim, called *indigo*, has an inhibitor effect on PCR.

Extraction methods have been developed to remove commonly encountered PCR inhibitors and, for example, the silica binding methods that are commonly used in forensic analysis are effective at removing most inhibitors whereas the methods that produce a cruder extract such as the Chelex resin are more prone to inhibition. When it is not possible to remove all the potential inhibitors from a DNA extract, the addition of the protein *bovine serum albumin* (BSA) to the PCR can in many cases prevent or reduce the inhibition of the *Taq* polymerase. The BSA acts as a binding site for some inhibitors and can competitively remove or reduce the concentration of the inhibitor. The action of inhibitors can be detected, for example by spiking a PCR with a known amount of DNA, this alerts the analyst that further purification steps are required.

Sensitivity and Contamination

The great advantage of PCR is that it will amplify DNA from a template of only a few cells. This high level of sensitivity can also be a potential disadvantage, as DNA from incidental sources can be present and contamination can be introduced. Throughout the handling and analysis of DNA samples extreme care needs to be taken to minimize the chance of introducing this extraneous DNA.

When samples are collected from the scene of an incident, there may be cellular material from persons who had been present at the scene prior to the incident and hence DNA profiles will be generated from people unconnected with the incident. This type of DNA can be termed as incidental as it is not a contamination of the samples. At the time of the incident there is an opportunity for transfer from the perpetrator and it is this cellular material that is pertinent to the investigation. Consider an event such as theft from a house.

Prior to the incident there will be cellular material from the owners and from any recent visitors. At the time of the break in there may be transfer from the thief. If the incident is discovered by a neighbour then they will introduce their cellular material after the incident and prior to the scene being secured. When the police are called they have the potential to introduce their cellular material. Once the scene is secured then those entering should be wearing full protection to minimize the opportunity for transfer of their cellular material. If there is any introduction of DNA from those at the crime scene, during collection and transportation, or from laboratory staff, then this is considered as contamination.

PCR Laboratory

Once evidential samples have reached the forensic laboratory there is further potential to introduce contamination. A fundamental feature of PCR laboratories, to reduce the possibility of introducing contamination, is that they are clearly divided into pre- and post-PCR areas.

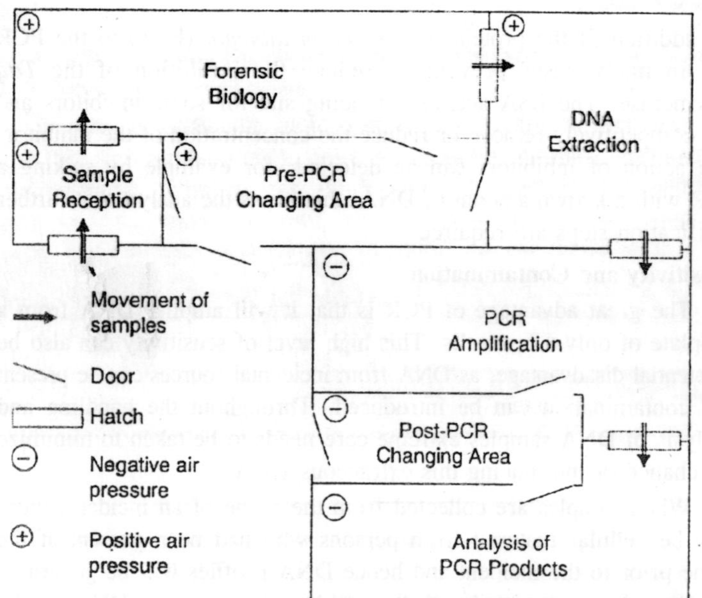

Fig. 5.3. The PCR laboratory is designed so that the work flows through the different processes in one direction starting with sample reception and forensic biology and finishing with the post-PCR analysis.

Pre-PCR

Once the samples reach the laboratory, potential contamination comes from the reagents, equipment and the forensic scientists undertaking the analysis. To prevent contamination being introduced from the scientist, protective clothing is worn, including a lab coat, gloves, a face mask, safety glasses/visor and a head cover. Even with these precautions it is still possible to get the scientist's DNA profile showing up – a database of all the people who enter/work in the laboratory can be used to detect when contamination could have been introduced within the laboratory.

When laboratories are engaged in analysing both samples from suspects and from crime scenes it is common to have dedicated areas for the two classes of sample; this prevents any potential cross-contamination of crime scene and suspect DNA. Special dedicated facilities may also be used when dealing with samples that contain very small amounts of DNA, such as hair shafts. DNA extraction and PCR set-up are commonly carried out in specialized clean hoods that provide a very controlled environment. The hoods have stainless steel surfaces and are easy to keep clean; they have filtered air to prevent any dust or other contaminant getting into the reaction, and they are fitted with a UV-light source that is used to remove any contaminating DNA effectively. The pipetting of any liquids involved in the extraction and PCR set-up is performed using pipette tips with barriers to prevent any DNA carry over. During the DNA extraction process negative control extractions must always be carried out to monitor for contamination; positive controls that involve extracting material similar to the casework samples, for example buccal swabs or blood stains, can be carried out to monitor that the extraction and amplification procedures are working efficiently. The PCR set-up introduces another positive and negative control: the positive control involves setting-up a PCR with DNA of known origin and whose profile is known. Successful analysis demonstrates that the reaction worked. In the negative control PCR, water replaces the DNA to monitor for contamination in the reagents or introduced during the PCR set up.

Post-PCR

The most potent source of contamination is previously amplified PCR products. Following a PCR there are millions of copies of the target sequence that can potentially contaminate subsequent reactions. Each time a PCR tube is opened there is some aerosol spray and a single droplet of aerosol will contain thousands of copies of the amplified target, resulting in transfer of some of the amplified product. The fundamental feature of any laboratory that engages in PCR analysis is that there must be physical separation of the pre-PCR and the post-PCR analysis to minimize the possibility of contaminating DNA extractions and PCR set-ups with amplified material. In addition to the two physical spaces there should also be dedicated equipment, protective clothing and reagents for each area. There must be a unidirectional work flow through the laboratory - PCR products must never be brought back into the pre-PCR part of the laboratory. There must also be temporal separation of tasks - it is not possible for a scientist who has been working in the post-PCR to then work in the pre-PCR area without the possibility of introducing contamination; an overnight break before returning to the pre-PCR area is normally recommended. Larger laboratories will have scientists who are dedicated to only the pre- or the post-PCR analysis.

Rapid Assessment of PCR Product Quality and Quantity by Capillary Electrophoresis

With the growing applications for the *polymerase chain reaction* (PCR) in human identity testing, a need exists for more rapid and automated forms of assessing amplification success. Methods that allow the characterization of a sample without consuming much material are helpful, especially in forensic cases. In addition, information regarding the quality and quantity of PCR product can be valuable in some applications. This chapter will focus on quantitating PCR products using *capillary electrophoresis* (CE). This CE method has proven effective prior to sequence analysis of polymorphisms in the D-loop region of mitochondrial DNA.

Traditional means of analyzing PCR products are often limited in the amount of information that can easily be obtained. For example, the most common method of PCR-product detection involves gel electrophoresis and subsequent staining for detection purposes. Although the quality of the same may be assessed (i.e., Do extra bands appear besides the target sequence?), quantitation of the PCR product requires an extra step (e.g., densiometric scanning). Likewise, many procedures that provide quantitative information, such as hybridization to immobilized probes or fluorescence spectrophotometry, fail to provide qualitative information. Performing multiple characterizations of the sample in order to obtain both qualitative and quantitative information is time consuming, labor-intensive, and more importantly, may consume significant portions of the sample. Thus, a method that consumes only a small portion of the sample and provides both qualitative and quantitative information would be valuable to characterizing PCR products.

CE can serve as an effective tool for PCR-product analysis because it is a rapid and quantitative technique in addition to being automated. Direct, on-column detection may be performed with *laser-induced fluorescence* (LIF) of an appropriate intercalating dye placed in the run buffer. No precolumn derivatization is necessary because the DNA fragments bind the dye when traveling through the column. High sensitivity is possible because the dye alone gives rise to very little signal. On interacting with the DNA fragments, a significant enhancement of fluorescent signal is observed. The use of an intercalating dye allows the PCR products to be tested with high sensitivity without having fluorescent tags already attached, which may interfere with future characterization of the sample (e.g., sequencing). Using LIF and intercalating dyes, CE has recently been applied to quantitating PCR products from HIV-1 DNA, the polio virus, the hepatitis C virus, and mitochondrial DNA. The method described in this section uses an internal DNA standard of known concentration to correct for variation between injections. By comparing the peak area of the PCR product to the peak area of the internal-standard DNA fragment, the relative amount of the PCR product may be calculated.

When using a PCR product as the DNA template in a sequencing reaction, the DNA fragment's concentration and purity can impact on the quality of the sequencing itself. Knowledge of a poor DNA template, prior to sequencing, can thus save time, effort, and expense. For example, when polymorphisms are examined in the D-loop of mitochondrial DNA, contaminating PCR products can generate a mixture of signals at positions throughout the chromatogram where the sequence of the contaminant differs from the template of interest. In addition, failure to remove unreacted PCR primers following the initial PCR reaction may result in mispriming of the DNA template during cycle sequencing.

Both of these scenarios increase the noise in a sequence chromatogram, which makes it more difficult to unambiguously determine the sequence. Thus, it is desirable to have a presequencing method that can detect any contaminating DNA fragments (e.g., nonspecific PCR products) along with showing the presence of excess PCR primers and the concentration of the PCR product of interest. Wilson et al. noted that an optimum template concentration of 205 ng exists for PCR-product templates used in sequencing the D-loop region of mitochondrial DNA. The CE method described here has been used to rapidly assess the quality and quantity of the PCR-amplified mitochondrial DNA prior to cycle sequencing.

Materials

1. The work described in this section was performed on a Beckman P/ACE 2050 with a Laser Module 488 argon ion laser. System Gold software was used to collect and integrate the peak information.
2. Capillary column, 50 μm id × 27 cm, DB-17 coated. The distance from injection to detection is 20 cm because the detection window is located 7 cm from the outlet end of the capillary.
3. Sieving buffer: 100 m*M* Tris-borate, 2 m MEDTA, pH 8.2, with 1% hydroxyethyl cellulose (HEC), HEC viscosity: 8613 cP for a 2% solution at 25°C. The HEC (5 g) was typically stirred overnight at room temperature in 500 mL of the Tris-borate-EDTA solution.
4. Intercalating dye: 50 ng/mL YO-PRO-1, 3.2 μL of the 1-m*M* stock solution into 40 mL of buffer solution. Fresh dye-containing buffer solutions were typically prepared every 2d to avoid problems with

degradation. The dye is light-sensitive and a possible carcinogen and should be treated appropriately.

5. Internal DNA quantitation standard: 200 bp DNA fragment (QS-200) at a concentration of 100 ng/μL.
6. Methanol, HPLC grade.
7. The PCR products came from the D-loop region of mitochondrial DNA. The primer sequences for the hypervariable regions HV1 and HV2 are shown below

   HV1
   L15997 5'-CAC CAT TAG CAC CCA AAG CT-3' (A1)
   H16395 5'-CAC GGA GGA TGG TGG TCA AG-3' (B1)
   HV2
   L047 5'-CTC ACG GGA GCT CTC CAT GC-3' (C1)
   H408 5'-CTG TTA AAA GTG CAT ACC GCC A-3' (D1)

   The combination of primers A1 and B1 generates a PCR product over the HV1 region that is 437 bp in length. Likewise, the combination of C1 and D1 produces a 402 bp DNA fragment for HV2. The entire D-loop region can be amplified by combining A1 and D1 for a 1021-bp amplicon.
8. Vials: both amber and clear, 4 mL wide-mouth with threads.
9. Sample vials: 0.2-mL MicroAmpTM Reaction tubes.

Methods

1. Prepare the capillary by cutting it to the desired length and removing approx 5 mm of the polyimide coating for the detection window. Place the capillary in an LIF capillary cartridge. The cartridge will allow liquid to flow around the capillary and maintain a constant-temperature environment.
2. Using a transfer pipet, fill three 4-mL amber vials with the HEC buffer containing the intercalating dye. Be sure to remove all bubbles from the solution surface because they may interfere with the flow of electrical current. Two buffer vials will be used as the inlet and outlet vials during the separation. The third vial will be used to fill the capillary with fresh separation media between each run.
3. Dilute the 200-bp quantitation standard. Typically, the 100 ng/μL 200-bp fragment was diluted to 0.400 ng/μL by placing 2 μL of the 200-bp standard into 498 μL of deionized water. The diluted quantitation standard was prepared in 500-μL volumes so that it could be used in multiple analyses (e.g., up to 20 CE samples) and thus facilitate better reproducibility between runs.

4. Prepare the CE sample by adding 1 μL of the DNA sample generated by PCR into 24 μL of the 0.400 ng/μL diluted 200-bp standard. Mix the sample well by drawing it into and out of the pipet tip several times.
5. Place the sample vial on a spring inside a 4-mL wide-mouth vial. Screw a silicon rubber cap on the 4-mL vial (to prevent evaporation) and load the samples into the autosampler.
6. Program the method for CE analysis:
   (a) Set the detector to collect data at a rate of 10 points/s.
   (b) Set the column temperature at 25°C.
   (c) Rinse the capillary for 1 min with methanol.
   (d) Fill the capillary with run buffer containing the entangled HEC polymer and YO-PRO-1 intercalating dye for 2 min.
   (e) Dip the tip of the capillary inlet in a vial of deionized water for 5 s.
   (f) Inject the sample under 0.5 psi (low pressure on Beckman P/ACE unit) for 45 s.
   (g) Apply a separation voltage of 15 kV (556 V/cm). The current should rise to ~20 μA.
7. Enter the sample names into the computer to relate the sample with the appropriate autosampler position.
8. Start the sample sequence. During application of voltage to the first sample (step g above) watch to see that the current rises to ~20 μA and remains stable. If, within the first minute, the current does not rise, the capillary is plugged and needs to be further rinsed with methanol and run buffer.
9. Following the completion of the CE separations (or while the next sample is being processed), data analysis may be performed:
   (a) The data-collection software will integrate the area of each peak. Use this peak information in the equation shown below. The primer peaks should pass the detector around 2 min, the 200-bp internal standard at ~2.5 min, and the HV1 or HV2 DNA fragments at ~3 min.
   (b) Calculate the concentration of the PCR product (in this case, HV1 or HV2 regions ofmtDNA):

   $$[\text{PCR Product}] = (25\ \mu\text{L}/1\ \mu\text{L}) \times (\text{Area PCR product})/(\text{Area 200 bp Stnd}) \times (0.384\ \text{ng}/\mu\text{L})$$

   where (0.384 ng/μL) is the amount of 200 bp DNA in the CE sample.

Notes

1. The capillaries may be purchased in 10-m rolls and cut to size by the user. In this case, the polyimide outer coating of the fused silica capillary must be removed to allow on-column detection. This detection window may be made by etching a short section of the polyimide coating with hot fuming sulfuric acid and cleaning with ethanol. This method protects the integrity of the inner-wall coating. Alternatively, some researchers use the flame from a match to remove the polyimide outer coating. Precut capillaries are also available and may be purchased with detection windows already prepared, albeit at a higher price.
2. Glass sample vials are commercially available. However, modified PCR tubes work well and can be disposed of after use. To make the CE sample tubes, carefully remove the top portion of a 0.2-mL MicroAmp Reaction Tube with a scalpel.
3. A long injection time benefits reproducibility and sensitivity. A 10-s pressure injection of water, prior to injecting the sample, may be used to improve resolution. Hydrodynamic (pressure) injections are more reproducible than electrokinetic injections and are thus preferred in quantitative work.
4. Separation speed in CE is directly related to the applied voltage and the capillary length. A shorter capillary would permit faster separations, but the Beckman instrument design is limited to 20 cm (injection to detection distance; 27 cm total length).
5. A regular check of column resolution is recommended to maintain good-quality results. Running a daily standard restriction digest works well. The 4-min method described here should split the 271 and 281 bp fragments of the ϕX174 *Hae*III restriction digest. Occasionally a capillary may not be adequately coated on the inside, which leads to electro-osmotic flow and affects both reproducibility and resolution. In addition, after extended use (typically over 1000 runs if the capillary is maintained well), the inner coating of the capillary may degrade, which leads to a rapid decrease in column performance. In either case, simply replace the capillary with a new one.
6. The methanol wash and buffer rinse between each run help to maintain column integrity. In addition, storing the capillary in deionized water overnight or during periods of instrument inactivity benefits column lifetime. Following the final run of the day, water may be pushed through the capillary for several minutes. Both

capillary ends should be left in water vials to prevent the tips from drying out.

7. The piercing levers, which come in contact with the HEC buffer, may become sticky with extended use. They should be cleaned once a week, or as needed, to remove any HEC residue. Likewise, the silicon vial caps need to be regularly cleaned. Failure to keep the instrument clean will result in buffer vials sticking, which may prematurely halt a run sequence.
8. It is important to keep in mind that when using intercalating dyes for detection, the fluorescent-signal intensity is related to the number of fluorophores bound to the DNA rather than the actual quantity of DNA present. Peak heights and areas increase incrementally as DNA size increases because more intercalating sites exist for larger DNA fragments.

   Thus, the length of the DNA fragments should be considered when noting the limit-of-detection or when absolute measurements are being made. A factor may be included in the quantitation equation shown above to adjust for differences between internal standard and the PCR-product fragment lengths. However, this factor was circumvented in this work since the PCR-product concentration was always determined relative to the internal standard concentration.
9. Buffer vials used for quantitative work should be replaced approximately every 20 runs to avoid problems from buffer depletion. A gradual loss of intercalating dye and other buffer ions from the outlet buffer vial can lead to a loss in signal intensity over a series of multiple injections. With lower levels of fluorescent intercalating dye available in the buffer, less dye will bind to the DNA and result in a lower fluorescent signal. Frequent changes of the buffer vials minimize this problem.
10. In determining the number of samples that can be processed in a certain period of time, the rinse steps between separations must be considered. Thus, the time to completely process a sample in a routine fashion is 8 min (1 min methanol wash + 2 min buffer fill + 45 s injection + 4 min run).
11. Other PCR products can also be rapidly analyzed with this same method to verify amplification or to evaluate/optimize a multiplex PCR reaction. With the quantitative capability of CE, primer concentrations and PCR conditions can be easily modified to balance amplification of multiple systems.

Kinship Testing

The application of DNA profiling to kinship analysis is widespread and offers an easy means of establishing biological relationships. Not surprisingly, paternity testing is the most common form of kinship testing, with hundreds of thousands of tests being performed worldwide each year. Since the first DNA based kinship test in 1985, DNA analysis has been applied to larger numbers of kinship tests, to the testing of more complex relationships and to the identification of highly compromised human remains.

Paternity Testing

PCR-based STR profiling has now become the standard tool and the PowerPlex 16 and AmpF*l*STR Identifiler STR kits that can analyse 15 loci simultaneously are routinely used. Laboratories that undertake kinship testing often have over 20 genetic markers at their disposal, including STR markers on the X and Y chromosomes, that allow for the testing of complex relationships.

The sensitivity of STR analysis, while not essential for most forms of paternity testing, allows samples to be routinely collected using buccal swabs and has expanded the possible scenarios where it can be used, for example, the analysis of low amounts of DNA recovered from foetal cells.

The methodology used to produce DNA profiles for paternity testing is identical to the analysis of material recovered from crime scenes. The interpretation of results is more complex than when comparing profiles from crime scenes and suspects. If the tested man does not possess the alleles that have been inherited from the biological father we can conclude that he cannot be the biological father. However, because mutations between the father and child could lead to a false exclusion at any given loci, it is standard practice is to require an exclusion at three or more loci before a test is declared negative.

If we cannot exclude the tested man as being the biological father then we have to assign a value to indicate the significance of non-exclusion. Likelihood ratios, which consider two competing, and mutually exclusive hypotheses are used. The hypotheses are:

$$\frac{\text{The tested man is the biological father}}{\text{The tested man is not the biological father}} \quad \begin{matrix} = H_p \\ = H_d \end{matrix}$$

The symbols H_p and H_d were put forward by the prosecution (H_p) compared with the hypothesis put forward by the defence (H_d), although in many civil cases the terms prosecution and defence are not appropriate. This likelihood is called a *paternity index* (PI) and can be assessed using equation.

$$\text{Paternity index} = \frac{\Pr(G_c \mid G_m, G_{tm}, H_p)}{\Pr(G_c \mid G_m, G_{tm}, H_d)}$$

where Pr is probability.

To calculate this likelihood ratio, we compare the probability of the child's genotype (G_c) given the mother's (G_m) and tested man's genotype (G_{tm}), if the tested man is the biological father (H_p) and the probability of the child's genotype given the mother's and tested man's genotype, if the tested man is not the biological father (H_d).

The numerator and denominator are conditional on the genotypes of the mother, child and tested man. They can be derived using a '*Punnet square*'.

Punnett square

The equations are not difficult to understand, particularly if derived from a Punnett square and converting to text form. Consider the case where the mother is genotype a, b and child is genotype b, c and the alleged father is c, d. If he is the father then the mother must pass on allele b, and the father must pass on allele c. If he is not the father then the mother must still pass on allele b but some other man must pass on allele c. This is given in the Punnett square below.

		Alleles from alleged father	
		c	d
Alleles from	a	a, c	a, d
mother	b	b, c	b, c

If the alleged father is the biological father then this can happen one in four ways, with a probability of 0.25.

If the alleged father is not the biological father, then the mother must pass on allele b with probability of 0.5 and the chance that a male other than the alleged father is the father is dependent upon the frequency of allele c (P_c) in the population. This gives a likelihood ratio of:

$$PI = \frac{0.25}{0.5p_c} = \frac{1}{2p_c}$$

The same process can be used for any of the possible combinations. Consider the version where the alleged father is homozygous (b, b) and the mother heterozygous (a, b) and the child is heterozygous (a, b)

		Alleles from alleged father	
		b	b
Alleles from	a	a, b	a, b
mother	b	b, b	b, b

If the alleged father is the biological father then this can happen in two ways, with a probability of 0.5.

If the alleged father is not the biological father then the mother must pass on allele b with probability of 0.5 and the chance that a male other than the alleged father is the father is dependent upon the frequency of allele b (P_b) in the population. This gives a likelihood ratio of:

$$PI = \frac{0.5}{0.5p_b} = \frac{1}{p_b}$$

Consider a case when the mother is a, b, the child is a, b and the alleged father is a, c.

		Alleles from alleged father	
		a	c
Alleles from	a	a, a	a, c
mother	b	a, b	b, c

Allele a or b could be passed from the mother. Note that if she passed on allele a then this would be an exclusion and therefore it would need to be allele b that is passed from mother to child if the man is the biological father. Considering the numerator (H_p) genotype a, b occurs in only one of four ways (0.25). Considering the denominator (H_d) the mother passed on either allele a (0.5) or allele b (0.5) and the chance that either event took place, allele a or allele b, is the sum of the probabilities. This results in the equation below:

$$PI = \frac{0.25}{0.5p_a + 0.5p_b} = \frac{1}{2(p_a + p_b)}$$

In Table 5.1 all the potential combinations of alleles from a mother, child and tested man are shown along with the resulting numerator, denominator and PI equation.

The combined PI is calculated by applying the product rule and multiplying the PI from each locus in this case the PI is 2920823. This can be represented by this statement:

> *Statement of positive paternity* The results of the DNA testing are 2920823 times more likely if the tested man is the biological father of the child than if the biological father is another man, unrelated to the tested man.

Table 5.1 The numerator and denominator that should be used when calculating a paternity index are determined by the genotypes of the child (G_C), mother (G_M), and tested man (G_{TM}).

G_C	G_M	G_{TM}	*Numerator*	*Denominator*	*PI*
A_iA_i	A_iA_i	A_iA_i	1	p_i	$1/p_i$
		A_iA_j	1/2	p_i	$1/2p_i$
		A_jA_k	0	p_i	0
	A_iA_j	A_iA_i	1/2	$p_i/2$	$1/pi$
		A_iA_j	1/4	$p_i/2$	$1/2p_i$
		A_iA_k	1/4	$p_i/2$	$1/2p_i$
		A_jA_k	0	$p_i/2$	0
A_iA_j	A_iA_i	A_jA_j	1	P_j	$1/p_j$
		A_iA_j	1/2	P_j	$1/2p_j$
		A_jA_k	1/2	P_j	$1/2p_j$
		A_kA_l	0	P_j	0
	A_iA_j	A_iA_i	1/2	$(P_i + P_j)/2$	$1/(p_i + p_j)$
		A_iA_j	1/2	$(P_i + P_j)/2$	$1/p_i + p_j$
		A_iA_k	1/4	$(P_i + P_j)/2$	$1/2(p_i + p_j)$
		A_jA_k	1/4	$(P_i + P_j)/2$	$1/2(p_i + p_j)$
		A_kA_l	0	$(P_i + P_j)/2$	0
	A_iA_k	A_jA_j	1/2	$P_j/2$	$1/p_j$
		A_iA_j	1/4	$P_j/2$	$1/2p_j$
		A_jA_k	1/4	$P_j/2$	$1/2p_j$
		A_jA_l	1/4	$P_j/2$	$1/2p_j$
		A_kA_l	0	$P_j/2$	0

The significance of likelihood ratios can be difficult for lay people to evaluate and the results are often presented as a probability of paternity, making the results more accessible. To calculate a probability of paternity requires Bayesian analysis and takes into consideration non-genetic evidence: the likelihood ratio (LR) is multiplied by the prior odds of paternity that are determined by non-genetic evidence, such as the testimony of the woman. It can be calculated by using the equation given below:

Probability of paternity =

$$\frac{\text{LR} \times \Pr(H_p \mid \text{non-genetic evidence})}{\text{LR} \times \Pr(H_p \mid \text{non-genetic evidence}) + [1 - \Pr(H_p \mid \text{non-genetic evidence})]}$$

Taking the above paternity test it is possible to turn the likelihood ratio into a probability of paternity for any prior odds of paternity; for example:

Prior probability = 0.1

$$\text{Probability of paternity} = \frac{2920823 \times 0.1}{(2920823 \times 0.1) + (1 - 0.1)} = 0.999996919$$

When this figure is used to report the results of a test it is often quoted as a percentage, which is more accessible to non-scientists. In this case the probability of paternity would be quoted as 99.9997%.

The value that is attributed to the prior odds of paternity is, of course, subjective. In civil cases, the value of 0.5 is commonly used, although there is little scientific merit to this value. In criminal cases, probabilities of paternity are often not presented because it is the duty of the jury/judge to assess the prior odds of paternity. If results are presented as a probability of paternity, a range of values calculated using different prior odds is often quoted.

With low paternity indexes the impact of prior odds can be significant. However, with the possibility of analysing a large number of STR loci, the PIs are typically in the millions and the posterior probability of paternity is therefore extremely high, even when the prior odds are very low. In the paternity test presented above, even with the prior odds as low as 0.001, the probability of paternity is still 99.9966 %.

In addition to the standard paternity testing where the mother, child and alleged father are available, testing can also be carried out when the mother is not available. More complex relationships can be examined, such as determination of sibship and paternity tests to discriminate between close relatives. Calculations can also incorporate correction factors to allow for deficiencies in allele frequency databases, in particular, the effects of subpopulations. Fortunately, computer programs have been developed to deal with both routine and complex scenarios.

Identification of human remains

The first application of DNA analysis to the identification of human remains was in 1987, when skeletal remains were profiled using single nucleotide polymorphisms in the DQα locus. Unfortunately, this system did not have high powers of discrimination and it was not until the early 1990s that DNA profiling was successfully applied to the identification of human remains. As DNA profiling technology and methodology have evolved to be more robust and powerful, it has been applied to increasingly complex situations including the identification of people killed in air crashes; fire; terrorist attacks; natural disasters and war. STRs are the most commonly used tool but mitochondrial DNA and SNPs have also been employed on occasion.

The matching of human remains can be through comparison to personal objects that belonged to the missing person, such as combs and toothbrushes, or by comparison to close family members.

In cases that involve hundreds of victims, the statistical analysis becomes very complex. Because of the high number of pair-wise comparisons that are made between the victims and relatives, the potential for coincidental matches that result in false positives and ultimately misidentifications is significant. The existence of relatives within the population of victims also complicates the analysis and there are limitations as to what can be achieved.

6

Role of 'X' and 'Y' Chromosomes

X Chromosome in Forensic Science

The sex chromosomes or gonosomes, chromosome X (ChrX) and chromosome Y (ChrY) are unique and differ in several aspects from the other chromosomes, which are referred to as *autosomes* (AS). Both ChrX and ChrY are unique with regard to the major content of their genes and sequences. In the cells of normal human males not affected by chromosomal aberrations, sex chromosomes do not occur in pairs. Males carry one X and one Y chromosome. Hence, most ChrX and ChrY regions are hemizygous in males. However, blocks of sequence homology between X and Y chromosomes suggest a common origin. During male gametogenesis, recombination between X and Y chromosomes occurs in small sub-telomeric regions of the X and Y chromosomes called the *pseudoautosomal regions*. These segments are homologous. Genes and markers in the pseudoautosomal region are not sex-linked. Recombination frequencies in this region are 20 times higher than on autosomes.

There are two pseudoautosomal regions - the Xp and Xq telomeres - referred to as PAR1 and PAR2. Furthermore, ChrX and ChrY show several regions of homology in addition to the common pseudoautosomal regions. In females ChrX is present as a homologous pair and resembles autosomes in this respect. However, even individuals with more than one ChrX possess only one active ChrX per cell. According to the Lyon Hypothesis additional copies are inactivated, which explains why ChrX monosomies, trisomies and polysomies are compatible with life.

Functional ChrX inactivation is connected with the formation of a morphologically visible heteropycnic chromatin that is also called *sex chromatin*. Inactivated ChrXs are visible in many but not in all female cells as Barr bodies or 'drum-sticks'. The latter are structures in the nuclei of polymorphonuclear leucocytes. Chromosome X monosomies, trisomies and other polysomies occur in different forms of appearance and may be connected with serious handicaps and infertility. Triple X (trisomy X) females frequently have a nearly normal development.

For parental generations, such gonosomal irregularities can usually be excluded since they would be associated with infertility. Unexpected and undetected aberrant gonosomal karyotypes in an offspring may however occur and affect the accuracy of kinship testing using ChrX markers. Gonosomal genotype X0, for example, which is associated with Ullrich-Turner syndrome, occurs at an incidence of 1 in 2500 female live-births. Both complete and partial monosomies have been observed. Another unexpected situation is when an XY-karyotype occurs in phenotypic females. This happens in context with androgen insensitivity or XY gonadal dysgenesis. Such disturbances cause genetic males to present with an unobtrusive female phenotype, although the present of ChrY can easily be detected by an amelogenin test. The posterior probability of a full or partial ChrX monosomy, or an XY female, increases when several closely linked ChrX markers appear to be homozygous. In the way that they perturb kinship testing, karyotypes XO and female XY are formally equivalent to autosomal uniparental disomy. As with AS markers, paternity exclusion that relies upon ChrX marker homozygosity thus requires independent experimental verification.

A gonosomal aberrant male karyotype with XXY (or XXXY, XXXXY, etc.) develops Klinefelter syndrome and shows a prevalence of about 1:500 males. Klinefelter syndrome may be detected in kinship testing when ChrX markers show heterozygosity. Ethical aspects are discussed below.

History of Forensic Utilization of the X Chromosome

The fundamental idea for extensive usage of X-chromosomal markers in forensic practice came from the experiences made during the second half of the last century in the field of clinical genetics. There are many well-known diseases and traits such as haemophilia, Duchenne muscular dystrophy, Lesch-Nyhan syndrome, G6PD deficiency, colour blindness, etc. that follow X-chromosomal inheritance. If a male patient is fertile, all his daughters possess the defective paternal X chromosome and transmit it to half of the next generation. Half of all daughters are again gene carriers and also half of their sons inherit the defective allele and exhibit the trait due to the hemizygote state of their ChrX. Furthermore, when a male exhibits two or more ChrX-linked traits it is obvious that alleles of all relevant loci are unified to one haplotype. This explains why ChrX linkage analysis is fairly easy. It is obvious that knowledge of such simple contexts is valuable not in clinical genetics only but also in kinship testing. However, cognition of sex-linked genetic markers usable in forensic genetics rose very slowly.

In the course of forensic kinship testing, which started in the middle of the last century, initially only blood group markers played a role. These were later supplemented by serum protein and enzyme variants. However, all of them were of autosomal inheritance. Regarding X-chromosomal markers, the first significant achievement was made when the Xg^a blood group was detected by the team of Race and Sanger. Chromosome X linkage of Xg^a could easily be recognized by comparing the frequencies of the Xg^a/Xg phenotypes in males and females (males: 0.62/0.38; females: 0.86/0.14). The blood group Xg^a is a fairly weak antigen. This may be the reason why Xg^a testing could not be established as a significant method in kinship testing practice. However, some questions of scientific interest, such as identification of the origin of X chromosomes in chromosome aberration syndromes such as Klinefelter and Ullrich-Turner syndrome have been solved using serological Xg^a testing. Later Ellis *et al.* (1994) identified the Xg^a antigen derived from the N-terminal domain of a candidate gene, referred to earlier as PBDX.

Two further ChrX loci encoding gene products with polymorphic appearance and therefore with a potential for usage in kinship testing are known. Glucose-6-phosphate dehydrogenase (G6PD) and phosphoglycerate kinase (PGK) show considerable diversity on the protein level in some geographical regions. However, to our knowledge, with rare exceptions, X-linked enzyme variants do not play any role in forensic contexts.

In the pre- DNA-technique era forensic scientists used sex chromatin tests for gender assessment in human tissues or single cells. Later this technique was complemented by fluorescence microscopic demonstration of male heterochromatin. It can be shown as a quinacrine mustard-stained part of ChrY in metaphases and even in metaphase cell nuclei.

In the early 1980s clinical geneticists started with genomic linkage analysis aimed at gene carrier detection and prenatal diagnosis. Some X-linked diseases, such as Duchenne muscular dystrophy and haemophilia, were in the focus of interest. In the first stage typing targets mainly were *single nudeotide polymorphisms* (SNPs), which could be detected by the Southern technique and were called *restriction fragment length polymorphisms* (RFLPs) according to the detection technique involving restriction enzymes. Later SNP linkage markers were supplemented by CA repeat polymorphisms and the minisatellite St14 (DXS52). Investigation of the latter kind of polymorphism was enabled by creating the *polymerase chain reaction* (PCR) technique. Whilst usage of dinucleotide repeats is shunned by the forensic community, minisatellite marker DXS52 clearly fulfills the forensic requirements for markers. Nevertheless, DXS52 appeared in the forensic literature only very sporadically. The first two ChrX microsatellites that played a significant role were HPRTB and ARA. Kishida *et al.* (1997) and Desmarais *et al.* (1998) almost at the same time created formulas for the calculation of useful parameters such as *mean exclusion chance* (MEC), which considers the unique inheritance of ChrX. Thirty years before Kruger *et al.* (1968) had created the MEC for AS.

One of the challenges in kinship testing is to establish techniques that can bridge large pedigree gaps. We know from observation in clinical genetics that persons who share a very rare genetic feature can be unified to a common pedigree. The famous monarchic haemophilia pedigree can be demonstrated as an example. Some members of the European high nobility show the trait of haemophilia, which leads to the term '*royal disease*'. Typing of the haemophilia gene would enables us to show that all affected persons with a certain mutation belong to the same pedigree descending from Queen Victoria (1837–1901). Two reasons ban us from doing this. Firstly, typing of harmful mutations in kinship testing would violate our ethical principles. Secondly, very rare traits would contribute to kinship only very seldomly. However, this example can demonstrate the power of rare alleles. Fortunately, the same effect can be achieved in another way: substituting *short tandem repeats* (STRs) by haplotypes consisting of clustered STRs provides a comparable power and can be used systematically in kinship testing.

Chromosome X Short Tandem Repeats

Microsatellites or simple sequence repeats are tandemly repeated DNA sequences found in varying abundance in all human chromosomes.

In forensic science the term *short tandem repeat* (STR) is ingrained. Including ChrX the overall STR density is comparable in all chromosomes. Within the chromosomes the density of STRs, however, shows significant variations. Tri- and hexanucleotide repeats are more abundant in exons, whereas other repeats are more abundant in non-coding regions. Moreover, as has been shown, a striking enrichment (>10-fold) of $[GATA]_n$ is revealed throughout a 10 Mb segment at Xp22 that escapes inactivation, and is confirmed by fluorescence *in situ* hybridization. A similar enrichment is found in other eutherian genomes. These findings clearly demonstrate sequence differences relevant to the novel biology and evolution of the X chromosome. Furthermore, they implicate simple sequence repeats, linked to gene regulation and unusual DNA structures, in the regulation and formation of facultative heterochromatin.

The analysis of tri-, tetra- and penta-STRs has become widespread in forensic medicine and STRs located on autosomes were used long before application of Y-chromosomal and X-chromosomal STR markers. Although the existence of ChrX STRs, i.e. HPRTB and ARA and DXS981, was reported relatively early, the desire to use such markers as tools for forensic application came up later.

The International Society for Forensic Haemogenetics guidelines for the forensic use of microsatellite markers apply to both AS and ChrX STRs. However, some specific molecular and formal genetic aspects need to be taken into account when dealing with ChrX markers. The forensic application of microsatellite markers can be done in practise if they are in Hardy-Weinberg equilibrium and have a high enough degree of polymorphism. The application of coding STRs such as ARA should be avoided.

Figure 6.1 review the main forensic ChrX repeat markers known to date. Most of them show no specific peculiarities in terms of their handling and some are routinely used by our own group and others. Solely DXS10011 should be singled out. This tetranucleotide repeat marker occurs in two sequence variants, type A and B. Whereas the type B allele mutation rate is comparable with other STRs, type A alleles mutate with very high frequencies. In general, mutation rates of ChrX STRs seem not to differ from microsatellites of other chromosomes. An early report on a high rate of mutation in DXS981 could not be confirmed in kinship testing and seems to be a misinterpretation of results obtained when working with lymphoblastoid cell lines of CEPH families.

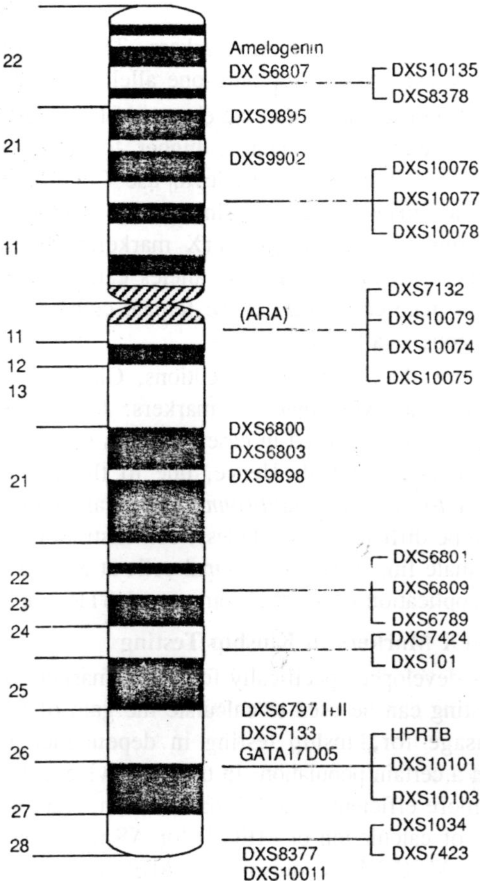

Fig. 6.1. Chromosome X ideogram with STR markers.

Typical STRs show regular structure with constant length differences between different alleles, i.e. 3, 4 or 5 bp steps. However, several markers such as DXS7130 and DXS6803, DXS10011 and DXS981 are composed of different repeat units resulting in 2 or 1 bp differences between alleles. Consequently, typing of such markers essentially requires gene scanner equipment and advanced carefulness.

Power of ChrX Markers in Trace Analysis

The *power of discrimination* (PD) value of ChrX markers varies according to gender. When female traces are to be matched to female individuals the ChrX markers equal those for AS. For the matching of male traces to male suspects, the PD value of ChrX markers is generally smaller than that of AS markers. This is due to the fact that male ChrX analysis utilizes only one allele per STR.

In a mixed female/male stain, the chance of having all male alleles included in the female component is higher for ChrX than for AS markers, therefore it is not advisable to use ChrX markers to test male traces in a female background. In order to identify female traces in male contamination, however, ChrX markers are more efficient than AS markers because the female alleles can only be completely included in the male component if the female coincidentally happens to be homozygous at all loci.

We conclude that, with few exceptions, ChrX markers are less powerful in stain analyses than AS markers. Furthermore, if more than four ChrX STRs are used in casework it is unavoidable that two or more of them are linked. Hence, due to the possibility of the existence of a *linkage disequilibrium* (LD), calculation of identity likelihood can be difficult. Nevertheless, demonstration of female skin debris under male finger nails or vaginal cells at a penis, etc. may be an issue for application of an X-chromosomal STR amplification kit.

Power of ChrX Markers in Kinship Testing

Formulas developed specifically for ChrX markers in the context of kinship testing can be used to calculate the gain of the concerning marker in usage for kinship testing in dependence of the allele distribution in a certain population. In trios involving a daughter, ChrX markers are more efficient than AS markers. This fact is reflected by the formulas for calculation of MEC(I) for AS markers and MEC(II) and MEC(III). MEC(III) is equivalent to MEC(II). MEC(I) for AS is not suitable for ChrX markers except for deficiency cases in which the paternal grandmother is investigated instead of the alleged father. If MEC(I) is compared to MEC(II) and MEC(III), the latter are consistently larger. Finally, Desmarais *et al.* (1998) introduced formulas for the mean exclusion chance of ChrX markers involving father/daughter duos lacking maternal genotype information, MEC(IV), which is also appropriate for maternity testing of mother/son duos.

Paternity testing in trios and duos

Paternity cases involving the common trio constellation of mother, offspring and alleged father can usually be solved with AS STRs alone, and do not seem to require any additional or alternative markers. When father/son relationships are to be tested, ChrX markers can contribute nothing anyway. However, when father/daughter relationships are in question it may be worthwhile including ChrX markers in testing.

This is especially the case when difficult-to-analyse template materials are involved, such as DNA from exhumed skeletons, historical or prehistorical samples, etc. Despite primer sets for typing degraded DNA now being available, in such instances sufficient statistical power has to come from a small number of low-size STRs. Fortunately, ChrX STRs are normally characterized by relatively high MECs, even at a low to medium degree of polymorphism. In those contexts, ChrX markers may be superior to AS markers in some instances. As an example I would like to mention a case that we have solved recently. We were requested to prove a father/daughter relationship by typing only the daughter's and the alleged father's saliva. The paternal saliva trace was taken from a stamp licked 30 years ago. The paternity likelihood could be established to be 99.93 by DXS8378-DXS7132, HPRTB and DXS7423 alone. Autosomal systems had contributed only little in solving this question.

Paternity cases involving blood-relatives

In paternity cases involving close blood-relatives as suspects, the exclusion power of STRs is substantially reduced and ChrX STRs may be superior to AS markers. For example, if two alleged fathers are father and son, they would not share any X-chromosomal alleles identical by descent (ibd) so that ChrX markers would be more efficient than AS markers. Brothers, in contrast, share a given maternal ChrX allele with probability 0.5, which corresponds to the probability of exactly one allele shared identical by descent at an AS locus.

For four unlinked ChrX loci, the chance of sharing alleles identical by descent would be 0.54 = 0.0625. Unfortunately, since the ChrX length is not more than 198 cM this chromosome can host a maximum of four, but strictly only three unlinked marker regions. When the markers are closely linked, they do not segregate independently. As with AS markers, they would instead represent a single haplotype that is shared with a probability of 0.5. The ChrX contains four linkage groups located at Xp22.2, Xq12,Xq26 and Xq28 that can provide independent genotype information. At present, we propose that it is preferable to use clusters DXS10135-DXS837, DXS7132-DXS10074, HPRTB-DXS10101 and DXS7423-DXS10134 to define haplotypes in forensic practise. Typing of these four marker pairs can be done by using the PCR kit Mentype Argus X-8 that is now commercially available. Alternatively, other cluster haplotypes such as DXS101-77424, DXS6801-DXS6809-DXS6789 and DXS10076-DXS10077-DXS10078 may be chosen.

Paternity testing using abortion material in incest and rape cases

After incest or criminal sexual assault, pregnancies may be terminated by suction abortion. An aborted 6–8 week product of conception consists of small amounts of non-identifiable foetal organs as well as maternal blood and other tissues. In such cases, microscopic detection of embryonic organs or chorionic villi is not generally successful and samples will contain a mixture of foetal and maternal DNA. By typing the simple amelogenin dimorphism, the appearance of a ChrY signal can clarify the sex. For male foetuses, further ChrY testing can easily help to assess the paternity. In incest cases in which a father is charged with abusing his daughter, however, ChrX testing of the abortus cannot demonstrate paternity since all foetal alleles would necessarily coincide with alleles of the daughter. In such cases, ChrX testing of mixed abortion material can only be used for the purpose of exclusion, not inclusion. The highest certainty may be provided by a typing strategy using AS and ChrX markers simultaneously. A quite different situation occurs when incest has to be investigated and clean foetal material can be obtained by chorion biopsy. In the case of a female foetus, ChrX testing would prove the fathering by a father–daughter incest when all foetal alleles coincide with alleles of the pregnant woman. Recently, we have reported a case of prenatal exclusion without involving the putative father of an incestuous father–daughter parenthood.

Maternity testing

There are some situations in which mother/child testing is requested. For example, public authorities responsible for aliens often allow family reunion only after proved kinship. Maternity can also be demonstrated by sequencing mitochondrial DNA (mtDNA), however this technique would not always yield the same level of certainty. For example, mtDNA sequences are identical not only to those of their own children but also to nephews and nieces in a maternal line. Furthermore, due to the high rate of illegitimate paternity in modern societies, the identification of skeletons or carcasses by mother/child testing is more reliable than through the assessment of father/child relationships.

Typing of ChrX STRs may thus represent a sensible alternative option to assess maternity. For testing mother–daughter relationships, ChrX markers are equivalent to AS markers and do not provide any specific advantage. Testing mother–son kinship, however, is more efficiently performed using ChrX markers. As discussed above, the option for ChrX marker typing using short amplicons should be considered, especially when skeletal human remains or other difficult samples have to be analysed. The exclusion chance in such cases is identical to that of ChrX STRs in father/daughter tests.

Chromosome X Marker Mapping and Haplotype Analysis

Genetic investigations in paternity trio cases should involve at least 12 STRs located on 10 chromosomes. However, solving complex kinship cases needs additional effort and ChrY and ChrX haplotyping is proving to be a powerful tool in solving difficult questions. The simultaneous analysis of STRs located on the same chromosome requires knowledge about the extent of pairwise linkage and linkage disequilibrium between them. Comprehensive studies on ChrX sequencing have determined 99.3% of the euchromatic sequence of the X chromosome. Hence, for a short time physical mapping of most ChrX markers, given as distance from the Xp telomere (measured in base pairs, bp), can be performed using internet databases such as the UCSC Genome Browser Database. Unfortunately, however, genetic and physical distances are not strictly correlated.

The classical approach to studying linkage between markers is via pedigree analysis. Based upon LOD ('logarithm of the odds') scores calculated from family data, meiotic recombination fractions are estimated for pairs of markers and transformed into genetic distances (measured in centimorgan, cM) using appropriate mapping functions. Due to the hemizygosity of sex chromosomes in males, linkage analysis is particularly efficient for ChrX loci. Nevertheless, for accurate mapping of very short distances, typing of a high number of meioses would be necessary. On the other hand, due to the limitations in typing very high numbers of meioses it may be justified to employ a simple rule of thumb: a physical distance of 1 Mb corresponds to a genetic distance of 1 cM, i.e. one expected recombination per 100 meioses. Genetic data resources available via the Marshfield and NCBI websites can be consulted to access genetic localization for many markers. Under practical aspects we have subdivided the ChrX into separate linkage groups 1–4. Under practical aspects, four STRs that are unlinked, i.e. DXS8378, DXS7132, HPRTB and DXS7423, have been chosen and can be seen as the cores of these four linkage groups. This set of four unlinked STRs (plus amelogenin) can be typed using the commercially available forensic ChrX typing kit (Mentype Argus X-Ul). In a second stage the kit is extended by further STRs. Mentype Argus X-8 provides a valuable tool for ChrX haplotyping. Each of the four

STR clusters spans less than 0.5 cM and therefore provides a stable haplotype. Consequently, the genetic risk of recombination within each of the four clusters will be less than 0.5%.

Generally, alleles of linked loci form haplotypes that recombine during meioses at a frequency corresponding to the inter-marker genetic distance. In kinship testing, haplotypes of closely linked STRs must therefore be analysed as a whole, rather than through their constituent alleles, if the meiotic stability of haplotypes is high enough. *Linkage disequilibrium* (LD), which refers to this '*non-random*' association of alleles at different loci, measures the deviation of population-specific haplotype frequencies from the product of the corresponding allele frequencies. For markers with strong LD, haplotype frequencies cannot be inferred from allele frequencies alone but instead have to be estimated directly from population data. Due to their higher mutation rate, STRs tend to show less LD than SNPs. However, LD can still occur between closely linked STRs and therefore has to be assessed prior to their practical application. In some ChrX regions we analysed the inter-marker LD of STRs by genotyping male DNA samples. Significant LD was observed for some very tight-linked marker clusters, namely DXS101 and DXS7424, DXS6801, DXS6809 and DXS6789, DXS10076, DXS10077 and DXS10078 and DXS10079, DXS10074 and DXS10075. For example, testing the latter mentioned cluster in an Eastern German population of 781 unrelated men revealed 172 different haplotypes. Due to a considerable LD the number of observed haplotypes is smaller than previously expected. Nevertheless, 72% of all observed haplotypes showed frequencies of <0.02. Hence, despite the existence of LD, these STRs and the other STR clusters mentioned are characterized by a high evidentiary power in kinship testing.

Deficiency paternity cases

When, in a case of uncertain paternity, a biological sample from a putative father is not available and DNA from paternal relatives has to be analysed instead, the situation is called a '*deficiency paternity test*'. This branch of kinship testing is the main field of ChrX marker application and the major advantage of ChrX markers can be demonstrated here. Again, as illustrated using the royal pedigree, X-chromosomal traits or ChrX marker testing can connect pedigree members through large distances with respect to X-chromosomal tracks, however they fail when X-chromosomal lines are interrupted by father–son relationship. The benefit of ChrX testing can be shown by the presentation of some examples.

When ChrX markers are investigated in a deficiency case, the mother of the unavailable putative father (i.e. the putative grandmother) is the key figure. Instances in which she is available for genotyping, strictly speaking, do not represent deficiency cases. All ChrX alleles of the putative father can be determined by investigating her, and the MEC can be calculated using the respective formula for AS markers. The ChrX marker genotype of the putative grandmother can also be reconstructed to some extent from her children. If she has several daughters, it is possible to determine the parental origin of most of their ChrX alleles and therefore the grandmaternal genotype. If brothers of the putative father are available, the data are even more informative. Then, the grandmaternal genotype must have been heterozygous for all ChrX loci for which brothers of the putative father carry different alleles. If they carry identical alleles, the constellation is uninformative: the mother can be either homozygous or heterozygous at the corresponding locus. If closely linked loci have already been identified as being heterozygous, the probability of homozygosity at the original locus can be assessed by haplotyping. This is exemplified for DXS6801, DXs6809 and DXS6789. In this case a woman 'Nora', and her putative uncles 'Jim' and 'Joe' were tested for kinship. We typed 18 ChrX markers, including the Xp21 cluster. For some loci the constellation is informative in the sense that it narrows down the set of possible alleles of the *putative grandmother* (PGM) and consequently of the *putative father* (PF). In the present case, single STR typing revealed such a pattern and a consequent exclusion of paternity for DXS8378 and DXS10011. However, since DXS10011 is strongly prone to mutation, the exclusion was still regarded as weak. Anyhow, whilst single STR results for the Xp21 cluster were uninformative, haplotyping showed that the necessary paternal allele combination of 14–31–14 could not have been inherited from the PF. For the PF to have received this haplotype from the PGM, two recombinations would have been required. Since the probability of such a double recombination is only $0.051 \times 0.046 = 2.35 \times 10 - 3$, i.e. of the same order of magnitude as the mutation rate of most STRs, the PF could unequivocally be excluded from paternity.

When female individuals have the same father, they also share the same paternal ChrX. An investigation of ChrX markers of two sisters or step-sisters can thus exclude paternity even when none of the parents are available for testing. The AS markers cannot provide such information. A positive proof of paternity is also possible with a lack of maternal genotype information, but is generally less reliable. This is due to the fact that sisters usually inherit only partially matching haplotypes from their mother. The co-inheritance of two identical maternal ChrXs without a recombination is not impossible, but rare. With a total genetic length of approximately 198 cM there are several virtually uncoupled regions on the ChrX. Assuming that the number of recombination breakpoints between two ChrX loci follows a Poisson distribution with parameter λ equal to the genetic distance between the loci, the chance of inheriting a non-recombined ChrX equals $e^{-2} = 0.135$ (200 cM = 2 M, the basic unit of genetic distance). Therefore, the probability of two sisters inheriting two identical, non-recombined maternal ChrXs is $2 \times 0.1352 = 0.036$. This implies that, if two step-sisters share an identical haplotype A in addition to individual haplotypes B and C, the likelihood ratio of shared paternity vs. non-shared paternity equals

$$f(A) \cdot \frac{1}{2} \cdot 2f(B)f(C) / 0.036 \cdot f(A) \cdot f(B) \cdot f(C) = 27.8$$

In other words, the probability of full sisterhood, assuming equal prior odds, cannot exceed $27.8/(1 + 27.8) = 0.965$.

Grandfather–grandson kinship is an excellent field for X marker usage. Passing the daughter generation, the grandpaternal X-chromosome normally underlies a recombination. However, typing haplotypes consisting of closely linked markers provides a high chance to indicate kinship. Since the two questionable cousins exhibit the ChrX haplotype with respect to two STR pairs, we were able to demonstrate that putative cousins share a common grandfather.

Chromosome X–chromosome Y Homologue Markers

The ChrX–ChrY homologue non-recombining region are unique in the genome. Hosted on the ChrY this region can be transmitted only from father to son whereas the ChrX counterpart is inherited in the typical X-chromosomal mode. Doubtless, the most utilized locus of this type is the diallelic indel-polymorphism amelogenin, which is located at Yp11.1; Xp22.2 and is well-established for molecular gender assessment. Cali *et al.* (2002) described the locus DXYS156, which is located at Yp 11.3 and Xq21.2-3. This marker is multi-allelic at both ChrX and ChrY. A Y-chromosome-specific nucleotide insertion in the duplicate STR allows males to be distinguished from females, as does the commonly used amelogenin system, but with the advantage that this locus, due to their multiple alleles, may contribute towards DNA fingerprinting of a sample. Yet another bonus is that both the X and the Y copies of DXYS156 have alleles specific to different parts of the world, offering separate estimates of maternal and paternal descent of that sample. It is of interest that some further markers of this kind have been published, namely DXYS241, DXYS265 and DXYS266. However, since they are dinucleotides they are sub-optimal in their use for forensic casework. Nevertheless, ChrX–ChrY homologue markers should attract more attention from the forensic community.

Chromosome X STR Allele and Haplotype Distribution in Different Populations

The ChrX marker differences of allele distribution are marginal when nearly related populations are compared. However, when considered worldwide they may show noteworthy allele frequency differences. *Linkage disequilibrium* (LD), or the non-random association of alleles, is not completely understood in the human genome. However, studies of LD between microsatellites and, more recently, between SNPs have provided new insights into the origin and history of human populations. For example, LD levels are much higher in non-African than in African populations and this may reflect a population bottleneck that is associated with the origin of non-African populations. In particular, LD between ChrX markers can indicate ethnic differences with high effectiveness. Thus, ChrX marker LD investigation may complement ChrY and mtDNA studies on human world migration.

Ethical Considerations in ChrX Marker Testing

Detection of gonosomal aberrations and testicular feminization ChrX marker testing

In the most countries, such as Germany, forensic scientists follow the principle that forensic DNA testing should not disclose diseases or genetic risks. This principle fully complies with STR typing strategies using well-established autosomal STRs, such as CODIS markers, ChrY markers, mtDNA analysis and nearly all established ChrX markers. Both ChrY and mtDNA typing may reveal some general information as to a person's ethnic origin, however, this cannot be considered as an intervention into the person's privacy. In principle, the same applies to gender identification typing with ChrX and ChrY markers. However, chromosomal aberrations such as Klinefelter syndrome and Ullrich-Turner syndrome may be recognized when ChrX markers are used. This may be diagnosed when females show (virtual) homozygosity in all the ChrX STRs investigated. Furthermore, androgen insensitivity syndrome (known also under the alternative titles of 'testicular feminization syndrome, androgen receptor deficiency or dihydrotestosterone receptor deficiency') can be recognized when a person's female phenotype is linked not with a female genotype (XX) but with the male counterpart XY.

When gonosomal aberrations or instances of androgen insensitivity or XY gonadal dysgenesis are detected, ChrX typing is no longer a valid means of kinship testing. In any case, it appears worthwhile emphasizing that such findings, when inadvertently obtained during kinship testing, fall under the premise of confidentiality. Disease-relevant information should not be revealed to an affected individual unless they explicitly ask for it.

HumARA trinucleotide repeat

Notwithstanding the fact that HumARA is one of the best-established forensic STR markers, our group has recently announced that we no longer consider HumARA to be a suitable DNA marker in forensic casework. From the very beginning of HumARA testing it has been known that, in contrast to all other forensic DNA markers, the HumARA CAG repeat is located in a coding region (androgen receptor gene, exon 1). This means that the repeat codes for a polyglutamine tract proved that X-linked *spinal and bulbar muscular atrophy* (SBMA) is attributable to a mutation at this locus. This disease occurs at trinucleotide repeat lengths longer than 43. Apart from the SBMA disease, HumARA typing can detect a number of further health risks, e.g. increased risk of impaired spermatogenesis, prostate cancer and many more.

Since sex chromosome markers are especially efficient for solving deficiency cases, an increasing usage can be expected. A specific demand for kinship tests in which only remote relatives are available for testing can be expected to arise, particularly from the need to rejoin families in the context of war and worldwide migration. Here, ChrX marker testing may also prove helpful. Furthermore, the proportion of non-marital children is constantly increasing in modern industrial societies and, for example, accounts for approximately 50% of all births in the eastern federal states of Germany. In many of these instances, paternity may be disputed at some stage and, when the putative father dies early or unexpectedly, the need for a paternity test may only be recognized after the interment.

Y-Chromosomal Markers in Forensic Genetics

Analysis of the human Y chromosome in forensics has three main applications: male sex identification, male lineage identification and identification of the geographical origin of male lineages. A male individual is identified, based on DNA evidence, by detecting male-specific parts of the Y chromosome in crime scene samples. Male lineage identification (a male lineage is defined as a male individual together with all his paternal male relatives) is performed by typing male-specific Y-chromosomal DNA polymorphisms in the crime scene samples and searching for matching profiles in suspects. The geographical origin or, in other words, genetic ancestry of male lineages is revealed by using Y-chromosomal markers with specific geographical distributions, as determined from reference databases. The value of Y-chromosomal markers for male identification in forensics is underlined by the fact that the vast majority of violent crimes are committed by males and that almost all cases of sexual assault involve males as perpetrators. Consequently, Y-chromosomal markers are increasingly being used by forensic laboratories. This is reflected in the large increase in the number of publications dealing with Y-chromosomal markers in the forensic science literature over recent years. A number of milestone discoveries in human genetics made it possible to use human Y-chromosomal markers for forensic applications. In this section we will describe the applications of Y-chromosomal markers to modern forensics, together with some of the key discoveries in human molecular and population genetics that have allowed such applications, and finally we will give a brief outlook on the future of Y-chromosomal markers in forensics.

Identification of the Male Sex

Up until the beginning of the last century it was generally believed that in humans sex was determined by environmental factors such as maternal nutrition. With the discovery of the human X and Y chromosomes in the early 1920s it was first assumed that the number of X chromosomes determined the sex of a human individual. It took an additional 36 years to establish that sex determination in humans and other mammals is independent from the number of X chromosomes and that the presence of the Y chromosome is responsible for the male sex. During more than three decades of continued, intensive research into the molecular basis of human male sex determination, a series of putative candidate sequences on the human Y chromosome have been established, e.g. simple repetitive sequences. Finally in the early 1990s the so-called '*sex determining region Y*' or SRY gene was identified and it was subsequently shown that the transfer and expression of SRY in female mouse embryos led to the development of testicles. Today it is generally accepted that the SRY gene expresses the testis-determining factor and is the key gene responsible for male sex formation in humans and other mammals.

These (and other) discoveries in human genetics opened the door for forensic DNA-based human sex identification. In the 1970s luminescence microscopy was used for detection of the human Y chromosome in forensic material. Later, advances in molecular genetics allowed more sensitive detection of the Y chromosome using, for example, Y alphoid DNA. The breakthrough for DNA-based sex identification in forensics came with the introduction of the *polymerase chain reaction* (PCR) for the sensitive detection of various regions on the human Y chromosome, including the amelogenin gene.

Although the detection of DNA from the non-recombining region of the Y chromosome identifies the presence of male material, not detecting Y-specific DNA does not mean that a sample contains only female material. This is because a negative result in a Y chromosome DNA test can have other reasons than there being no Y chromosome present in the sample being investigated, e.g. technical failures, no amplifiable DNA, etc. For this reason, combined tests to detect both Y-chromosomal and X-chromosomal DNA were developed. Of these, the amelogenin gene test has become the most established in forensic laboratories. The amelogenin gene is present on both the X and the Y chromosome and the test is based on a length polymorphism within the gene itself differentiating the Y-chromosomal from the X-chromosomal copy. Nowadays this test is included in many commercial kits for the DNA-based identification of human individuals. However, it should be noted that the reliability of the test has been criticized due to the occurrence of Y-chromosomal deletions that can include the amelogenin gene. Although the frequency of such deletions is generally low, their incidence can be increased in certain populations due to events in the population history. Furthermore, due to the highly repetitive molecular structure of the Y chromosome, deletions are known from many Y-chromosomal regions. Therefore, the reliability of DNA-based sex tests can be improved by increasing the number of Y loci tested. Naturally, the detection of Y-chromosomal DNA polymorphisms as used to identify male lineages because of their property to carry genetic variation between male lineages is informative for male sex identification.

Identification of Male Lineages

Most of the human Y chromosome (i.e. the non-recombining region of the Y chromosome, NRY) is male specific and is inherited unchanged from fathers to sons, unless a rare mutational event occurs. DNA recombination, a genetic process that reshuffles genetic material between homologue chromosomes to create additional variation, is not acting on the NRY because of the absence of a homologue chromosome. Due to the lack of recombination, a Y-chromosomal mutation creating a new allele is always inherited by male offspring in subsequent generations. On the other hand, the lack of recombination also means that all male relatives carry the same Y chromosome, independent of the degree of paternal relationship. This makes Y chromosome polymorphisms very useful for male identification but also means that male lineages (i.e. groups of paternally related males), but not individual males, can be identified, at least with the currently available Y markers.

The use of Y-chromosomal polymorphisms for male identification in forensics started 40 years ago with the analysis of whole Y-chromosome length polymorphisms to detect exclusion constellations in paternity cases, even though the molecular basis of the underlying polymorphisms was unknown at the time. Later, and with increased knowledge about the molecular biology of the human Y chromosome, the use of whole Y-chromosome length differences was abolished from forensic applications due to the discovery of Y-chromosome length differences between cells from the same individual. The real breakthrough came in the early 1990s with the identification of the first Y-chromosomal microsatellite or short tandem repeat (Y-STR) polymorphism, DYS19, and its immediate application to a rape case, revealing an exclusion constellation. However, as known from the application of autosomal STRs to forensics, the value of a single marker for human individualization is limited. Instead, many STRs are needed to achieve high resolution and confidence. In 1997 a first attempt towards the forensic application of Y-STR haplotypes was made by the Forensic Y-Chromosome Research Group coordinated by Lutz Roewer from the Humboldt University in Berlin with the characterization of 13 Y-chromosomal STRs in 3825 unrelated males from 48 population samples. This study was recently rated as the second most highly cited publication in the five leading forensic science and legal medicine journals, according to the ISI Web of Science database, but in fact it is the most cited paper ever published in a leading forensic journal (306 citations) based on a database query in July 2006, reflecting the success of Y-STR markers, especially in forensic science.

By 1997, 13 Y-chromosomal STRs were available for forensic applications. Of these, nine describe the so-called '*minimal haplotype*' recommended by the International Forensic Y User Group as the minimal set of Y-STRs to be used for human male individualization in forensics. The advantage of genetic markers from the non-recombining part of the Y chromosome compared with those from any other chromosome is that single marker information can be combined as haplotype information since the male-specific part of the Y chromosome is inherited completely linked from fathers to sons. For forensic applications this means that the multiplication of single locus allele frequencies for obtaining combined DNA profile matching probabilities cannot be applied to Y-chromosomal markers, but instead compound haplotype frequencies must be used for establishing matching probabilities in cases of non-exclusions. The combination of single loci in compound Y-chromosomal haplotypes, such as using the nine Y-STRs from the minimal haplotype, leads to an enormous increase in informativity. Consequently, the number of individuals that need to be investigated for obtaining representative haplotype frequencies is expected to be enormous and much larger than needed for autosomal markers. This has led to the establishment of Y-STR haplotype databases for obtaining more accurate and reliable haplotype frequencies. The largest database is the 'Y-Chromosome Haplotype Reference Database, YHRD'. This database started out as a European initiative, was later expanded by mirror databases for U.S. populations, and Asian populations and today exists as a combined and further expanded database with 40,108 haplotypes in a set of 320 populations worldwide, including population samples from all continental regions.

Numerous laboratories, mostly from the international forensic genetics community, have contributed Y-STR haplotype data under controlled quality criteria to the YHRD and the number of contributed haplotypes is constantly increasing. The YHRD allows complete and partial Y-STR haplotype profiles to be searched for population-based and region-based frequencies, and provides useful graphical representations of the geographical distribution of the respective haplotypes, as well as lists with the number of matches per population sample. In addition to the search function, information about typing methods, molecular characteristics, including mutation rate estimates, and several statistical tools, including a haplotype frequency surveying method, are available through the public-domain website of the database. This makes the YHRD unique not only in size but also in data authenticity, compared with databases established from published Y-STR data or other databases without quality control requirements. Due to the introduction of various commercial Y-STR kits, company-based

Y-STR haplotype databases have become available recently, mostly collecting data from individuals living in the USA:

In the future it would be desirable if all data could be included in a single database allowing user-friendly single access for a comprehensive Y-STR haplotype frequency search.

The number of scientifically known Y-STRs has dramatically increased over recent years. In 2004, results from a comprehensive survey of Y-STRs were published using the nearly complete Y chromosome sequence for a systematic search for all useful Y-STR markers. In this study, 166 previously unknown Y-STR markers were found, increasing the total number of verified Y-STRs to 215. Although the 9–11 commonly used Y-STRs provide high haplotype diversity, and thus high probability of male lineage identification, additional Y-STRs will increase the haplotype discrimination, depending on the marker added and the population analysed. Furthermore, studies have reported population samples with a high number of identical 9–16 loci Y-STR haplotypes as a result of severe bottlenecks in the history of those populations, e.g. 14% of males in a Pakistani population sample and 13% of males in a Finish population sample share the same 16-loci Y-STR haplotype. Therefore, in cases of matching haplotypes, typing additional Y-STRs can be useful for forensic applications, and currently many of the newly described Y-STRs are investigated with respect to their haplotype discrimination potential, population genetic diversity, mutation rates, as well as their suitability for multiplex analyses.

A number of Y-STR markers are located in multicopy regions of the Y chromosome and thus consistently show more than one male-specific allele. These multicopy Y-STRs, although often very variable due to the simultaneous detection of multiple polymorphic loci, are less useful for forensic stain analyses since they might cause interpretation difficulties in mixed stains with more than one male involved. Some of these multicopy markers are located in Y-chromosomal regions where the number of copies is assumed to be associated with male fertility problems (such as AZF). Consequently, a Y-STR profile including these loci can potentially be informative for the fertility status of a man. Such loci should be omitted from forensic tests because of the additional information they potentially reveal.

The most important application of Y-chromosome markers for male lineage identification in forensics is in cases of sexual assault. The nature of the material available from sexual assault cases, usually mixed stains from the female victim's epithelial cells and the male perpetrator's sperm cells, makes autosomal STR profiling challenging. Normally, to separate the male and female genetic components, differential lysis is applied to extraction DNA from mixed stains. Often, and especially when the number of sperm cells is low, this approach fails, resulting in potential overlap of the victim's and perpetrator's autosomal STR profiles, making male perpetrator identification impossible. Recent technological advances, e.g. using laser dissection microscopy to specifically collect sperm cells, are promising but the success of autosomal STR analysis from such material depends on the number of sperm cells collectable in each particular case. If the number of sperm cells is low, technical problems of *low copy number* (LCN) analysis are expected, and the approach will not be successful when no sperm cells can be collected. However, the specific detection of male DNA by analysing Y-chromosomal STRs in principle avoids the problem of profile overlap (since females do not carry a Y chromosome) and additionally is much more sensitive. Mixing experiments have shown that Y-STRs can still be amplified successfully and reliably up to male–female DNA mixtures of 1 : 2000. In addition, even in the absence of sperm (i.e. in cases of oligospermic or azoospermic males involved) but the presence of mostly or only male epithelial cells in a mixed stain, Y-STR analysis has proven to be highly successful. It has also been shown that Y-STR haplotype profiling in rape cases can be successful from cervicovaginal samples recovered up to 4 days post-coitus.

The use of Y-STR markers in forensics is regulated by two recommendations of the DNA Commission of the International Society of Forensic Genetics in collaboration with expert Y chromosome scientists. Because of the above-mentioned advantages and the enormous research effort that has been undertaken, Y chromosome markers (especially Y-STRs) are routinely used for male lineage identification in many forensic laboratories all over the world, and have been for many years already. One case shall be mentioned as an example to demonstrate the power of Y-STRs in forensic male lineage identification. To identify a serial rapist who had raped 14 young women and murdered one of them in north-western Poland, Y-STR haplotype profiles were obtained from >400 suspects as part of an elimination process. A man was identified with a Y-STR haplotype profile identical to that obtained from the crime scene, but with an autosomal STR profile matching that of the crime scene in only 9 of 10 markers. This finding suggested that the perpetrator must be one of this man's close relatives and DNA analysis of his brother revealed a complete match of both the autosomal STR and Y-STR profiles, identifying the brother as the perpetrator. It should be pointed out that Y chromosome (or mtDNA)-based mass screenings (which are on a voluntary basis) are also seen critically since legislation in many countries provides the right to refuse testimony in cases where close relatives are involved. However, Y chromosome (and mtDNA)-based male (and female) lineage identification is able to identify close and distant male (and female) relatives.

Although there is general agreement on the use of Y-STR markers to exclude suspects, there is still an ongoing discussion about how to use Y-STR haplotype information in the courtroom when a match between the crime scene sample and a suspect is established. Usually it is common practise to place some significance on the probability of such a match. This can be achieved by a method that extrapolates frequency estimates based on observed data stored in a database such as the YHRD. This '*haplotype surveying method*', available via the YHRD website, generates estimates of the prior and posterior frequency distributions of Y-STR haplotypes. A simplified use of Y-STR haplotype databases for obtaining confidence in the statistical meaning of a haplotype match can be obtained from mismatch distribution analysis, whereas a more conservative approach is to simply count the number of times the haplotype exists in the database and establish a confidence interval by taking into account the size of the database. However, some scientists argue that existing Y-STR databases are not representative of real populations because of their limited size and because the databases are normally based on unrelated individuals, whereas real populations are not only bigger in size but also do contain related individuals. The latter is especially important for Y chromosome markers since close and distantly related men can share the same Y-STR haplotype. Such a perspective leads to the most conservative use of Y-STR haplotype information in cases of established matches, stating that the suspect cannot be excluded from being the donor of the crime scene sample. It is noteworthy that official recommendations by the DNA Commission of the International Society of Forensic Genetics on the estimation of the weight of the evidence of Y-STR typing have not yet been provided but are expected in the near future, as announced elsewhere.

Identification of a Male's Paternity

The second forensic application offered by Y chromosome markers is in testing for the paternity of male offspring. Already in 1985, and therefore seven years before the first hypervariable Y-STR marker was discovered, it was suggested based on statistical considerations that the use of polymorphic Y markers should increase the chance to detect non-paternity compared with their autosomal counterparts. Polymorphic Y-chromosomal markers are especially useful in deficiency cases where the alleged father of a male child is deceased. Such cases can only be solved via autosomal STR profiling with a high degree of certainty if both parents of the putative father are available for DNA analysis. Only the complete genotypes of the grandparents allow a reliable reconstruction of the STR alleles inherited from the deceased putative father to his child, given the mother's profile. However, many cases are brought to paternity testing where none or only one parent of the deceased alleged father is available for DNA analysis. In those cases involving a male child, Y-STR haplotyping can identify the biological father if a biological male relative of any grade of relationship is available for testing to replace the deceased alleged father in the Y chromosome DNA analysis. Since Y-chromosomal STR haplotypes are identical between male relatives (unless rare mutation events occur), finding matching haplotypes between the male child and any biological paternal relative of the putative father will provide evidence in favour of the biological paternity of the deceased putative father (or any of his contemporary male relatives). Conversely, finding haplotype differences between the child and the male relative will exclude the deceased alleged father from paternity. However, the number of generations that separate the alleged father from his male relative used for Y chromosome analysis will increase the probability that mutations will introduce differences between the male relative and the child, despite the deceased male being the true father of the child. Thus, mutation rate estimates of the Y-STRs used for testing need to be taken into account in calculating paternity probabilities. Therefore, knowledge about mutation rates for the Y-STRs used in forensics is important.

The first study to estimate mutation rates for Y-STRs used in forensics applied deep-rooting pedigrees and revealed an average rate of 2.1×10^{-3} mutations per locus per generation. In principle, mutation rate estimates should include the uncertainty caused by potential non-biological paternity, being especially crucial in pedigree studies where paternity cannot be established directly. However, in this study the biological paternal relationships within the pedigrees used for Y-STR mutation rate estimation were confirmed by additional analysis of the

Y-chromosomal minisatellite MSY1. The first comprehensive study establishing Y-STR mutation rates based on father–son pairs of (autosomal) DNA-proven biological paternity revealed an average rate of 2.8×10^{-3} mutations per locus per generation. Subsequent, additional studies using father–son pairs confirmed previously obtained mutation rates and a summary of mutation rate estimates for Y-STR markers commonly used in forensics is available from the YHRD website. Given the hypervariability of Y-STR haplotypes with sufficient loci included (e.g. the minimal haplotype), paternally unrelated males normally show differences at many Y-STRs. If two minimal haplotypes show differences at only one or two loci involving only one or two repeats, a relationship between the two respective male individuals needs to be considered, given the available knowledge about Y-STR mutation rates. It has been suggested that exclusion constellations at three or more Y-STRs need to be established before an exclusion of paternity can be concluded. Mutations at STRs, independent of whether they are located on the autosomes or on the sex chromosomes, are results of errors during DNA replication and mismatch repair. Single-strand slippage within the repetitive sequence of the STR locus can lead to a gain or a loss of repeats, usually of single repeat units.

Another feature of Y-STRs that is of relevance for forensic applications (although not for paternity testing) concerns the rare occurrence of additional Y-STR alleles. Two mutational events lead to the observation of additional Y-STR alleles: first, a Y-chromosomal duplication including the STR locus occurs, and subsequently a slippage mutation results in allelic differences between the original STR and the copy. Additional Y-STR alleles were observed at almost all Y-STRs used in forensics and can be misinterpreted as the involvement of multiple males when detected in a crime scene sample.

In principle, the absence of recombination between Y specific markers allows the identification of non-biological paternity after many (male) generations in pedigree analysis. Thus, disputed paternity cases from historical times involving male offspring can be resolved today by testing Y-chromosomal polymorphisms in true paternal male descendants. This has been done in many cases, with the most prominent being that of the former U.S. President Thomas Jefferson and the children of Sally Hemmings, one of his slaves. It could be shown that Y-chromosomal profiles based on Y-SNPs, Y-STRs and a Y mini-satellite of a fourth-generation male descendant of Easton Hemings Jefferson, one of Sally Hemmings sons, and four sixth- and seventh-generation descendants of Field Jefferson, Thomas Jefferson's father's brother, were identical. From the Y-chromosome data it was concluded that either Thomas Jefferson or one of his contempory male-line relatives, including his brother Randolph, had fathered Easton Hemings Jefferson. Unfortunately no living male descendants of Randolph Jefferson were available for testing.

In the same way that Y chromosome DNA analysis can be used for paternity testing and forensic stain analysis, it can also be used for identifying the biological remains of missing persons, including cases of mass disasters. Reference material of known living relatives is needed, as for autosomal DNA analysis, but the advantage of Y (and mitochondrial DNA) markers over autosomal markers is that relationships can be established and individuals identified, even if only reference samples of distant relatives are available for analysis. This can be highly relevant in mass disasters such as the 2004 Tsunami disaster in Southeast Asia, where entire families died and close relatives were therefore not available as references for autosomal DNA testing.

Identification of a Male's Geographical Origin

The third forensic application of Y-chromosomal DNA polymorphisms is in the identification of the geographical origin or genetic ancestry of an unknown male individual. Since this is the most recent application of Y-chromosomal markers to forensics, it deserves a somewhat more detailed summary. Geographical origin or, in other words, genetic ancestry identification is important in forensic cases with no known suspects. In such cases it would be helpful for the police to be able to concentrate their investigation towards finding suspects from specific groups of individuals, i.e. people of a particular geographical origin (often the terms '*ethnic group*' or '*ethnic identification*' are used but are unfortunate since ethnicity is determined by more factors than geography). Genetic testing can, to a certain extent, provide such information, at least for some geographical regions of the world. However, in order to trace the suspect(s), the police would usually extrapolate information on particular externally visible characteristics from the DNA data providing information about the geographical origin. Assumptions about a suspect's looks based on his DNA-based geographical origin are strictly indirect and the entire approach is feasible only when a high correlation between a geographical region and an externally visible trait exists. For instance, there is a high correlation between human skin colour and latitude also leading to continental differentiation. As result, European geographical origin is usually strongly associated with light skin colour, whereas African genetic ancestry usually is with dark skin colour. Because of this strong association, it is somewhat justified to conclude a light skin colour appearance of a donor of a DNA sample when DNA typing reveals a European genetic origin, and a dark skin colour appearance from a DNA test revealing a African genetic origin. However, similarly strong correlations involving other phenotypic traits and geographical regions are rare.

DNA-based identification of geographical origins is usually performed by testing markers where a specific allele or haplotype is restricted to a certain geographical region or shows significant and large frequency differences between geographical regions. In general, frequency distributions of genetic markers arise when a mutation occurs in a single individual living in a particular geographical region and inherits the mutations to produced offspring who subsequently spread/migrate to other geographical regions or remain where they are. There can be several reasons why a marker increases in frequency so that it can be used for geographical origin identification. For instance, the mutation can have a beneficial effect on the individuals carrying it, resulting in reproductive success. Such effects of positive selection causing high marker frequencies are known, for instance, from genes responsible for or associated with resistance towards certain infectious diseases but can be expected from all genes with close environmental interactions and severe influence on survival and reproduction. In the case of resistance towards infectious diseases, the marker frequency depends on the strength of selection (benefit) but also on the frequency of the disease-causing organisms (e.g. mutations in genes expressed in red blood cells provide malaria resistance and are frequent in regions with a high incidence of malaria because of the high frequency of malaria-causing *Plasmodium* spp.). However, based on existing knowledge, positive selection is unlikely to have shaped Y chromosome diversity and the frequency distribution of Y markers basically depends on the mutation rate, the geographical region of occurrence of the mutation, cultural factors influencing the degree of male reproduction (i.e. residence and marriage patterns, warfare, etc.) and the migratory history of the respective (male) population.

With the availability of the first population data of Y-STRs it was noticed that – albeit rarely – some Y-STR marker alleles show a highly restricted geographical distribution, e.g. short DYS390 alleles in the Pacific region. Also, significant differences in the Y-STR haplotypes were found between geographically distant populations as well as between geographically close populations, such as the Germans and the Dutch, although not between many other European groups. Within Europe at least three different groups of populations (called *metapopulations* in the YHRD) – Eastern Europeans, Western Europeans and Southeastern Europeans – were identified in the YHRD. Thus, based on the minimal Y-STR haplotype, information about which European region a male and his paternal ancestors originated from can be obtained, at least for some of the most characteristic haplotypes and those that show a more restricted distribution.

With the recent expansion of the YHRD to additionally include non-European population samples, continental information can also be obtained from Y-STR haplotype data, although such conclusions are still preliminary because of the low (but growing) number of non-European samples. There are a number of Y-STR haplotypes that show a continentally restricted frequency distribution. For instance, a YHRD search in August 2006 revealed that the Y-STR haplotype most characteristic for the Eastern European population cluster (DYS19, DYS389I, DYS389II, DYS390, DYS391, DYS392, DYS393, DYS385a-b: = 17, 13, 30, 25, 10, 11, 13, 10–14) is found in 192 out of 40108 individuals in a set of 320 worldwide populations of which 186 (97%) are European. From the remaining six matches, one (0.5%) is in Turkey, one (0.5%) in Kazakhstan and four (2%) in Hungarian Gypsies. This haplotype was not observed elsewhere in the world. Of the 186 European matches, 123 (66%) are found in the Eastern European metapopulation, as expected, 53 (28.5%) in the Western European metapopulation, 7 (3.8%) in the South-Eastern European metapopulation, 2 (1%) in US Americans and 1 (0.5%) from Argentina – the latter three men are of self-declared European descent.

The Y-STR haplotype most characteristic for the Western European metapopulation (14, 13, 29, 24, 11, 13, 13, 11–14) was found in 820 out of 40108 individuals in a set of 320 worldwide populations, of which 731 (89%) are Europeans. From the 89 remaining matches 85 are of likely European ancestry through European admixture: 30 are from the USA, UK, Brazil or Columbia but from individuals of self-declared African ancestry, 3 are from African countries, 2 are from the UK but from individuals with self-declared Asian ancestry, 13 are from Reunion Creoles, 7 are from Ecuador Mestizos, 2 are from Ecuador Quichuas – all of these most likely indicate European Y-chromosomal admixture – and 28 are from U.S. Hispanics. Thus, altogether this haplotype is found in 99.5% of the matches in individuals with European ancestry; the remaining four matches are from Turkey, China, Georgia, and Hungarian Gypsy. This haplotype was not observed elsewhere in the world. As expected, this haplotype is most frequent in the Western Europeans with 466 (57%) matches, and was also found with 16 matches (2%) in the Eastern European metapopulation, 16 matches in the Southeastern European metapopulation (2.3%) and 233 matches (28.4%) in Europeans from Argentina, Brazil, Colombia, South Africa and US Americans of European descent. In contrast, the Y-STR haplotype that is most frequent in US African Americans (15, 13, 31, 21, 10, 11, 13, 16, 17) was found with 41 matches in the YHRD, of which 38 (92.6%) are Africans or men with known African descent: Cameroon, Bantu South Africa, Guinea, Mozambique, Egypt, African Americans from the USA, Brazil, Ecuador, Colombo and UK Afro-Caribbeans. The remaining 3 matches are from one Argentinean European, one US Hispanic and one Reunion Creole, most likely indicating African Y-chromosomal admixture.

Although, as can be seen, at least some Y-STR haplotypes are informative for geographical origin identification, the relatively high mutation rate of Y-STRs tends to randomize genetic ancestry signals over a large number of generations/long time span. Therefore it is often stated that Y-STRs are more informative for detecting recent rather than ancient events in the genetic history of populations, whereas ancient events can be identified more reliably using Y-chromosomal single nucleotide polymorphisms, or SNPs, which have mutation rates 100,000 times lower than Y-STRs. One of the first studies describing a geographically restricted distribution of a Y-SNP marker, and its use for investigating human population history, appeared in 1997. Today, a large number of Y-SNP markers are known and many of them show a continent-specific distribution. A comprehensive summary of the distribution and applications of Y-chromosome SNP markers can be found elsewhere. Here, we want to illustrate the suitability of Y-SNP markers for detecting geographical origins using three continent-specific examples:

African origins

The Y-SNP marker SRY_{4064} (or one of its phylogenetic equivalents, M96 or P29) defining haplogroup E appears at high frequency almost everywhere in Africa but is absent from all regions outside Africa, except those in close geographical proximity to Africa. This is because the mutation probably arose in Africa some time after humans migrated out of Africa, about 150,000 years ago, but before the major human migrations within Africa.

European origins

The Y-SNP marker M173 defining the haplogroup R1 has a high frequency in Europe and a low to non-existent frequency outside of Europe, except those areas with known records of European immigration, e.g. due to the European colonizations starting about 500 years ago carrying the marker to regions such as Polynesia, together with more recent European admixture, e.g. in New Zealand. This mutation most likely has an ancient origin in Eurasia but its current frequency distribution is believed to be the result of a postglacial expansion starting 20,000–13,000 years ago from a refugee population somewhere on the Iberian peninsula, explaining the gradual frequency decline from Western to Eastern Europe.

East asian origins

The Y-SNP marker M175 defining the haplogroup O, has a high frequency in East Asia where it most likely originated, but does not exist elsewhere, except in regions with known East Asian influences, e.g. due to the expansion of Austronesian speakers starting about 6000 years ago in east Asia and carrying the marker to regions such as Polynesia.

Some cases are known where a high correlation between Y-STRs and Y-SNPs has been observed, such as the statistically significant Y-chromosomal differentiation between Polish and German populations, which is assumed to be a genetic consequence of politically forced population movements during and especially after World War II. Furthermore, some European metapopulations, as identified by their Y-STR haplotypes, correlate well with specific Y-SNP haplogroups, e.g. the most characteristic Eastern European Y-STR haplotype (17,13,30,25,10,11,13,10–14), together with its close relatives, is associated with Y-SNP haplogroup R1 (xR1a1), whereas the most characteristic Western European Y-STR haplotype (14,13,29,24,11,13, 13,11- 14), together with its close relatives, is associated with Y-SNP haplogroup R1a1. Although in cases of close correlation, Y-STRs and Y-SNP markers alone will reveal the same geographical information, a combination of both marker types can be more informative due to the additional information provided by closely related Y-STR haplotypes (e.g. one-step neighbours) existing on a particular Y-SNP background.

To use any type of genetic marker to identify the geographical origin of an individual, large reference databases are required to establish the marker's geographic distribution. Such a database exists for Y-STR haplotypes, with the YHRD. Unfortunately, however, a similar resource for Y-SNP data is not yet available. Ideally, for Y-chromosome-based geographical origin identification, Y-SNPs and Y-STRs should be combined in a single reference database in order to maximize male-specific ancestry information. Efforts to include Y-SNP data in the YHRD database are currently underway.

There is one severe problem with using Y-chromosomal markers for genetic ancestry identification, namely in cases of individuals with mixed genetic heritage (genetic admixture). For example, a Y chromosome DNA analysis of the son of a European man and an African woman will reveal a European geographical origin in the son in spite of his, most likely, African appearance. A similar analysis in all his male relatives will also reveal European (Y-chromosomal) genetic ancestry, even if all of them produce offspring with African women. In such cases, testing Y-chromosomal markers will be completely misleading if conclusions about a person's appearance are to be drawn from the test results. Continental and population-wide genetic admixture is known from North and South America but in principle can be expected in individuals everywhere, with an increased probability in regions with a known history of influences from people of different continental origin, e.g. due to the European expeditions to the Americas and the Pacific, or as a result of the African slave trade to the Americas. Therefore, to reveal a person's geographical origin with a high degree of accuracy, ancestry-informative markers from the Y chromosome need to be combined with those from both mitochondrial DNA and autosomal DNA.

Future of Y-Chromosomal Markers in Forensics

Due to the unique properties discussed above and the expected increases in the data content of Y-chromosome reference databases it can be expected that Y-chromosomal markers will be increasingly used in forensic casework in the future, particularly in cases where autosomal STRs do not provide useful information. If an autosomal STR profile can be obtained, e.g. in difficult cases through LCN analysis in combination with laser dissection microscopy, the existing national DNA databases together with essentially individual identification provided by autosomal STRs will always make autosomal STR profiles more informative than those from Y-STRs (given their lack of identifying individuals). However, if no interpretable autosomal STR profile can be obtained from a crime scene sample, Y-STRs are the markers of choice for male lineage identification, including low male and multi-male components in mixed stains.

The forensic use of Y-chromosomal markers for geographical origin identification is also expected to increase but will depend not only on the construction of enlarged worldwide reference databases, but also on non-scientific issues such as the adaptation of national DNA laws or the practical interpretation of existing laws. The forensic application of DNA markers to geographical origin identification is not in agreement with the legislation in those countries where the use of DNA for law enforcement purposes is restricted towards markers that allow DNA identification based on non-coding number codes, as usually obtained from autosomal STRs, and do not allow the use of markers that can reveal other kinds of information. Such countries will have to adjust their legislation if they wish to take advantage of the new scientific possibilities offered by new Y-chromosomal (and other genetic) markers. The Netherlands is one (if not the only) country that has modified its DNA legislation and, since 2003, under specific conditions allows the use of DNA markers for genetic ancestry identification as well as for the identification of externally visible characteristics. However, assumptions about the externally visible characteristics of an individual based on geographical origin identification will always be indirect. Furthermore, the accuracy of the assumptions is highly dependent on the level of correlation between the geographical region and the visible trait and therefore such tests are currently limited to a small number of geographical regions where a high correlation exists. In the future it will be important to understand the genetic basis of externally visible human characteristics, which is challenging due to the complex nature of many genes as well as environmental factors being most likely involved. Such research might provide DNA markers to be used by forensic laboratories as direct predictors of human appearance and thereby help to trace unknown suspects.

Finally, the Y-chromosomal markers available today only allow male lineage but not male individual identification. Not being able to differentiate between members of the same male lineage is clearly a major limitation when a Y-chromosomal profile match is obtained (although excluding male individuals is highly valuable too and can be done with a high degree of certainty based on existing Y markers). Future research will determine whether it will be possible to find Y chromosome markers that allow differentiation between close male relatives and thus allow the identification of male individuals and not 'only' groups of male relatives as possible today.

7

Single Nucleotide Polymorphism

One of the most significant outcomes of the Human Genome Project has been the identification of large numbers of *single nucleotide polymorphisms* (SNPs). The application of SNPs to forensic analysis is currently limited to some specialist cases. However, with advances both in our knowledge of SNPs and in the technology used to detect the polymorphisms, SNP analysis may play an increasingly important role in the future.

SNPs – Occurrence and Structure

'SNPs are single base pair positions in genomic DNA at which different sequence alternatives (alleles) exist in normal individuals in some population(s), wherein the least frequent allele has an abundance of 1% or greater'. The structure of a SNP is very simple.

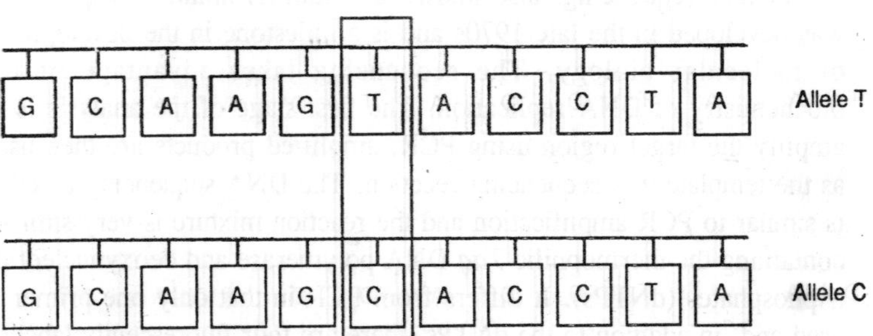

Fig. 7.1. SNPs are created when the DNA replication enzymes make a mistake as they copy the cell's DNA during meiosis.

SNPs are found in the human genome about once in every 1000 bp. Given that the human genome is 3.2 billion bp long, we can estimate that there will be approximately 1 million differences between two genomes that are due to SNPs: this represents approximately 85% of human genetic variation.

The biallelic state of the vast majority of polymorphisms intrinsically limits the information that can be gained from the analysis of any given SNP, and this has been the major factor limiting their application to forensic analysis: between 50 and 80 SNPs are required to achieve the same levels of discrimination as the current STR based methods. However, the vast numbers of SNPs within the genome (currently over 10 million SNPs have been placed in public databases) can compensate for the limited information carried by any individual SNP, and make them a tempting polymorphism to exploit. The technology that is being used for SNP detection is evolving and SNP analysis is becoming possible in many forensic laboratories.

Detection of SNPs

There are many techniques available for the resolution of SNPs. In the 1970s it was established that particular enzymes produced by bacteria can be used to cut the DNA molecule by recognizing specific sequences. Restriction digestion can be used to genotype SNPs when the SNP either creates or destroys a particular restriction enzyme recognition sequence but the method is limited for forensic casework because it needs a large amount of DNA and is a long and laborious process.

Sanger Sequencing

Sanger sequencing, also known as *chain-termination* sequencing, was developed in the late 1970s and is a milestone in the development of molecular biology. The sequencing takes advantage of the biochemistry of DNA replication. The first stage of the analysis is to amplify the target region using PCR; amplified products are then used as the template in a sequencing reaction. The DNA sequencing reaction is similar to PCR amplification and the reaction mixture is very similar, containing the thermophilic *Taq* DNA polymerase and deoxynucleotide triphosphates (dNTPs). It differs from PCR in that only one primer is used and, in addition to the dNTPs, there are four fluorescently labelled dideoxyribonucleotides (ddNTPs); each ddNTP is labelled with a different coloured dye. The ddNTPs do not contain the hydroxyl group on the 3' carbon, which prevents any extension of the DNA molecule.

```
5'                                                  3'
AGCTGTAAGTCTATACGTATCGTTAGTGCCTTGACTATGTCCGTA  -- Template
                           CGGAACTGATACAGGCAT  -- Primer
                          ACGGAACTGATACAGGCAT  -- 1
                         CACGGAACTGATACAGGCAT  -- 2
                        TCACGGAACTGATACAGGCAT  -- 3
                       ATCACGGAACTGATACAGGCAT  -- 4
                      AATCACGGAACTGATACAGGCAT  -- 5
                     CAATCACGGAACTGATACAGGCAT  -- 6
                    GCAATCACGGAACTGATACAGGCAT  -- 7
                   AGCAATCACGGAACTGATACAGGCAT  -- 8
```

Fig. 7.2. A primer anneals to the template strand. This is extended by Taq polymerase until a ddNTP is incorporated.

The concentration of dNTPs is higher than ddNTPs and therefore in most cases a dNTP is added. The ddNTPs are incorporated at random intervals along the molecule. This produces a range of different sized molecules. The products of the sequencing reaction are analysed using capillary gel electrophoresis systems, such as the ABI PRISM 310 Genetic Analyzer, that separates DNA to single base pair resolution and can simultaneously detect four different fluorescent labels.

Sequencing is not a practical option for the analysis of SNPs in a forensic context. Most SNPs are widely dispersed around the genome and a separate reaction is required for each SNP. An exception is the mitochondrial genome, where a number of SNPs are concentrated into a small area and can be analysed in a small number of reactions. Sequencing has also been a powerful method to type SNPs within rapidly evolving regions of DNA in the HIV virus.

SNP Detection for Forensic Applications

Restriction digestion and sequence analysis are not viable methods to use for most forensic cases that might require the analysis of 50 to 80 SNPs dispersed around the genome. A number of methods have evolved that can be applied to the detection of multiple SNPs. Methods that are based around the concepts of either primer extension or primer hybridization are the most widely used.

Primer Extension

Primer extension is a robust method for discriminating between different alleles and several methodologies have been developed. One of the commonly used methods is the *mini-sequencing reaction*. The basis of the reaction is very similar to Sanger sequencing. The first part of the procedure is to amplify the target region using PCR. An

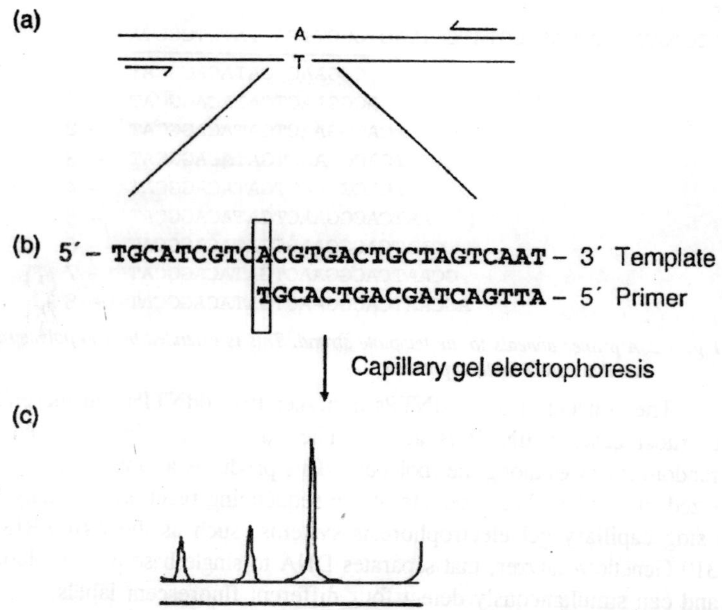

Fig. 7.3. The primer extension assay. (a) The target sequence is amplified using PCR and the products are used as the template in the extension assay; (b) an internal primer hybridizes to the target adjacent to the SNP and a single fluorescently labelled ddNTP is added by Taq polymerase; (c) the reaction is analysed by capillary electrophoresis.

internal primer then anneals to the denatured PCR product; the 3' end of the primer is adjacent to the polymorphic site. The primer is then extended by *Taq* polymerase but only ddNTPs that are labelled with fluorescent dyes are provided; the primer is only extended by one nucleotide. The extended primer can be analysed using capillary gel electrophoresis and the colour of the detected peak allows the SNP to be characterized. A widely used commercial kit called *SNaPshot* is based on this methodology. By using different sized primers and different fluorescent tags for each of the four bases, a large number of SNPs can be simultaneously detected.

Variations on the primer extension technique include pyro-sequencing; microarrays, where the extension primers are attached to a silicon chip; and allele specific extension, when the primer is only extended if it is 100% complementary to the target sequence.

Allele Specific Hybridization

Under stringent conditions, even one nucleotide mismatching between a template and primer can differentiate between two alleles.

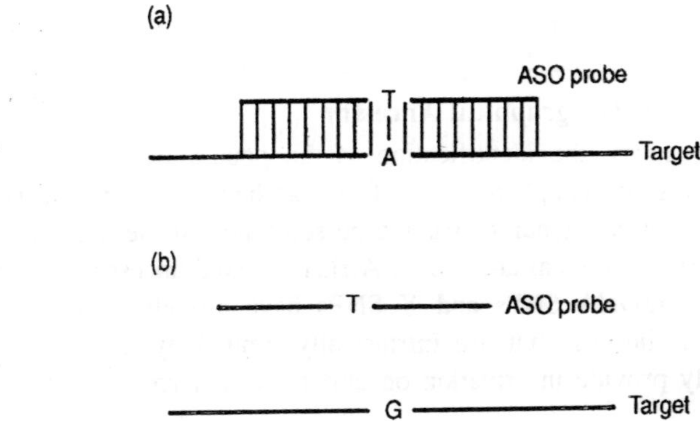

Fig. 7.4. Allele specific hybridization. Allele specific oligonucleotide (ASO) probe that include the SNP are hybridized with the target DNA. (a) Under highly stringent conditions only perfectly matched sequences will form stable interactions; (b) with one mismatch in sequence the ASO will not hybridize.

There is a large number of methods that exploit the hybridization of probes, including reverse dot blots; Taqman assays; LightCycler assays; molecular beacons; and GeneChips.

Forensic Applications of SNPs

A vast amount of data is available on the different SNPs in the human genome and one of the biggest tasks when applying SNPs to forensic applications is to select the most appropriate SNPs from the overwhelming numbers that are available. The choice of SNPs is very much dependent on the application.

Forensic Identification

The vast majority of forensic DNA analysis involves the characterization of biological material recovered from the scene of a crime. Several panels of SNPs have been developed that are designed to provide maximum discrimination powers for forensic identification. These contain SNPs that are polymorphic in all major population groups.

A panel, containing 52 SNPs was developed by the SNP for ID Consortium. Using this panel of SNPs produced match probabilities that ranged from 5.0×10^{-19} in an Asian population to 5.0×10^{-21} in a European population. When applied to paternity testing, average paternity indices of between 336000 in Asian populations and 550000 in European populations, were achieved.

However, even with the high discrimination power, the effort involved in analysing 50 SNPs is greater than when undertaking standard STR analysis. The major attraction of using SNPs with the current technology is that SNP analysis can provide results from highly degraded DNA when conventional STR profiling has failed.

Prediction of the Geographical Ancestry

In many cases, the identification of the population group from which a crime scene sample has come from can be valuable intelligence for the investigating agencies: was the person who left the material at the crime scene of Caucasian, Asian, African, mixed ancestry? Panels consisting of mtDNA SNPs and Y SNPs have already been found useful for this purpose but are intrinsically limited by the fact that they can only provide information on either the maternal or paternal ancestry.

Autosomal SNPs that have different frequencies in different major population groups can provide valuable information on geographic ancestry. Many of the SNPs selected for this purpose are associated with coding regions that have been subjected to selection pressures. These include pigmentation genes and genes involved with the metabolism of xenobiotics. The pigmentation genes, in addition to providing information on geographic ancestry, can also give information on phenotype of the person who deposited the biological material at a crime scene, including skin, hair and eye colour.

SNPs Compared to SIR Loci

Current STR-based multiplex kits like AMPF*l*STR Identifiler and PowerPlex 16 can amplify 15 STR loci and the amelogenin locus. Using the current technology it is difficult to co-amplify and detect any more STR loci. Also the size of the amplicon for each STR is quite large. The great advantage STRs have over SNPs is their power of discrimination due to the large number of alleles they have in comparison with biallelic SNPs. In contrast to STRs, around four-times more SNPs are required to reach the discrimination power equivalent to STR loci.

Another major disadvantage to using SNPs is that mixtures of two or more people might be either problematic or impossible to interpret since SNPs are biallelic markers. Also current DNA databases consist of profiles comprising STR loci and therefore SNPs cannot be used in that context. At the same time it is possible to analyse hundreds of SNP loci and, due to their structure, the amplicon size can be much smaller, typically less than 100 bp. This allows the detection of DNA templates that are highly degraded and may generate data when standard STR typing fails to generate a result.

In the foreseeable future, STRs will be the most commonly used genetic polymorphism analysed. They are tried and tested in most judicial systems and also form the basis of most forensic DNA databases. Even so, the use of SNPs in forensic genetics is likely to increase in the coming years and may at some point in the future replace the analysis of STR polymorphisms. The application of SNPs to specialized applications, for example, SNP based blood grouping and molecular autopsy (looking for mutations that can explain sudden death), is likely to become more widespread.

8

Biological Acids and Steroid Analysis

Sequencing of biological or synthetic peptides has sparked interest in the separation and quantitation of amino acids by *capillary electrophoresis* (CE). Because amino acids comprise a group of negatively charged, positively charged and neutral molecules, it has been difficult to separate and quantitate all amino acids using a single procedure. Today many proteins and peptides that require sequencing are frequently available in only microgram (μg) quantities necessitating quantitation of the amino acids at extremely low concentrations. Although a few amino acids contain aromatic groups that strongly absorb in the *ultraviolet* (UV) range, the majority lacks strongly absorbing chromophore groups. This lack of sensitivity further complicates the ability to separate amino acids.

CE does offer advantages in solving some of these problems. Specifically, CE requires only a small sample size, although nanomolar (n*M*) are still required, and the separation can be finished quickly, sometimes within minutes.

Amino Acid Analysis

Jorgenson and Lukacs first used CE to separate and detect amino acids in 1981. They demonstrated rapid separation and fluorescent detection of both peptides and amino acid derivatives. After derivatization with 5-dimethylaminonaphthalene-1-sulfonyl chloride (dansyl) they were able to separate a mixture of dansylated amino with a separation efficiency of approx 250,000 theoretical plates. They also demonstrated that the separation was proportional to voltage applied and that by increasing the voltage up to 30 kV, efficiencies exceeding 400,000 theoretical plates can be achieved within 10–30 min. This pioneering work demonstrated that the simple, rapid separations found with CE can be an alternative to *high-performance liquid chromatography* (HPLC).

Amino acid identification and quantification is of prime importance for medical diagnosis as well as biomedical and industrial research. Thus, as methods and instrumentation have become available throughout the 1980s, the use of CE for amino acid separation and identification has expanded.

Detection

Derivatization to produce either a strongly UV absorbing or fluorescent chromophore prior to injection onto the capillary have been investigated to enhance the detection of amino acids.

Ultraviolet

In early studies, UV absorption was the most common method to detection amino acids or amino-acid derivatives separated by CE. There were, however, several drawbacks. The short pathlength of the capillary and the low molar absorptivities of the amino acids or derivatives limited the detection limits. Even so, the strong UV absorbance of the coenzyme pyrroloquinoline quinone was shown to provide sensitive detection of derivatized amino acids. Additionally, cyclic 3-phenyl-2-thiohydantoin derivatives that absorb strongly at 254 nm are produced by the reaction of phenylisothiocyanate and amino acids. However, the formation of the thiohydantoin derivatives from the amino and carboxylic acid groups of the amino acid eliminates one of the properties (the zwitterionic charge) that helps in the separation of many of the amino acids.

Fluorescence

Fluorescence, both lamp based and laser induced, has been found to be more useful for the highly sensitive detection required for amino acids separated by CE. During the 1980s, most investigators used lamp based fluorescence. Albin et al. described a lamp-based fluorescence detector to measure amino acid derivatives of 9-fluorenylmethyl chloroformate at concentrations as low as 10 ng/mL. Lui and coworkers synthesized 3-(4-carboxybenzoyl)-2-quinolinecarboxyaldehyde to produce fluorescent isoindole products and were able to effectively detect 17 amino acids with lamp-based fluorescence.

Laser-induced fluorescence (LIF) dramatically improved sensitivity but because of the limited number of commercially available lasers the number of derivatizing agents were limited to those with excitation spectra that match those of commonly used lasers. The argon ion laser has been the most popular in LIF because of its output at 488 nm that matches the excitation maxima of fluorescein isothiocyanate. Lui et al. used a chiral reagent, 4-(3-isothiocyanatopyrrolidin-1-yl)-7-nitro-2,1,3-benzoxadiazole to produce fluorescent diastereomeric derivatives with a 488 nm excitation maximum. A helium-cadmium laser with emission lines at 325 or 442 nm has been used in some applications. Tetramethylrhodamine isothiocyanate amino-acid derivatives have been sucessfully detected using a helium-neon laser. In additon, laser modifications have resulted in a semiconductor laser and diode laser, both of which are reported to improve efficiency. Timperman et al. have also reported a highly sensitive LIF wavelength-resolved detection system.

A sheath flow cell was used as a post-column reactor for fluorescence derivatization by Cobel and Timperman. They described a simple laser-induced fluorescence detection method for proteins and amino acids in which fast-reacting o-phthaldialdehyde-2-mercaptoethanol was added to the sheath fluid for derivatization. Fluorescent excitation using a helium- cadmium laser (325 nm excitation) allowed emissions to be collected with a microscope objective and focused through a slit to a photon-counting photo-multiplier tube. Lowest limits of detection were for glycine which showed detection limits at 2.3×10^{-8} *M*. A UV (krypton fluoride) laser (244 nm excitation) was used by Chan and associates for measurement of native tryptophan fluorescence after separation by *micellar electrokinetic chromatography* (MEKC).

Indirect fluorescence

Some investigators reported measurement of native amino acids by indirect fluorescence detection. The principle of this method of detection is dependent on the presence of a strongly fluorescing background electrolyte to produce a high background signal. The nonflorescent analyte passing through the detector displaces some of the fluorescing-background electrolyte, resulting in a decrease in background signal. Indirect detection was described by Bruin et al. using salicylate at pH 11.0 as the background electrolyte to detect underivatized amino acids. The method was reported to be more sensitive for low electrolyte concentrations. Ma and coworkers also studied the use of quinine sulfate as the background electrolyte for detection of cationic amino acids. In addition, Lee and Lin studied nine different background electrolytes for detection of underivatized amino acids. They found π-amino salicylic acid and 4-(*N,N*-dimethyl)aminobenzoic acid in a basic solution to be the most useful. They also found that adding cationic surfactants reduced the electro-osmotic flow. In a later study, they added cyclodextrins in reduce electroosmosis and enhance selectivity.

Nuclear magnetic resonance (NMR)

Sweedler et al. found proton *nuclear magnetic resonance* (NMR) a useful detection system. They circumvented the inherently low sensitivity of NMR, which requires the use of large diameter flow cells, by wrapping a microcoil directly around the capillary to construct a 5.0 nL cell. Even though the sensitivity was less than that of UV detection systems, NMR detectors can provide an alternative for on-column detection.

Mass spectroscopy (MS)

Electrospray ionization to create gas phase ions from the nonvolatile components separated by CE allowed structural analysis through *mass spectroscopy* (MS). This combination of CE and MS was reported by Garcia and Henion. They attempted to overcome the incompatibilities between the two systems by the use of gel-filled capillaries to decouple the electrophoresis buffer from the ionization source. They provided much structural information on separated dansylated-amino acids.

Electrochemical

Although most underivatized amino acids are not electroactive, some reports of electrochemical detection methods do appear promising. Underivatized amino acids were detected by electrochemical detection using a copper electrode above pH 12.0. Dinitrophenyl-derivatized amino acids have also been detected using a reductive electrochemical system. O'Shea et al. described the use of carbon-fiber electrodes with an electrical isolation circuit. Using this system, they were successful in detection of glutamic acid and aspartic acids, which are easily oxidized following reaction with naphthalene-2,3-dicarboxaldehyde.

Other techniques

Waldron and Dovichi reported a thermooptical detector system that used a krypton fluoride laser as the energy source. The method was found to be sensitive at the 1 μM level for 3-phenyl-2-thiohydantoin-amino acids. Other workers investigated chemoluminescence and nucleation light-scattering detection.

Derivatization

Although derivatization alters the electrophoretic properties of amino acids, it has been the only method to detect amino acids at the concentrations required (p*M*). This has led to a plethora of derivatizing agents.

Table 8.1. Common agents for amino acid derivatization

Derivatizing agent
5-dimethylaminonaphthalene-1-sulfonyl chloride (dansyl)
Fluorescein isothiocynate
Fluorescamine
Pyrroloquinoline quinone
3-phenyl-2-thiohydantoin
o-phthaldialdehyde
Naphthalene-2,3-dicarboxaldehyde
9-fluorenylmethyl chloroformate
(+)- and (–)-1-(–fluroenyl) ethyl chloroformate
3-(4-carboxybenzoyl)-2-quinolinecarboxaldehyde
4-(3-isothiocyanatophrrolidin-l-yl)-7-nitro-2, 1 ,3-benzoxadiazole
6-aminoquinoyl-*N*-hydroxysuccinimidyl carbamate
Tetramethylrhodamine isothiocyanate
Pyronin succinimidyl ester
Dicarbocyanine succinimidyl ester
o-phthaldialdehyde in tandem with dicarbocyanine succinimidyl ester
1-methoxycarbonylindolizine-3,5-dicarbaldehyde
2-(9-anthry)ethyl chloroformate
Tetramethylrhodamine thiocarbamyl
(S)-1-(1-naphthyl)ethyl isothiocyanate
(S)-1-phenylethyl isothiocyanate
N-tert-butoxycarbonyl
N-acetylcysteine and *o*-phthaldialdehyde
2,3,4,6-tetra-*O*-acetyl- 1-thio-β-D-glucopyranose to *o*-phthaldialdehyde
(+)-*OO*-dibenzoyl-L-tartaric anhydride
o-phthaldialdehyde-2-mercaptoethanol
Phenylthiocarbamyl
Monobromobimane
4-aminosulfonyl-7-fluoro-2, 1 ,3-benzoxadiazole

Pre-column

The dansyl amino acids derivatives, as described by Jorgenson and Lukacs, have been the most frequently reported, especially in early studies. The dansyl derivatives are still used as the standard to assess the utility and efficiency of new techniques or modifications of previous methods. The fluorescence is easily detected and, although quantum yields are reduced in the aqueous environment of CE, results are reproducible.

Fluorescein, another popular fluorescent label for biochemical molecules in early CE studies, has both excitation and emission spectra in the visible wavelength range allowing for easy detection. However, undesirable side reactions of *fluorescein isothiocynate* (FITC) used in the derivatization process have prevented its widespread use when the molecule of interest is at low concentration. Another fluorogenic molecule, fluorescamine, which has similar properties to FITC has also been used. The problem with this label was that the sensitivity was insufficient for many applications.

A substituted isoindole ring, formed through the reaction between anime group on an amino acid and o-phthaldialdehyde, results in derivatives that show both a strong absorbance at 260 and 340 nm and also fluoresce at 475 nm. Unlike FITC, o-phthaldialdehyde does not produce florescent side products, making it a more usable reagent. However, when compared to another popular fluorogenic derivatizing agent, naphthalene-2,3-dicarboxaldehyde, the derivatives formed with o-phthaldialdehyde are much less stable. Naphthalene-2,3-dicarboxaldehyde derivatives, like fluorescein, have excitation and emission spectra in the visible range, 462 nm and 490 nm, respectively. They became popular in chiral separations even though the narrow Stokes shift presented a potential source of error on some instruments.

The fluorogenic label, 9-fluorenylmethyl chloroformate, forms amino derivatives that strongly absorb at 265 nm and fluoresce at 315 nm. Both primary and secondary amines can be derivatized with this reagent. Wan and associates used a related agent, (+)- and (–)-1-(-fluroenyl) ethyl chloroformate, in the analysis of amino-acid enantiomerics. Liu and others reported a highly sensitive method for separation of primary amines derivatized with 3-(4-carboxybenzoyl)-2-quinolinecarboxaldehyde. They used LIF as the method of detection. In another study these same investigators separated amino-acid residues labeled with the reagent, 4-(3-isothiocyanatopyrrolidin-l-yl)- 7-nitro-2,1,3-benzoxadiazole, which has an excitation maximum of 480 nm.

Many of these amino-acid derivatives are unstable, which prevented long-term storage of the compounds, thus limiting the ability to have purified standards for unknown identification. Improved stability was achieved using 6-aminoquinoyl-*N*-hydroxysuccinimidyl carbamate as the derivatizing agent. Amino-acid derivatives were prepared with this reagent using protein or peptide hydrolysates were much more stable in both HPLC and CE applications.

LIF because of its sensitivity, sparked investigations with many fluorophores was used to produce amino-acid derivatives. The 540 nm optimal excitation wavelength of Tetramethylrhodamine isothiocyanate, produced by a helium–neon laser, allowed a low-cost detection method. A synthesized label, pyronin succinimidyl ester, was excited with a semiconductor laser. Mank and Yeung labeled amino acids with the dicarbocyanine using dicarbocyanine succinimidyl ester. A diode laser (667 nm emission) was used in this study to produce the excitation wavelength along with a low-cost detection method.

On-column

Although most derivatizations have been developed using pre-column techniques, on-column and post-column derivatizations have also been investigated. On-column derivatization has been achieved at the inlet of the capillary column where derivatizing reagent and sample were allow to react for a period of time before the electrophoresis was begun. Two variations have been described. In one method, the tandem mode, a plug of the derivatizing reagent was injected into the capillary inlet preceding a plug of the sample solution. In the sandwich mode, a plug of derivatizing reagent was injected at the capillary inlet, followed by a plug of the sample solution and then by another plug of the derivatizing reagent.

Taga and Honda used o-phthaldialdehyde in a tandem mode with dicarbocyanine succinimidyl ester that capitalized on the mobility differences in of the two reactants. Although derivatization was enhanced, there was a loss in resolution. Another fluorescent-derivitizing reagent, 1-methoxycarbonylindolizine-3,5-dicarbaldehyde (excitation at 409 nm and emission at 482 nm), has been used in a sandwich mode to produce a highly sensitive method.

Gilman and Ewing demonstrated amino-acid, on-column derivatization and detection of separated amino acids from injected intact cells. Single cells were injected into the column inlet. Once in the capillary, the cells were lysed and the released amino acids derivatized with naphthalene-2,3-dicarboxaldehyde. The amino acids within the cells were able to be detected and quantitated at attomole concentrations.

Post-column

Pre-column and on-column derivatization allows for several potential errors. For example, the derivatizing agent may react more efficiently with one amino acid than another, thus quantitative errors may occur. At the same time derivatized standards may not directly relate to the same level of amino acid in an unknown mixture because of matrix differences and/or differences in affinity of the derivatizing agent. Derivatized amino acids may show different migration rates relative to each other as compared to their underivatized form, allowing possible qualitative problems. By using post- column derivatization, many of the potentially erroneous results of pre-column and on-column derivatization can be eliminated.

As with other derivatizing modes, the most extensively studied post-column agents have been fluorogenic. Albin and workers introduced o-phthaldialdehyde by differential electroosmotic flow at a gap junction reactor, which was further modified by Gilman and Ewing to allow introduction of the derivatizing agent by diffusion. Both o-phthaldialdehyde and naphthalene-2,3-dicarboxyaldehyde, along with LIF, were used to develop a highly sensitive analytical method for glycine. Zhu and Kok introduced o-phthaldialdehyde through a porous tube connecting the capillary and the reactor tube. Using a lamp rather than LIF, they were able to detect amino acids at concentrations of 2 μm. Using a coaxial design, Zhang and Yeung constructed a reactor that used a power source separate from that used by the CE instrument. Using o-phthaldialdehyde as the post-column derivatizing agent and LIF, they were able to detect concentrations of 2.2×10^{-8} M for six amino acids. These and other post-column derivatization methods for fluorescence and chemiluminescence detection was reviewed by Zhu and Kok.

Methods of Separation

Micellar electrokinetic capillary chromatography (MEKC)

Pure mixtures have been used in the great majority of the studies involving separation of amino acids. However, low-peak capacity of the methods used limited the use of CE in separating more complex mixtures. Using *micellar electrokinetic capillary chromatography* (MEKC), separation of neutral along with charged components was possible based on their partitioning between the aqueous phase and a pseudo-stationary phase. MEKC was shown very effective in separation of complex mixtures of amino acids. Ong and coworkers successfully separated 15 dansylated amino acids in less than 30 min using 40 m*M* *sodium docecyl sulfate* (SDS) in a phosphate-borate buffer. The first separation of all 20 natural amino acids was reported by Skocir and coworkers using 102 m*M* SDS in 20 m*M* borax buffer, pH 9.2, and a column temperature of 10°C. Matsubara and Terabe subsequently resolved 24 dansylated amino acids in 70 min at pH 2.4 using a neutral surfactant and a Tween 20-phosphate buffer.

Terabe and his coworkers also showed that addition of urea to SDS buffers enhanced separation of amino acids derivatized by 3-phenyl-2-thiohydantin. Using this derivatizing agent, Castagnola and associates studied the effect of various buffer conditions, SDS concentrations, and amount of derivatizing agent added. By optimizing the conditions, they were able to resolve 18 amino acids simultaneously in 15 min. Furthering this work, Kim and coworkers compared the surfactants, SDS and dodecyltrimethyl ammonium bromide, and indicated that SDS gave the best separation for analysis of Edman degradation products using 3-phenyl-2-thiohydantin as the derivatizing agent. Using a 50 m*M* SDS in 25 m*M* phosphate buffer, they could resolve all natural amino acids except leucine and isoleucine. Still another study demonstrated the use of mixed cationic-anionic micelles for separation of these derivatized amino acids.

MEKC separation and resolution of other derivatized amino acids were also investigated. Ueda and coworkers found that using naphthalene-2,3-dicarboxaldehyde they were able to separate the derivatized amino acids in about 25 min using SDS buffer to which β-cyclodextrin was added. DeSilva and Kuwana subsequently used cyclodextrin-modified MEKC to separate several amino acids using naphthalene-2,3-dicarboxaldehyde. They assessed the importance of SDS for the separation in addition to the effect of neutral hydroxypropyl beta-cyclodextrin and charged carboxy-methyl beta-cyclodextrin on the resolution. Chan and associates separated 18 amino acids derivatized with 9-fluorenylmethyl chloroformate using a SDS-borate surfactant at pH 9.2. Wan et al. used a SDS-phosphate-borax-urea system to separate 2-(9-anthry)ethyl chloroformate derivatized amino acids. Mank and Yeung separated 18 amino acids derivatized with dicarbocyanine using SDS-borate-MeOH at 30 kV.

Although fused silica capillaries work well and are easier to use, coated capillaries have the potential to improve the separation of derivatized amino acids. In this regard Sun et al. synthesized and evaluated anionic-polymer-coated capillaries with a pH-independent electroosmotic flow to separate dansylated amino acids. In addition, Janini et al. developed a technique called reversed-flow MEKC in which polyacrylamide coated capillaries were used to suppress the *electroosmotic flow* (EOF). Reversing the polarity of the instrument was necessary because the SDS micelle migration was anodic and the EOF was negligible under these conditions. Using this system with SDS-acetate, pH 4.2, was used to separate 15 dansylated amino acids. They also studied the effect of cetyltrimethyl ammonium bromide.

Other modifications have been reported to improve separation and resolution of amino acids that were difficult to analyze. Culbertson and Jorgenson used flow-counterbalanced CE to control the analyte migration to separate components with closely related mobilities, such as leucine and isoleucine derivatized with tetramethylrhodamine thiocarbamyl. Simultaneous pH and ionic-strength effects and buffer selection were investigated by Camillari and Okafo, who reported improved separation of dansylated amino acids when using D_2O to increase the viscosity.

Chiral separations

Amino acids have at least one chiral carbon and, with few exceptions, exist in two optically active enantiomeric forms, dextrorotatory (D) and levarotatory (L). These optical isomers behave differently in biological systems. For example, enzyme activity is often specific for a particular optical isomer and different enantiomeric forms of a drug may produce different therapeutic effects. In living organisms, proteins contain the D-enantiomeric form of amino acids, whereas nucleic acids contain the L form. The fact that the enantiomeric amino acids have different properties and functions of enantiomers make their separation critically important. Separation and quantitation of these forms has been achieved by a variety of methods, such as anionicpolymer-coated capillaries, addition of an optically active molecule to the migration buffer, which acts as a chiral selector, and by chiral derivatization prior to analysis creating a diastereomer.

Studies by Wan and associates using (+)- and (–)-1-(-fluroenyl) ethyl chloroformate, showed that after converting enantiomers of amino acids into diastereomers, separation, identification, and quantitation of the optical isomers was possible at 3×10^{-8} *M*. In another set of experiments Liu and others used CE to separate D- and L-amino acid residues using the fluorescent chiral reagent 4-(3-isothiocyanato-

Table 8.2. Common chiral selectors used for separation of enantiomers of amino acids

Chiral selector
L-histidine/Cu II complex
L-asparatamine/Cu II complex
Didecyl-L-alanine
α-cyclodextrin
β-cyclodextrin
γ-cyclodextrin
Heptakis-(2,6-di-o-methyl)-β-cyclodextrin
γ-cyclodextrin and sodium deoxycholate
β-cyclodextrin and urea
Heptakis-2,3,4-tri-*O*-methyl-β-cyclodextrin
Hydroxypropyl-β-cyclodextrin
Hydroxypropyl-γ-cyclodextrin
n-alkyl-β-D-glucopyranosides
Sulfobutyl ether-β-cyclodextrin
Bovine albumin and dextrins
Restocetin
Vancomycin
Sodium-*N*-dodecanoyl-L-valinate
Sodium-*N*-dodecanoyl-L-serine
β-escin
Digitonin
Sodium-*N*-dodecanoyl-L-glutamate
Digitonin and sodium taurodexycholate
Digitonin and sodium dococyl sulfate
Seriodal-glycoside surfactant-borate complex
L-phenylalanine anilide and methacrylic acid
L-phenylalanine anilide and 2-vinylpyridine
Triethanolamine-phosphoric acid with α-cyclodextrin
Teicoplanin

pyrrolidin-l-yl)-7-nitro-2,3- benzoxadiazole. Using 25 m*M* acetate buffer, pH 4.0, 10 m*M* Triton X-100 they were able to separate derivatized D,L-proline and D,L-valine. Without the addition of Triton X-100, no separation was seen; thus, they suggested that the partitioning coefficients for the various diasteromers between the micelles and the solution was of prime importance in their separation. They applied this method to the determination of D- and L-amino acids using the peptide, gramicidin D, as the test case. This study demonstrated that CE showed higher efficiencies than HPLC under the same conditions.

Gassmann and associates separated dansylated D- and L-amino acids by the interaction between the respective amino acid and a Copper (II) complex of L-histidine present in the support electrolyte. They reported separation and detection of femtomole amounts of racemic mixtures of dansylated amino acids within 10 min. In a later study, Copper II-L-aspartamine in the run buffer was also shown to be an effective chiral selector. Direct chiral resolution of underivatized amino acids by ligand-exchange *capillary zone electrophoresis* (CZE) was described by Vegvari and coworkers. Using *N*-(2-hydroxy-octyl)-L-4-hydroxyproline/Cu (II) as a selector, amino acids containing aromatic residues and histidine were resolved. In all the cases, *in situ* diasteromers were formed enhancing separation. Cohen et al. was also able to separate dansylated D- and L-amino acids using the chiral detergent, didecyl-L-alanine, dissolved in a solution of SDS, forming mixed micelles. The chiral detergent incorporated in the SDS micelles with the hydrophilic chiral L-alanine regions orientated to the surface where an interaction with chiral amino acids could occur.

Early studies of Snopek et al. showed the simple and robust utility of cyclodextrin as stereospecific selectors or electrolyte modifiers. They showed that α-, β- and γ-cyclodextrin as well as heptakis-(2,6-di-o-methyl)-β-cyclodextrin were effective in chiral separation for both CZE and isotachophoresis. They used a poly(tetrafluoroethylene) capillary and a conductivity detector to resolve model isomeric compounds. Terabe et al. advanced this work by a modification of the MEKC technique for enantiomeric separation by adding a mixture of β-cyclodextrins and γ-cyclodextrins. They then applied this technique for the separation of 10 pairs of dansylated-amino acids. The best separations, however, were achieved using a mixture of both cyclodextrins in SDS. Good separations were also achieved with addition of β-cyclodextrins, γ-cyclodextrins, and with mixtures of γ-cyclodextrin and sodium taurodeoxycholate. Penn and coworkers also studied the mechanisms involved in micelle-assisted separations using β-cyclodextrins in SDS to separate dansylated amino acids.

The use of urea was also found to enhance the separation of dansylated amino acids with β-cyclodextrins. In addition, Bonfichi et al. achieved efficient chiral separations using heptakis-2,3,6-tri-*O*-methyl-β-cyclodextrin and β-cyclodextrin. These workers used (*S*)- 1-(1-naphthyl)-ethyl isothiocyanate and (S)-1-phenylethyl isothiocyanate for derivatization prior to separations.

Chiral separations of dansylated amino acids have also been accomplished by adding high molecular weight anionic and cationic surfactants to cyclodextrins. The modified cyclodextrins, hydroxypropyl-β-cyclodextrin and hydroxypropyl-γ-cyclodextrin, were also shown to improve the chiral separations of *N*-tert-butoxycarbonyl amino acids. In addition, Wan and associates studied various combinations of SDS, 2-propanol, β-cyclodextrins, and γ-cyclodextrins in the enantiomeric separation of 2-(9-anthry)ethyl chloroformate derivatized amino acids. They were able to resolve 12 and 13 amino acids with various surfactant combinations. Riester et al. reported on the chiral separation of 9-fluorenylmethyl chloroformate derivatives of amino acids using γ-cyclodextrins along with SDS. Swartz et al. described the simultaneous MEKC separation of a mixture of six amino-acid enantiomers derivatized with 6-aminoquinoyl-*N*-hydroxysuccinimidyl carbamate. The use of n-alkyl-β-D-glucopyranosides to separate enantiomers has described by Desbene and Fulchic.

Many variations of MEKC have been used to separate enantiomers of dansyl-amino acids. For example, negatively charged sulfobutyl ether-β-cyclodextrin was found to be useful by Desiderio and Fanali to separate the enantiomers of dansylated amino acids. Similarly, Janini et al. used sulfobutyl ether-β-cyclodextrin to separate enantiomers of 12 dansylated amino acids. In addition, Sun and coworkers explored the use of affinity interactions between macromolecules and amino acids using bovine albumin and dextrins to separate dansylated amino acids. Dansylated amino acids have also been separated with *N*-methylformamide and β-cyclodextrin.

Armstrong et al. introduced the use of the macrocyclic antibiotic, ristocetin, as a chiral selector. Using this antibiotic the chiral separation of a large groups of amino acids derivatized with 5-dimethylamino-aphthalene-1-sulfonyl chloride, 6-aminoquinoyl-*N*-hydroxy succinimidyl carbamate, or 9-fluorenylmethylchloroformate was possible. Resolutions equal to or greater than those of cyclodextrin were achieved. Another macrocyclic antibiotic, vancomycin, was also found to be an effective chiral selector.

Amino acids derivatized with 3-phenyl-2-thiohydantoin have also been separated in MEKC using chiral surfactants, such as sodium-*N*-

dodecanoyl-L-valinate, sodium-*N*-dodecanoyl-L-serine, and sodium-*N*-dodecanoyl-L-glutamate. The formation of mixed micelles using sodium-*N*-dedecanoyl-L-glutamate along with a mixture of digitonin and sodium taurodexycholate or digitonin with SDS effectively separated phenylthiohydantoin-amino acids. Others showed that chiral micelles consisting of steriodal-glycosides borate complexes could also be used. Additionally, Lin and coworkers reported on the highly specific separation of amino-acid enantiomers using an on-column prepared molecular imprinted polymer. L-Phenylalanine anilide was used as the print molecule and methacrylic acid and/or 2-vinylpyridine as the functional monomers to prepare the on-column polymer.

Investigators have also designed procedures that produce derivatized amino acids that were diastereomers, thus separation did not need to be chiral selective. Houben et al. used N-acetylcysteine and o-phthaldialdehyde to derivatize D,L-valine forming diastereomers prior to separation. Tivesten and Folestad produced diastereomers by adding 2,3,4,6-tetra-*O*-acetyl- 1-thio-β-D-glucopyranose to the o-phthaldialdehyde for precolumn-labeling of D- and L-amino acids. They added polymer modifiers to achieve optimal conditions for the separation of 17 labeled amino acids. Scheutzner et al. optimized conditions by adjusting pH and solvent composition to separate diastereomer derivatives of (+)-*OO'*-dibenzoyl-L-tartaric anhydride in CZE.

The critical need to determine optical purity of raw materials as well as final products prompted the chiral separation and quantitation of tryptophan, a frequent starting material in pharmaceutical synthesis. In this regard Altria et al. not only detected but quantitated 0.1% L-tryptophan in the presence of the D-enantiomer using a triethanolamine-phosphoric acid containing-cyclodextrin. Tesarova et al. also compared separation of *N*-tert-butyloxycarbonyl (t-Boc) amino acids, important precursors in peptide synthesis, and their nonblocked analogs on a teicoplanin-based chiral stationary phase. The mobile-phase composition was optimized using various ratios of acetonitrile and 1% triethylamine/acetate buffer to achieve separation in 8–12 min. The retention and enantioresolutions were compared and the investigators concluded that native unblocked amino acids have better interaction with the teicoplanin stationary phasse, were better enantioresolved than blocked amino acids, and finally that the amino group plays an important role in the steroselective stationary phase-analyte interaction.

Direct chiral resolution of underivatized amino acids by ligand-exchange CZE was described by Vegvari and coworkers. Using *N*-(2-

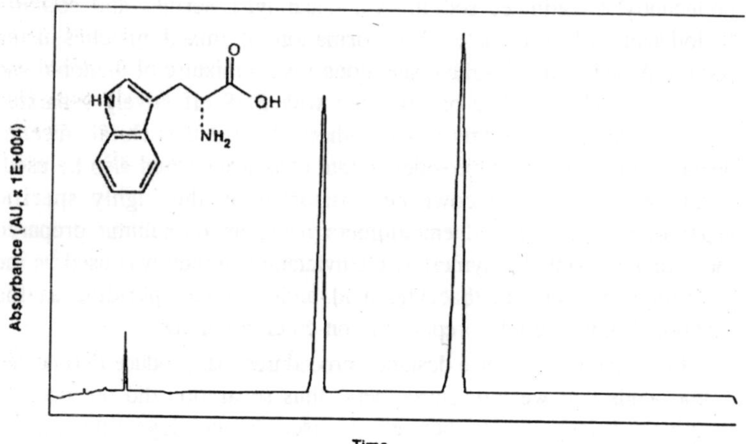

Fig. 8.1. Separation of tryptophan in the presence of highly sulfated α-cyclodextrin.

hydroxyoctyl)-L-4-hydroxyproline/Cu (II) as a selector, amino acids containing aromatic residues and histidine were resolved.

Microchip Technology

The challenges of microchip technology have also been applied to CE analysis of amino acids. By fusing a cover glass over glass or quartz plates into which small channels were micromachined, tiny capillary channels are formed. Such channels function as open-tubular capillaries on the microchip and was used by Seiler et al. to rapidly separate phenylthiocarbamyl amino acids in <2 min. Amino acids, derivatized with o-phthaldialdehyde have been separated within a few seconds using either a chip-based precolumn or a chip-based postcolumn derivatization reaction. The micromachining of CE injectors and separation on glass chips has also been studied by Fan and Harridan by studying the flow at the capillary junction under various defined conditions. Von Heeren and associates have used MEKC on microchips. They were able to separate six FITC-labeled amino acids in a few seconds. On-column sample gating was described by Monning and Jorgenson. In their system most of the sample, which was continuously introduced into the capillary, was destroyed by photolysis, but that which survived became the sample plug. FITC-labeled amino acids were separated in about 1.5 s. In a later study, 5-FITC-labeled amino acids were separated in 120 ms.

Clinical and Biomedical Applications

The most useful application for CE in amino-acid analysis is elucidating the structure of both natural and laboratory-synthesized proteins and polypeptides. In 1991, Bergman and associates demonstrated the utility of CE for preparative purposes because of its reproducibility. These workers also demonstrated that amino-acid composition and sequence analysis of proteins could be achieved using phenylthiocarbamyl derivatized amino. Rapid, reliable results on extremely small sample accelerated industrial adaptations. For example, the aromatic amino acids in citrus juice were measured by Cancalon and Byran and in cheddar cheese by Strickland et al. using CE.

Although the utility of amino-acid identification and quantitation in biological samples is more limited than for industrial uses, their measurement in specific cases can give crucial information about the disease state. Separation of amino acids in biological fluids is also much more difficult than when using pure substances. There is the potential for matrix interference, such as the reaction of the derivatizing agent with other components, and in addition, difficulty in comparing solvent-based standards to amino acids in the samples. Thus amino-acid separation and quantitation in biological samples is more problematic than analysis of model laboratory mixtures. Methods developed using model mixtures frequently do not work when applied to biological samples, making assay modifications necessary. Dankava and Kaniansky assessed limitations of various modes of CZE in the separation of enantiomers in model and urine matrices. Tryptophan was used as the model analyte and a 90-component mixture of UV light-absorbing organic anions served as the model matrix. Using on-line coupled isotacophoretic sample pretreatment for high sample-load capacity, they were able to separate samples corresponding to 3–6 μL of undiluted urine.

Cerebrospinal fluid analysis to monitor amino-acid levels using MEKC was reported by Berquist et al. using an on-line derivatization and microdialysis sampling technique. Continuous in vivo monitoring of glutamate and aspartate in neurotransmitters of rats using CZE has been reported by Zhou and coworkers. An automated procedure for in vivo monitoring cysteine and glutathione in rat caudate nucleus was also reported by Lada and Kennedy. In this study, microdialysis was coupled on-line with CZE. The dialysates were derivatized on-line with monobromobimane and transferred to the capillary by a flow-gated interface. Separated thiols were measured on-line by a helium-cadmium LIF. Glutamate in microdialysates of striated muscle were measured with CE in an off-line procedure. Additionally, phenylthiohydantoin derivatives of 3- and 4-hydroxyproline were separated using MEKC in bovine skeletal muscle collagen.

Diagnostic applications of CE for amino-acid analysis have also expanded. Glutamine measured by CZE and LIF detection in cerebrospinal fluid of children with meningitis was reported by Tucci and coworkers. They found glutamine concentration was lower in children with viral and bacterial meningitis and proposed that the lower concentrations might be caused by glutamine use by the bacteria. They confirmed the diagnostic utility of this analytical method in the critical differentiation of meningitis.

Jellum and coworkers described a multi-component analytical system to determined diagnostic metabolites, such as cysteine and homocysteine, in urine of patients with various aminoacidopathies and other metabolic disorders. They used a diode-ray detector for fluorescence detection of metabolites derivatized with 9-fluorenylmethyl chloroformate and separated by CZE. They modified and expanded this study using *gas chromatography-mass spectroscopy* (GC-MS) in a study on sera of patients collected prior to disease symptoms and held in the Janus-bank. Kang et al. determined 4-aminosulfonyl-7-fluoro-2, 1,3-benzoxadiazole-derivatized homocysteine, glutathione, and cysteine in plasma. Causse et al. separated and determined homocysteine in plasma using FITC as the derivatizing agent and an argon ion laser for detection. The detection of this intermediary metabolite in the methionine pathway is useful to detect not only genetic metabolic disorders, but also the potential risk for atherosclerosis and some thromboembolic diseases.

Tagliaro et al. used CZE in the determination of serum phenylalanine in a rapid, inexpensive method for diagnosis of phenylketonuria. Also, cysteine in human blood, plasma and urine has been separated and quantitated at the attomole level using an end-column amperometric detection with a gold/mercury amalgam electrode. In addition, enantiomeric forms of amino acids derived from novel depsipeptide antitumor antibiotics were analyzed by a metal chelate MEKC method using a cyclodextrin. The amino acids were hydrolyzed and derivatized with either dansyl chloride for UV-absorbance detection or with FITC for LIF detection. Enantiomeric identities of serine, beta-hydroxyl-*N*-methy-valine were confirmed and a nonchiral aminoacid, sarcosine, was found.

Organic Acid Analysis

Organic acids are a heterogeneous class of low-mol-wt metabolites that contain at least one carboxylic acid group. Several hundred compounds may be included, depending on how expansive a definition is used. Normally, amino acids are not included, although some organic acids contain nitrogen. The wealth of clinical information obtained by analysis of organic acids has tended to be ignored for a number of reasons. The primary clinical application has been limited to the diagnosis of inborn errors of metabolism. Also, traditional analysis has been performed using *gas chromatography-mass spectrometry* (GC-MS), which is expensive and technically demanding. With the advent of less expensive methods of analysis such as *capillary electrophoresis* (CE), organic-acid analysis is finding many previously underutilized and unrecognized clinical applications. The current state of the art still requires organic acid profiling for inborn errors of metabolism by GC-MS analysis, however, this is unlikely to remain the case much longer. Already CE methods for the short-chain organic acids have been published and more comprehensive profiling methods are certain to be developed. The real promise of CE for organic acids, however, lies in fast and inexpensive assays for newer applications, several of which are discussed here.

Many of the CE applications for organic acids share a number of features to improve separation and detection. These include: (1) Flow reversal of the *electroosmotic flow* (EOF), (2) the use of indirect photometric detection or direct detection at short wavelengths, and (3) the need for specimen preparation, particularly at low concentrations of analyte.

Flow Reversal

In the standard configuration, cations pass the detector first, followed by neutral compounds and then anions. Reversal of the EOF produces much faster separations for anions such as organic acids. Although not all assays for organic acids use flow reversal, the majority do. Flow reversal is achieved by two basic methods, use of coated capillaries or uncoated fused- silica capillaries with a cationic surfactant added to the electrolyte. In general, coated capillaries require less conditioning and give more stable performance characteristics.

Detection Methods

Because commercially available instruments are equipped with photometric detection, many of the applications for organic acids use direct photometric detection at short wavelengths (185–200 nm) or indirect photometric methods. These detection methods are adequate and can be used for virtually any compound. One limitation is that identification depends entirely on the compound's characteristic migration time. Direct detection at longer wavelengths (>200 nm) offers more positive identification, but is limited to those organic acids that absorb strongly at these wavelengths. Other detection methods, such as fluorescence, have found fewer applications, mainly due to the limited number of organic acids that fluoresce or can be efficiently conjugated to a fluorogenic reagent, in addition to the cost of the detector. Electrochemical methods are just beginning to be applied to organic acids, and promise to provide good quality, sensitive, yet inexpensive detection methods in the future.

Specimen Preparation

Like many low-mol-wt compounds, organic acids may require specimen preparation to achieve adequate assay reproducibility. This may be critical when detection of levels on the order of μmol/L is needed. To account for variation in sample recovery, addition of an internal standard is highly desirable. Internal standards also allow for the calculation of a relative migration index, increasing the precision of the assay. Currently specimen preparation for organic acids remains relatively unsophisticated, often relying on dilution, filtration, and simple forms of extraction prior to injection onto the capillary. More efficient methods such as on-line analyte concentration will undoubtedly prove useful in the future.

Application for the Clinical Laboratory

The applications discussed in this chapter start with methylmalonic acid, since this is the one with which the authors have the most experience. An assay for urine methylmalonic acid has been operating on a routine basis in the first author's clinical laboratory since 1994. Several other applications share many characteristics with methylmalonic acid, and are discussed next, including succinic acid, oxalic and citric acids, and the simple short-chain organic acids. Most of these assays use either indirect detection or direct detection at short wavelengths. In contrast are the applications for orotic acid and xanthurenic acid, which rely on direct detection at longer wavelengths. Positive identification of these compounds can be enhanced by the use of diode array detection and spectral matching.

Methylmalonic acid

Measurement of methylmalonic acid levels in urine or serum is an excellent way to assess vitamin B_{12} (cobalamin) status. Vitamin B_{12} in the form of 5-deoxyadenosylcobalamin is an essential cofactor in the enzymatic conversion of methylmalonyl-CoA into succinyl-CoA. In vitamin B_{12} deficiency, methylmalonic acid rises early, often reaching

10–100 times the levels seen in normal individuals. In contrast, anemia and macrocytosis and even serum vitamin B_{12} immunoassays are relatively insensitive markers. Because of cost and availability of automation, immunoassays are routinely used as the preferred screening method, although it is well-established that low normal vitamin B_{12} levels do not exclude vitamin B_{12} deficiency. In contrast, assays for methylmalonic acid, the most sensitive marker for vitamin B_{12} deficiency, is many times more expensive, particularly when using GC-MS. Because vitamin B_{12} deficiency is now recognized as being more common than previously thought, an efficient and economic method for methylmalonic acid analysis is becoming increasingly important.

Methylmalonic acid is a deceptively simple dicarboxcylic acid (HOOC-CH-CH_3-COOH), but the analysis is challenging due to the number of closely related organic acids. Methylmalonic acid contains no strongly absorbing constituents, therefore, analysis by CE is currently based on two approaches, derivatization or indirect detection. Derivatization offers two advantages: (1) less specimen is required, and (2) the limit of detection is superior. Alternatively, indirect detection is faster and less expensive. This method does not have adequate sensitivity to detect levels found in normal individuals. Its use, therefore, is limited to the detection of inborn errors of metabolism.

Methylmalonic acid derivatization

Schneede and Ueland described a method using CE to quantitate levels of methlymalonic acid in serum. The assay used 1-pyrenyldiazomethane to react with acids present in serum producing a fluorescent 1-pyrenylmethyl monoester. After separation the products are detected by *laser-induced fluorescence* (LIF). Serum preparation requires addition of ethylmalonic acid as an internal standard, deproteinization with methanol, followed by a 12-h reaction with the derivatizing agent. Extensive dilution, needed to reduce matrix effects, is possible because of the sensitivity of the LIF method. Separation is based on a capillary (ID 75 μm) coated with a linear polyacrylamide to eliminate the EOF. The electrolyte consists of 30 mmol/L Tris-citrate buffer, pH 6.4. An organic modifier (50% dimethylformamide) and 0.1% hydroxypropyl methylcellulose are added to inhance separation and to suppress residual EOF. The specimen is introduced onto the capillary by pressure injection with a run time of about 26 min. The assay has a throughput of about 50 specimens per day. Reproducibility of the assay is acceptable with a *coefficient of variation* (CV) of 12% at 0.13 μmol/L and 5% at 4.3 μmol/L.

This method is adequate for routine analysis and the authors report having analyzed several thousand specimens at the time of publication. Although it represents a significant improvement over traditional GC-MS, the method requires a relatively lengthy specimen preparation and derivatization, in addition to an expensive method of detection. The HeCd laser is reported to be a major contributor to the cost. Use of ethylmalonic acid as an internal standard can also be problematic, since it can be found in some routine clinical specimens, although this is less of a problem for serum than for urine.

Methylmalonic acid by indirect detection

Methods for the indirect detection of methylmalonic acid have been described in assays for urine, and serum. These assays are similar, employing phthalic acid as the indirect detection agent, electrolyte, and buffer. Because the serum and urine assays use the same basic technology, only the serum assay will be described in the following paragraph.

Specimen (0.5 mL) preparation begins with addition of a dimethylsuccinic acid as the internal standard, acidification, and extraction with ethylacetate. The solvent is then evaporated, reconstituted in water, filtered, and injected electrokinetically (5 kV for 25 s). Separation employs an uncoated fused silica capillary (ID 75 μm). Flow reversal is accomplished by addition of cetyltrimethylammonium bromide (CTAB), a cationic surfactant. The electrolyte is composed of 3.3 mmol/L phthalic acid at pH 6.0, 0.46 mmol/L CTAB, and 35% acetonitrile (v/v). The organic modifier, acetonitrile, is added to improve resolution. The phthalic acid background signal is monitored by a diode array detector at 210 nm against a reference signal at 320 nm. Run time is about 6–7 min, and a batch of 15 specimens can be prepared and run in about 4 h. The *limit of detection* (LOD) is 0.2 μmol/L with a CV of $<10\%$ at 0.3 μmol/L.

The LOD of 0.2 μmol/L using indirect detection and phthalic acid is close to the reference limit of 0.4 μmol/L, the upper limit seen in normal individuals. Because methylmalonic acid rises dramatically (10–100 times normal levels) in vitamin B_{12} deficiency, the assay is adequate for clinical purposes. Indirect detection, however, depends entirely on migration time for identification. There is always the possibility that a coeluting compound could be hidden in the methylmalonic acid peak, falsely elevating the value. When methylmalonic acid is elevated, dilution should be used to reduce the possibility of interference by coeluting compounds. Also plasma specimens collected with citric acid

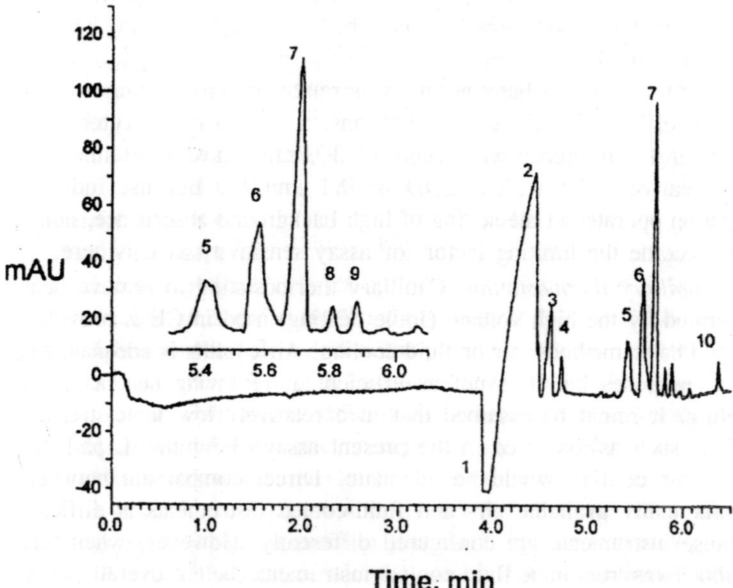

Fig. 8.2. Indirect photometric detection of serum methylmalonic acid using phthalic acid at pH 6.0 and monitored at 210 nm; the signal has been reversed to make descreased phthalic acid absorbance appear as peaks.

as the anticoagulant cannot be analyzed with this assay. The massive peak due to citric acid will overwhelm all other peaks in the vicinity, including the one for methylmalonic acid. EDTA plasma does not cause a similar problem. Specimen preparation is based on an organic phase extraction, representing a significant amount of the total assay time. Although the extraction method is acceptable, a more efficient method of specimen preparation would be a considerable improvement.

Indirect methylmalonic acid assay improvements

The assay of Franke et al. has undergone a number of improvements to make it more robust for routine operation. These include: (1) use of an amine-coated capillary rather than the combination of an uncoated capillary with surfactant, and (2) use of an electrolyte at pH 2.5 rather than the combination of an electrolyte at pH 6.0 with an organic modifier consisting of 35% acetonitrile. The reasons for these changes are discussed later, as are the advantages of using an instrument with a diode array detector and one with fluid-type cooling.

Diode array for indirect detection. Most often indirect detection is used with a simple single-wavelength detector. This type of detector tends to be more sensitive in absolute terms than a diode array detector.

in addition to being less expensive. However, it is the experience of the authors that a diode array produces better results when using indirect detection. In the assay described earlier, a single-wavelength detector (210 nm) produced a baseline that was relatively noisy giving a LOD of 1 μmol/L. Using the same conditions, a diode-array detector (210 nm against a reference wavelength of 300 nm), gave a baseline that was relatively flat with a LOD of 0.1 μmol/L. Because indirect detection operates in the setting of high background absorbance, noise may become the limiting factor for assay sensitivity as it is here.

Capillary thermostating. Capillary thermostating to remove heat generated by the high voltage (Joule heating) used in CE is provided by two basic methods, air or fluid cooling. Air cooling is adequate for many purposes but it is not as efficient at removing heat as fluid cooling. It might be assumed that in a relatively low ionic-strength buffer, such as that used in the present assay (3.3 mmol/L phthalic acid), air cooling would be adequate. Direct comparison between commercially available air- and fluid-cooled instruments is difficult because instruments are configured differently. However, when this method was run in a fluid-cooled instrument, better overall assay performance was found. The clearest example of this was that larger samples could be introduced onto the capillary before broadening of the analyte peaks occurred. Presumably, this was due to inadequate heat-induced dispersion in the air-cooled instrument.

Coated capillaries. Replacing the uncoated capillaries with an amine-coated capillary and removing the surfactant from the electrolyte improved migration time stability considerably. It is known that surfactants are excellent at coating surfaces. However, they can also be difficult to keep in solution. Thus the use of a surfactant inevitably gives an electrolyte that tends to change composition with time, causing stability problems with the migration time. Using an amine-coated capillary (ID 50 μm) improved the reproducibility and durability of the methylmalonic acid assay.

pH. When investigating methods to separate anions, it is known that lowering the pH reduces the number of compounds that are ionized. These unionized compounds will be swept along with the EOF, thus, fewer anions will be present to cause potential interferences. For this reason, separation in acidic environment has the potential to reduce interfering compounds to a minimum. Although this approach has obvious limitations, it works well with methylmalonic acid (pK_{a1} 3.07). At pH 2.5, methylmalonic acid showed an electropherogram with significantly fewer interferences. Succinic acid (pK_{a1} 4.60), for example, is found in the EOF at this pH. Phthalic acid (pK_{a1} 2.89), used as electrolyte and indirect detection agent, still retains significant buffering capacity at this pH.

Organic modifiers. In the original assay, an organic modifier consisting of 35% acetonitrile was added to the electrolyte to improve resolution between methylmalonic and succinic acids. Although organic modifiers can enhance resolution significantly, they can also cause unwanted side effects. One obvious problem is that the solution is prone to differential evaporation that can contribute to assay variability. When changing the pH from 6.0 to 2.5, succinic acid migrated with the EOF and an organic modifier was no longer required.

Succinic acid

Succinic acid (HOOC-CH_2-CH_2-COOH) is a closely related isomer of methylmalonic acid, although clinically, the utility of these two organic acids is much different. Succinic acid is a major metabolite in the tricarboxylic acid cycle and can be used to monitor mitochondrial function. Interestingly, succinic acid is also formed stoichiometrically as a product of the enzymatic synthesis of peptidyl hydroxyproline and it can be used to monitor increased collagen biosynthesis. As with many of the organic acids, analysis has been performed with GC-MS and studies on the clinical significance has been limited by the relatively high cost and difficulty of the analysis.

As expected from the similarity of the assays, many of the applications developed for methylmalonic acid and other related short-chain organic acids can also be used to detect succinic acid. The assay of Franke et al. for methylmalonic acid required little modification for use for serum succinic acid. Because the concentrations normally present are higher, succinic acid is a less demanding analyte. With the availability of a relatively easy and less expensive assay, increased investigations of the clinical utility of succinic acid can be expected in the future.

Oxalic and citric acids

Oxalic and citric acids are important analytes for the evaluation and treatment of urinary-tract calculi. The prevention of further stone formation is a major goal in the treatment of these individuals requiring an evaluation of the risk factors for calculi formation. Elevated oxalic-acid excretion is a risk factor for the formation of calcium oxalate stones and treatment includes removing sources of oxalic acid from the diet. In contrast, elevated citric-acid excretion is a protective factor that tends to prevent urinary calcium from precipitating. Thus, recurrent stone formers with low urinary citric acid may benefit from treatments to increase urinary citric acid levels.

Holmes describes an indirect detection method for oxalic and citric acid in 24 h urine collections. These compounds are also present on the electropherograms of many related assays. Because oxalic and citric acids are present at relatively high concentrations in urine, specimen preparation is minimal, and consists of acidification, centrifugation, and dilution (100-fold). Dilution is required primarily to reduce the chloride concentration, which is also detected by the indirect method used for this assay. Separation employs an uncoated capillary (ID 75 μm), an electrolyte and indirect detection agent consisting of sodium chromate (10 mmol/L), and a flow reversal agent consisting of 0.5 m*M* tetradecylammonium bromide (TTAB). The detection limit was 7 mg/L for both oxalic and citric acids, which compares favorably to standard enzymatic assays. Although standard enzymatic methods test for oxalic and citric acids separately, the method of Holmes measures both simultaneously. In addition, the assay can also be used to detect a number of related anions in urine, including chloride, sulfate, nitrate, phosphate, glycolate, and urate. All these components are potentially useful for the evaluation of the risks of urinary stone formation.

Profiling short-chain organic acids

The analysis of organic acids in urine is a well-established procedure for the diagnosis of inherited errors of metabolism. The large number of organic acids and the complexity of the urine matrix makes separation and quantitation difficult. Currently, GC-MS is the most reliable technique for this purpose. However, GC-MS is also expensive, labor intensive, and generally limited to referral laboratories. On the other hand, CE can provide a simple and rapid alternative. The benefits of a method, such as CE, that is widely available and that provides rapid analysis, is apparent in such situations as the critically ill newborn presenting with coma and metabolic acidosis. In such cases, rapid diagnosis facilitates appropriate treatment. Although CE is limited at the present time to the analysis of the short-chain organic acids, this is changing rapidly.

The methods for the small short-chain organic acids, originally developed from applications in the food sciences, share many characteristics, such as detection of similar compounds and migration orders. Both direct and indirect detection methods have been used.

Direct detection is generally based on wavelengths from 200 to 185 nm, and are generally less sensitive than indirect methods.

Indirect detection of short-chain organic acids

Chen et al. described an indirect detection assay for 14 short-chain organic acids in serum and urine. The migration order was oxalic, citric, malonic, tartaric, methylmalonic, ketoglutaric, succinic, ethylmalonic, methylsuccinic, glutaric, adipic, methylglutaric, lactic, and pyruvic acids. Serum (0.5 mL) preparation consisted of deproteinization with methanol, centrifugation, drying the supernatant, and redissolving in water (250 μL) to provide concentration. Urine preparation consisted of filtration to remove particulates and a fivefold dilution. Ethylmalonic acid was used as an internal standard in both specimen types. Of the capillaries evaluated, polyacrylamide-coated capillaries showed superior performance. Phthalic acid was used as the indirect detection agent in a carbonate buffer; however to avoid interferences seen at shorter wavelengths, 230 nm was selected as the monitoring wavelength. The limit of detection was between 6 and 28 μg/mL for citric, methylmalonic, succinic, glutaratic, and lactic acids.

Direct detection of short-chain organic acids

Shirao et al. described an assay for 12 short-chain organic acids in urine based on direct detection at 185 nm. The migration order was: oxalic, formic, malonic, fumaric, succinic, α-ketoglutaric, citric, acetic, pyruvic, lactic, isovaleric, and hippuric acids. The limits of detection were given as 5 μg/mL for all but hippuric acid, which was 100 ng/mL. Urine was centrifuged and passed through a C18 column prior to hydrostatic injection. Separation was based on an uncoated capillary (ID 75 μm), with an electrolyte and buffer of 50 m*M* borate at pH 10.0 with addition of a commercial flow-reversal agent.

Hiraoka et al. described a similar assay for cerebrospinal fluid based on direct detection at 185 nm. Compounds detected included (in migration order): oxalic, fumaric, acetic, pyruvic, lactic, and glutamic acids. However, unlike urine, ascorbic acid was also seen.

Jariego and Hernanz also described an assay for 10 short-chain organic acids in urine based on direct detection at 185 nm. The migration order was methylmalonic, glutaric, 3-methylglutaric, *N*-acetylaspartic, 2-aminoadipic, propionic, lactic, 2-oxoisovaleric, isovaleric, and homogentisic acids. The limits of detection were between 5–15 μmol/L. Urine was prepared by passing through a centrifuge-type filter, and diluted to a creatinine concentration of about 1 mmol/L prior to introduction of the sample onto the capillary by pressure. Separation was accomplished using a polyimide-coated capillary (ID 75 μm). The electrolyte consisted of sodium sulfate, calcium chloride, and a commercial additive for flow reversal.

Barbas et al. described an assay for 10 short-chain organic acids in urine employing direct detection at 200 nm. The migration order was: fumaric, malic, methylmalonic, citric, pyruvic, acetoacetic, propionic, lactic, butyric, and 3-hydroxybutyric acids. Urine preparation consisted of passing through a centrifuge-type filter, followed by introduction of the sample onto the capillary by pressure. Separation was achieved on a neutral- surface capillary (ID 75 μm) using an electrolyte of 200 mmol/L sodium phosphate buffer at pH 6.0 with 100 mL/L methanol. The organic modifier was added to resolve methylmalonic, propionic, and lactic acids.

Orotic acid

Orotic acid is an intermediate in the biosynthesis of pyrimidines and an important analyte in the examination of a number of inborn errors of metabolism. The disorder most associated with elevated orotic acid is ornithine transcarbamylase deficiency, an inborn error of the urea cycle. In contrast, orotic acid is normal in the urea-cycle defect consisting of carbamoyl-phosphate synthase deficiency. Orotic acid can also useful for the evaluation of a number of other conditions including hereditary orotic aciduria and lysinuric protein intolerance.

Orotic acid has a distinctive absorbance signal in the region of 200–320 nm that makes direct detection possible. Unlike indirect photometric detection (and direct detection at very short wavelengths), direct detection in the mid-range UV offers the advantage of matching the obtained spectra with a spectral library for a more positive identification. Like fluorescence, this type of detection is obviously limited to compounds having a suitable absorbance.

Franke and Nuttall describe an assay for orotic acid based on direct detection at 278 nm. Use of a diode-array detector allowed for automated spectral matching to monitor the purity of the orotic acid and internal standard peaks. Separation was on a polyvinyl alcohol-coated capillary (ID 50 μm), and an electrolyte consisting of 100 m*M* phosphate buffer at pH 3.0. Migration time at 20 kV was about 10 min at 35°C and about 14 min at 25°C. Above 20 kV, the Ohm's law plot deviated from linearity, although this was probably owing to the limitations of an air-cooled instrument. The migration time showed a coefficient of variation <1%. Urine-based control material showed a coefficient of variation <8% at 17 μmol/L (normal control).

Specimen preparation. Specimen preparation consisted of adding an internal standard (2,4- dinitrobenzoic acid) and barbituric acid buffer at pH 4.4 to the urine specimen, passing it through a single-use C1 8 reversed-phase column, and injecting the eluate. Although relatively complex, without preparation of the urine specimen, the migration time and assay precision did not have adequate reproducibility. Poor reproducibility resulting from minimal specimen preparation has been reported in a variety of circumstances, particularly when the concentrations are in the μmol/L range.

Coated capillaries. A polyvinyl alcohol-coated capillary was used to provide flow reversal, and performed well in this application. The capillaries were easily conditioned in under 10 min, required no additional conditioning between specimen injections, and proved to be durable. It is worth emphasizing that the performance of coated capillaries far outstripped that of uncoated capillaries, which required lengthy pre-conditioning in addition to re-conditioning between specimens.

Xanthurenic acid

Xanthurenic acid is a metabolite that can be used to evaluate vitamin B_6 status, much as methylmalonic acid can be used as a sensitive indicator of vitamin B_{12} status. Xanthurenic acid is a metabolite of tryptophan via the kynurenine pathway. This is also referred to as the tryptophan-niacin pathway. Several enzymes in this pathway require vitamin B_6 as a cofactor. As a result, high levels of several tryptohan metabolites, including xanthurenic acid, accumulate when vitamin B_6 is deficient. Xanthurenic acid also has a strong absorbance signal making it suitable for direct photometric detection. Significantly, xanthurenic acid has limited solubility below pH 8.0. This requires operating at higher pH, increasing the potential for interfering anions. However, as with orotic acid, direct detection and spectral matching can be used for positive identification of the xanthurenic acid peak.

Separation of serum xanthurenic acid was based on a polyvinyl alcohol- coated capillary (ID 50 μm), similar to the orotic acid assay. Instead of an acidic electrolyte, however, 200 m*M* glycylglycine was used to provide buffer capacity at pH 8.2. Specimen preparation started with 0.5 mL serum, addition of Tris acetate buffer at pH 9.0 (including an internal standard of 3-nitrobenzoic acid), and addition of urea and ethanol to completely solubilize xanthurenic acid. After mixing, this mixture was passed through a centrifuge-type filter, and pressure injected. A diode array detector was used to monitor peaks at 243 nm, and automated spectral matching was employed to monitor peak purity. The limit of detection for xanthurenic acid was 1 μmol/ L with a coefficient of variation was < 9% at 10 μmol/L.

Other applications

Many organic acid assays can be found in the literature. Many are useful for applications in the food sciences and for research purposes, but fewer have been developed with the specific needs of the clinical laboratory in mind.

1. *Ascorbic acid*. Koh et al. describe an assay for ascorbic acid (vitamin C) in fruit beverages using direct detection at 254 nm. Urine and plasma were also examined briefly.
2. *Bile acids*. Yarabe et al. describe an assay for the separation of 15 bile acids in serum based on indirect detection.
3. *Electrochemical detection*. DeBacker and Nagel describe a potentiometric method of detection for short-chain organic acids that may be useful for future studies.
4. *Fatty acids*. Assays for saturated and unsaturated fatty acids in food products use indirect detection.
5. *Nicotinic acid and metabolites*. Zarzycki et al. describe an assay for nicotinic acid and its metabolites in human plasma. Nicotinic acid is related to the tyrptophan pathway, and the assay shows some similarities with that of Weber et al. in that direct detection at 254 nm is used.
6. *Phenylketonuria*. Dolnik described the separation of the acids of phenylketonuria based on direct detection at 260 nm. The specific organic acids identified were phenylpyruvate, 2-hydroxyphenyl-acetate, phenylacetate, mandelate, 4- hydroxyphenylpyruvate, and phenylalanine.
7. *Profiling organic anions*. Schoots et al. described an assay based on direct detection at 254 nm for profiling organic anions in the serum of uremic patients. The quantitation of hippuric, p-hydroxyhippuric, and uric acids was emphasized. Specimen preparation consisted of deproteinization with centrifuge-type filtration, and dilution (10-fold). Separation was based on a Teflon capillary (ID 200 μm). Analysis required 8 min, which was a significant improvement over the 90 min required for similar HPLC methods. Petucci et al. described an assay for profiling organic anions in serum and hemodialysate fluid from uremic patients using direct detection at 210 nm. Compounds identified included hippuric acid, tryptophan and tryptophan metabolites (indican, kynurenic

acid, nicotinic acid), tyrosine, purine, and pyrimidine metabolites. Specimen preparation consisted of passing through a centrifuge-type filter to remove proteins. The filtrate was then pressure-injected. Separation was based on an uncoated capillary (ID 50 μm) and an electrolyte of 150 m*M* borate buffer at pH 9.0. Run time was about 16 min and did not use flow reversal.

8. *Quinolinic acid and other tryptophan metabolites*. Weber et al. described an assay for tryptophan and 10 of its metabolites in urine using direct detection at 254 nm. Tryptophan metabolites are an interesting group of compounds that have not been fully exploited for their diagnostic potentials, and include xanthurenic acid and quinolinic acid. Quinolinic acid appears to be toxic to neurons, and may have important implications for the development of some neurological diseases.

CE is a sensitive and versatile technique and represents an inexpensive and practical method for the determination of organic acids. Applications include far more than the traditional investigation of inborn errors of metabolism. From the applications discussed previously, several general conclusions can be drawn concerning organic-acid assays.

Given the complex nature of biological specimens and the stringent requirements of the clinical laboratory, significant specimen preparation prior to injection is often needed to achieve stable migration times and good analytic precision, particularly when low concentrations are involved. The use of more sophisticated specimen preparation will undoubtedly make many applications more practical.

The analysis of anions such as organic acids is faster when flow reversal is used. Flow reversal with coated capillaries performs better than uncoated fused silica capillaries in combination with cationic surfactants. Coated capillaries require less conditioning, and give more stable migration times. Relatively large-diameter capillaries (ID 75 μm) are being used in most applications, primarily to maximize the limits of detection. Air-cooled instruments are adequate for many applications, although fluid-cooled instruments dissipate heat more efficiently and may give better assay characteristics. This is particularly true when larger diameter capillaries are used to increase detection limits.

Assays for the organic acids also tend to be sensitive to small pH changes, and may therefore be more reproducible when there is adequate buffering. When possible, operating at an acidic pH tends to reduce the number of potentially interfering anions.

Steroid Analysis

Adrenal Glands

The adrenal glands are paired structures situated above the kidneys that are approx 2–3 cm wide and 6 cm long and weigh approx 5 g. The glands consists of a yellow, outer cortex that constitutes approx 80% of the adrenal gland and a gray, inner medulla. The adrenal cortex consists of three distinct layers or zones of cells. The outermost layer, the zona glomerulosa, is the site of aldosterone synthesis, the principal mineralocorticoid produced by the human adrenal cortex, and corticosterone synthesis. The wider, middle zone is the zona fasciculata, and the innermost layer is the zona reticularis. The two inner zones of the adrenal cortex can be considered a single functional unit, where cortisol, along with some corticosterone, and dehydroepiandrosterone (DHEA) are synthesized. The glucocorticoids have widespread effects on carbohydrate and protein metabolism. Androgens secreted by the adrenal cortex pay a less important role than the androgens, which are secreted by the gonads.

Steroid synthesis

The human adrenal cortex produces and secretes glucocorticoids (cortisol and corticosterone), a mineralocorticoid (aldosterone), biosynthetic precursors of three end products (progesterone, 11-deoxy-corticosterone, and 11-deoxycortisol) and androgenic substances (DHEA and its sulfate ester). The synthesis of adrenal cortical steroids begins with cholesterol, which is converted to pregnenolone. A cholesterol hydroxylase and desmolase mediate this rate-limiting step. ACTH stimulates this conversion and also increases the uptake of lipoprotein, which is the major source of adrenal cholesterol, by the adrenal cortex and stimulates the hydrolysis of cholesterol esters to free cholesterol. Many of the intermediates of steroid synthesis are secreted to some extent, but the steroids that are found in physiologically significant amounts are aldosterone, cortisol, corticosterone, DHEA, and androstenedione.

Physiological Effects of Glucocorticoids

Of the naturally occurring steroids only cortisol, corticosterone, cortisone, and 11-dehydrocorticosterone have appreciable glucocorticoid activity. Cortisol, which is found in the highest concentration, accounts for most of this activity. About 75% of plasma cortisol is bound to *cortisol binding globulin* (CBG, an alpha globulin), 15% is bound to plasma albumin, and 10% is unbound (free), representing the

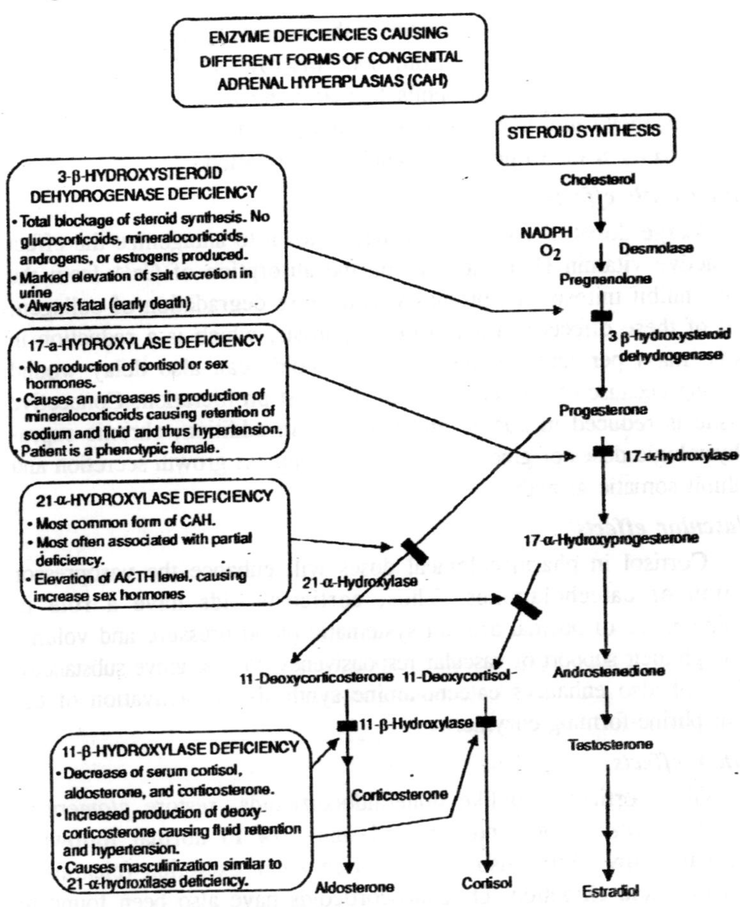

Fig. 8.3. Enzyme deficiencies causing different forms of congenital adrenal hyperplasias.

physiologically active portion. CBG also has a high binding affinity for progesterone, deoxycorticosterone, and some synthetic analogs.

Anti-inflammatory effects

Glucocorticoids inhibit inflammatory and allergic reactions. They do this by stabilizing the lysosomal membranes, inhibiting the release of proteolytic enzymes, and by increasing capillary permeability. This in turn reduces diapedesis of leukocytes. Glucocorticoids also reduce the number of circulating lymphocytes, monocytes, eosinophils, and basophils. The decrease in the number of basophils accounts for the fall in blood histamine levels and the reduction of the allergic response. There is also an increase in the number of inflammatory cells (neutrophils) caused by a decrease in the migration from the capillaries and an accelerated release from bone marrow. Glucocorticoids also inhibit the ability of neutrophils to marginate to the vessel wall. In addition, they cause impairment of the lymph nodes, thymus, and spleen that directly leads to decreased antibody formation.

Antigrowth effects

Large doses of cortisol have been shown to antagonize the effect of active vitamin D metabolites on the absorption of Ca^{2+} from the gut, inhibit mitosis of fibroblasts, and cause degradation of collagen. All of these effects can lead to osteoporosis, which is a reduction in bone mass per unit volume. Glucocorticoids can also delay wound healing because of the reduction of fibroblast proliferation. Connective tissue is reduced in quality and strength. In addition, chronic supra-physiologic doses of glucocorticoids will suppress growth secretion and inhibit somatic growth.

Vascular effects

Cortisol in pharmacological doses will enhance the vasopressor action of catecholamines. Thus, corticosteroids have a role in maintenance of normal arterial systematic blood pressure and volume through their support of vascular responsiveness to vasoactive substances. Cortisol also enhances catecholamine synthesis via activation of the epinephrine-forming enzyme.

Other effects

Glucocorticoids, unlike mineraldocorticoids, restore *glomerular filtration rate* (GFR) and renal plasma flow to normal following adrenalectomy. They also facilitate free-water excretion (clearance) and uric-acid excretion. Of Glucocorticoids have also been found to have psychoneural effects following chronic hyper- or hypo-cortisol secretion. In these cases patients may initially become euphoric and then psychotic, paranoid, and finally depressed. In addition, cortisol increases gastric flow and gastric secretion, while it decreases gastric mucosal-cell proliferation. The latter two effects can lead to peptic ulceration following chronic cortisol treatment.

Metabolic effects

Carbohydrate metabolism

Cortisol, the main glucocorticoid present in circulation, is a carbohydrate-sparing hormone exerting an anti-insulin effect, which can lead to hypoglycemia and insulin-resistance. In addition, glucocorticoids maintain blood glucose and the glycogen content of the liver by promoting the conversion of amino acids to carbohydrates and the storage of carbohydrate as hepatic glycogen.

Protein metabolism

The most important gluconeogenic substrates are amino acids that are derived from proteolysis in skeletal muscle. Cortisol enhances the release of amino acids from proteins in skeletal muscles and other extra hepatic tissues including the protein matrix of bone. The amino acids released are transported to the liver and then converted to glucose. This increased in glucose production via gluconeogenesis causes an increased urea production because of the conversion of amino-acid nitrogen to urea, accounting for the increased urinary nitrogen excretion. The proteolysis in skeletal muscle brings about a negative protein balance since the amino acids taken up by the liver that would have been used in the synthesis of new protein are instead used to form glucose or glycogen. This anabolic effect is an important exception to the overall protein catabolic effect of cortisol.

Fat metabolism

Glucocorticoids enhance the lipolytic actions of other hormones, such as growth hormone, catecholamines, glucagon, and thyroid hormone. Glucocorticoids also help in the mobilization of fatty acids from adipose tissues to the liver, where the metabolism of fatty acids inhibits glycolytic enzymes and promote gluconeogenesis. As a result of increased fatty acids oxidation, glucocorticoids may lead to increased ketosis, especially in patients with diabetes mellitus.

Congenital Adrenal Hyperplasia

Congenital adrenal hyperplasia (CAH) also known as the "*adrenogenital syndrome*" can be considered as a family of inborn error of steroidogensis. All CAH variants are inherited as autosomal recessive traits. Each member of this family is characterized by a specific enzyme deficiency that impacts cortisol production by the adrenal cortex, and if severe enough can lead to sexual ambiguity in both males and females. The enzymes usually affected are 21-hydroxylase (types I and II), beta hydroxylase (type III), 3 beta-hydroxylase (type IV), 17 hydroxylase (type V) and cholesterol 20-alpha hydroxylase (type VI). The most common syndromes are types I and II, which are caused by a 21-hydroxylase enzyme deficiency. The identification of the specific enzyme deficiency relies heavily on laboratory findings since all variants affect the glucocorticoid (cortisol) pathway in some manner. Although formation of cortisone and cortisol are blocked in type I and II CAH, precursors are still being manufactured, causing elevations of 17-hydroxyprogesterone. Normal basal serum 17-hydroxyprogesterone levels, however, cannot exclude late-onset CAH. Response to adrenocorticotrophic stimulation, however, clearly distinguishes this disorder from carriers of the classical disease.

In addition to being precursors of cortisone, many of the early intermediates are also estrogenic compounds. In the presence of abnormally high production of androgens, secondary sexual characteristics are affected. If this condition is manifested in utero, pseudohermaphroditism (masculinzation) of external genitalia occur in girls and macrogentisomia praecox (accentuation of male genitalia) occurs in boys. If the condition is not manifested until after birth, virilism (masculinization) develops in girls and precocious puberty in boys. In CAH variants IV, V, and VI, there is also some degree of interruption of the adrenal pathway, so that the external appearance of the female genitalia is not significantly affected and subsequent virilization is minimal or absent.

In CAH, the adrenal glands themselves increase in size because of hyperplasia of the steroid-producing adrenal cortex. This is because the level of cortisone and hydrocortisone produced by the adrenal gland controls normal pituitary production of ACTH through a negative-feedback mechanism. In variants of congenital adrenal hyperplasia, cortisone production is partially or completely blocked, prompting the pituitary to produce more ACTH in an attempt to increase cortisone production. This continues until the adrenal cortex tissue becomes hyperplastic under the continual ACTH stimulation. Also when the mineralocorticoid pathway leading to aldosterone is blocked (CAH types II, IV, VI), salt losing crises similar to those of Addison's disease occur.

In CAH, the correct identification of the enzyme affected is achieved by observation of clinical symptoms reflecting distinct hormonal patterns leading to the measurement cortisol, which should be low, as well as increased levels of steroids proximal to the suspected blocked step.

Two rounds of polymerase chain reaction (PCR) and *amplification-created restriction sites* (ACRS) analysis may provide important information for genetic counseling, prenatal diagnosis, and management of families at risk for CAH. The data from one study suggest that the steroidogenic acute regulatory protein amino acid replacement mutants that cause lipoid CAH are inactive because of fairly the inability of the enzyme to fold properly, which may be caused by the loss of salt bridges that stabilize the tertiary structure.

Some governments have done studies to evaluate the benefits of neonatal screening for CAH. One such study was done in Sweden from January 1989 to December 1994. The study concluded that the main benefits of screening was avoidance of serious salt-losing crises, earlier correct gender assignment in virilized girls, and detection of patients who would otherwise have been missed in neonatal period. Screening also prevented deaths due the decreased steroid production in the neonatal period.

Use of Capillary Electrophoresis (CE) in the Separation and Detection of Steroids

Clinically the evaluation of steroid levels is of great interest. There are many disorders that have been identified as being caused either by under or over secretion of steroids, e.g., CAH, Cushing's syndrome, Addison's disease, acromegaly, hirsutism, and adenomas. The ability to simultaneously measure multiple steroids in the urine and/or serum of these patients would be helpful in making the diagnosis of their disorder. However, the structural similarity and low concentrations of steroids have made rapid, yet accurate, analysis a problem. *Radioimmunoassay* (RIA), although extremely sensitive, requires extraction and purification by ***high-performance liquid chromatography*** (HPLC) to provide the required specificity. Thus, to analyze multiple steroids by RIA requires the same number of RIAs as steroids, limiting this application to specialized laboratories and, increasing the turnaround time. Other analytical methodologies based on chromatographic separation, such as *gas chromatography* (GC), *gas chromatography mass spectrometry* (GC-MS), and HPLC, have also been used for steroid testing. These procedures also require extraction, concentration, and derivation to enhance sensitivity and specificity, limiting their routine use because they are time-consuming and expensive.

Ideally, methodologies suitable for determination of steroids in clinical samples should meet the following criteria to be clinically justified. The methodology should:

1. Not require large sample volumes (typically <1 mL of plasma or serum should be used);
2. Have high sensitivity with detection limits in the 0.1–10 nmol/L range;

3. Be highly specific but retain the ability to detect and quantitate multiple steroids in the presence of other structurally similar compounds;
4. Have minimal derivation and/or prior sample preparation;
5. Provide a high sample throughput with a reasonable turnaround time;
6. Be relatively inexpensive; and
7. Be automatable.

In many ways *capillary electrophoresis* (CE) fit these criteria since it has the unique features high resolution, high mass sensitivity, low sample volume requirements, and over all versatility.

Serum

Steroids are neutral compounds and therefore would not be mobilized or separated when subjected to electrophoretic conditions. To overcome this inherent problem of neutral compounds, *micellar electrokinetic capillary chromatography* (MEKC), which uses ionic micelles to effect separation, was developed by Terabe et al. The separation principle of MEKC is similar to that of chromatography, except that MEKC utilizes electrokinetic phenomena to perform the chromatography instead of a liquid-delivery pump.

Using this technique, Abubaker et al. succeeded in developing a method to separate rapidly steroids whose measurement gives clinically useful information. They found excellent resolution for eight steroids by using a buffer of *sodium dodecyl sulfate* (SDS) and acetonitrile

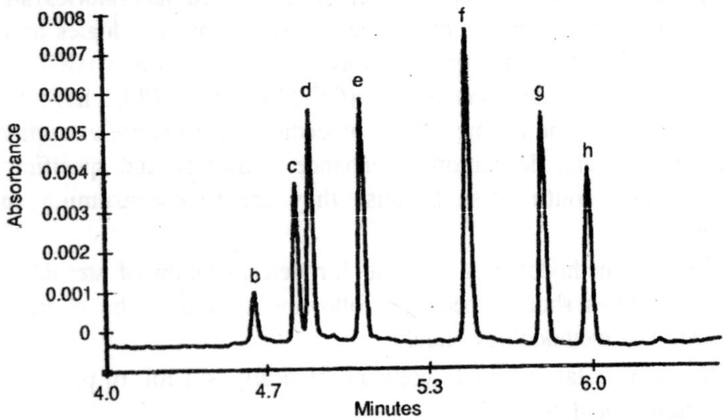

Fig. 8.4. Separation of testosterone propionate, progesterone, 17-hydroxy-progesterone, testosterone, 11-deoxycortisol, 21-deoxycortisol, cortisol, and cortisone from a serum ultrafiltrate.

with a neutral capillary. A similar resolution was achieved with a fused silica capillary using a *dodecyl trimethylammonium bromide* (DTAB) buffer, although the time required for separation was increased six- to seven-fold. The steroids separated were testosterone propionate, progesterone, 17-hydroxy progesterone, testosterone, 11-deoxycortisol, 21-deoxycortisol, hydrocortisone, and cortisone. Three of these hormones (11-deoxycortsol, 17-OH progesterone, and 21-deoxycortisol), are known to be important in helping to establish the diagnosis of CAH. Thus, using these methods to separate and quantitate these steroids could be very useful in screening newborns for CAH. However, the sensitivity was found to be inadequate without preconcentration.

The issue with sensitivity can potentially be overcome by using the on-line concentration techniques of stacking with reverse-migrating micelles or the field-enhanced sample injection with reverse migrating micelles developed by Quirino et al. Both techniques used the separation of ng/mL levels of testosterone and progesterone to demonstrate that this was a fast, effective, and easy way to concentrate neutral analytes inside the capillary. More work is still needed in this area to show its utility with serum.

Urinary-free cortisol

The total cortisol level in a 24-h urine represents the integrated or mean concentration of free cortisol in plasma over this 24-h period and provides an excellent diagnostic sensitivity and specificity for the detection of the increased secretion of cortisol by the adrenal glands (Cushing's syndrome). In contrast, total serum cortisol levels are not always an accurate measure of an overactive adrenocorticoid function and can be elevated in pregnancy, obesity, diabetes, or hyperthyroidism. *Urinary free cortisol* (UFC) measurement is therefore the most reliable single approach for screening patients for Cushing's syndrome. Currently the methods available for measuring UFC are associated with long turnaround times and interferences present in urine.

Lokinendi et al. used solid-phase extraction in conjunction with MEKC as a method for the separation and detection of UFC. The addition of an internal standard was found to be necessary for accurate and reliable quantitation of the free cortisol in urine. The internal standard, corticosterone, was chosen because it did not coelute with the various compounds present in the extracted urine. The authors evaluated the overall performance and feasibility of the method. In addition, they also evaluated linearity, recovery, and lower limit of detection of free cortisol in human urine and compared the results

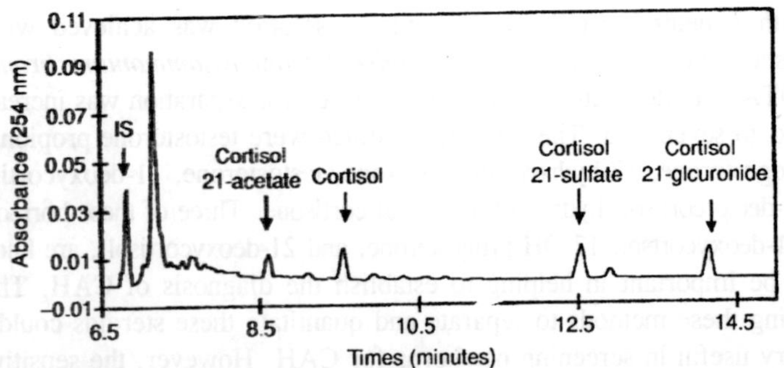

Fig. 8.5. Separation of Internal Standard (IS) (corticosterone) at 100 μg/dL and cortisol 21-acetate, cortisol, cortisol 21-sulfate, and cortisol 21-glucosidonate at 20 μg/dL in urine.

with a commercially available immunoassay. They found an excellent correlation (R = 0.95 and slope = 0.934) with the immunoassay with little, if any, interference from endogenous urine substances.

Congenital adrenal hyperplasia

CAH as discussed earlier is a group of autosomal recessive disorders involving the adrenal glands, in which the primary defect is a deficiency of one or more enzymes involved in the biosynthesis. The main three steroids that are measured to help in making the differential diagnosis are 17-hydroxy progesterone, 21-deoxycortisol, and 11-deoxycortisol. In frank CAH the serum levels of these steroids can reach levels such that detection by CE is possible. The real challenge, however, is in the detection of normal levels in order to differentiate between patients who have a partial blockage and normals. The highest levels that these steroids are normally found in serum are 138 ng/dL and 155 ng/dL for 17-deoxy progesterone and 11-deoxycortisol, respectively. MEKC can separate these structurally similar steroids rapidly, however, detection of normal serum levels is not currently possible with the conventional UV absorbance detectors available with most CE instruments. Using UV absorbance, the lower limit of detection for these steroids by MEKC is 0.05 mg/dL. Thus, a 3000-fold pre-concentration is needed to detect normal levels, which may be achieved using field-enhanced sample injection methods.

9

DATA PRESENTATION IN FORENSIC SCIENCE

Genetic information may be found in bone, teeth, skin and other soft tissue, tears, sweat, saliva, hair roots, earwax, semen, vaginal fluid, urine and blood. Examples would include saliva on a cigarette butt or drinking glass, or skin cells on a steering wheel or glass. About 95% of human nuclear DNA is non-coding DNA, the so-called '*junk*' DNA. These non-coding regions are the areas that are examined in DNA forensic testing. DNA forensic fingerprinting began in Leicester, UK, when in 1984 Alec Jeffreys discovered hypervarible loci made up of approximately 10 to 1000 tandemly repeated sequences, each typically 10-100 base pairs in length. Applications of molecular DNA analysis include criminal, immigration and civil cases. Murder, assault, rape, paternity testing and family and body identification are all issues that can be addressed with these techniques.

TECHNIQUES

Though the typing of *restriction fragment length polymorphisms* (RFLPs) was originally the primary method of DNA forensic analysis, the main forensic DNA analysis method of today uses autosomal *short tandem repeat* (STR) loci, which are usually typed by multiplex *polymerase chain reaction* (PCR) methods. The profiles from an STR multiplex analysis are displayed in a computer-generated graph called an *electropherogram*. The sources of ambiguity of an electropherogram profile are mixtures of samples, degradation of DNA, allelic drop-out, spurious peaks (technical artefacts) or false peaks.

In selected cases, such as degraded samples or when very small amounts of the sample are available for study, 'mini' STR markers that use shorter amplicons, autosomal *single nucleotide polymorphisms* (SNPs) or markers on the mitochondrial DNA or on the Y chromosome are more useful. The two largest DNA databases in the world, the UK National DNA Database (>3.4 million profiles) and the USA DNA database (>3.5 million profiles), use multiplex autosomal STR methods. Because SNPs have much lower heterozygosities than STRs, data from a larger number of SNP loci would be required to obtain the same discrimination potential. There is currently a 21-locus autosomal SNP multiplex that has been introduced.

Differential Lysis

In rape cases there may be a mixing of the victim's DNA and the rapist's DNA in the vaginal vault or other anatomical locations. Differential lysis is a technique used for vaginal fluid/semen mixtures that concentrates the sperm by lysing the victim's epithelial cells. This process thus eliminates the masking of the rapist's DNA by the victim's DNA. Though first described in 1985, the original protocol is still used today.

Autosomes (Nuclear DNA)

Currently, the most common method for forensic analysis of nuclear DNA is to use a multiplex system for STRs. There are about 20,000 known STR loci, however about 20 select loci are used in most forensic cases. The STRs that are commonly used were selected because they are independent: that is, the inheritance of one locus does not influence the inheritance of another locus. The 13 core loci used by the US FBI CODIS system are: TPOX, D3S1358, FGA, D5S818, CSF1PO, D7S820, D8S1179, TH01, VWA, D13S317, D18S51, D21S11 and D16S539. Along with these 13 core loci, the amelogenin locus for sex determination is also examined. For each locus, a genotype for the sample will be identified; then the frequency of such a genotype can be calculated using population genotypes.

At times the SNP approach may be utilized for nuclear DNA analysis, instead of the more popular (and discriminating) STRs, because SNPs are more useful in analysing degraded DNA than are STRs.

Y Chromosome

The Y chromosome is useful to trace relationships among males and to evaluate multiple males in a rape case and in male–female mixtures. There are at least 246 Y-chromosome SNP markers (Y-

SNPs) and at least 227 Y-chromosome STR markers (Y-STRs) described. Another author reports that there are at least 219 STR sites on the Y chromosome. The STR approach is the usual method utilized for DNA analysis of the Y chromosome.

Mitochondrial DNA (mtDNA)

Mitochondrial DNA is more durable and plentiful than nuclear DNA. However, it is less discriminating than nuclear DNA because it is transmitted only from mother to children, and has less variation between individuals than nuclear DNA. It is usually used when the nuclear DNA is degraded, such as when only hair, bone or teeth are present. There is a report of finding suitable mtDNA in guts of maggots (fly larvae) that have fed on human tissue and been collected in death investigations. There are many more copies of mtDNA than there are copies of nuclear DNA. There are usually 200–1700 copies of mtDNA per cell. Heteroplasmy is a special attribute of mtDNA. Heteroplasmy is when a person has two or more different mtDNA sequences present. Human mitochondria have 16,569 base pairs that comprise 37 genes. A region called the *discrimination loop*, or '*D-loop*' is a non-coding control region that has a fair amount of variation, and so is used for DNA testing of SNPs. The mtDNA D-loop region has two hypervariable areas called HV1 and HV2. The HV2 area has a region of length heteroplasmy identified as the homopolymeric *cytosine stretch* (C-stretch).

Investigations of the mtDNA coding region using an SNP method to increase forensic discrimination has been recently described. Statistical analysis of mtDNA is typically a '*counting method*'. Thus instead of calculating the match probability, which will typically be in the range of 0.005–0.025, a match is based on how many times a specific sequence is found in a population database.

Guidelines for reporting mtDNA analysis list three options as outcomes. These are:

1. *Exclusion* – the known and unknown samples have two or more nucleotide differences, thus the samples can be excluded as being from the same person or maternal lineage.
2. *Inconclusive* – one nucleotide difference between unknown sample and the known sample.
3. *Cannot Exclude* – sequences from known and unknown samples have a common base at each location or a common length variant in the HV2 C-stretch, thus the samples cannot be excluded as being from the same person or maternal lineage.

Messenger Ribonucleic Acid (RNA)

Messenger RNA (mRNA) appears to have a role in the identification of body fluids such as blood, saliva and semen. This approach may be utilized more in the future as a replacement for serological and protein analysis.

Laboratory Issues

Laboratories that run forensic tests should adhere to high-quality standards and be accredited. The laboratories should engage in proficiency testing and the results from such tests made available for review. A positive control, a negative control and a reagent blank sample should be run for all tests. Inadvertent transfer of DNA, chain of custody and contamination are major areas of concern for DNA forensic evidence and could contribute to undesirable variation in a case. Whenever possible, samples should be divided into two or more parts so that additional tests or repeat tests can be performed. If possible, any additional tests should be run by different personnel from those conducting the first test, and in a different laboratory if possible. The best opportunity for justice, for a wrongly implicated innocent person, is an independent re-test.

Statistical Analysis

Only about 0.1% (about 3 million bases) of a person's DNA differs from one person compared to another person. However, the amount of genetic material that is shared depends on the degree of relatedness that one person is to another person. Thus relatives share more genetic material or loci than non-relatives. Statistical methods for estimating the probability of a close relative matching the suspect's DNA profile are discussed in the literature. Using the 13 CODIS loci as an example, there is about a 10% chance that one of the 13 sites will match in two individuals. Two close relatives, such as a parent, child or sibling, will have about four or five sites that match out of the 13 loci. However, for people who are not close relatives there is less than one in a trillion that all 13 sites will match.

How are these probabilities calculated? The 10% per single site is based on population genetics. For example, if a Hispanic individual had a 10% match to the Hispanic population at each site, the probability that all 13 sites match another Hispanic individual would be:

$$0.1 \times 0.1 \times 0.1 \times 0.1 \times 0.1 \times 0.1 \times 0.1 \times 0.1 \times 0.1 \times 0.1 \times 0.1 \times 0.1 \times 0.1 = 0.1^{13}$$

= less than one in a trillion

The match probability (P_m) (or random match probability) is obtained by using the *product rule*. Multiplying the probability for each site by the probabilities for all the other sites is called the product rule. How do we calculate the probability that two or more people have the same genetic profile? Here is the process in five steps.

Step 1

Identify the STRs for the individual genotypes. An example of individual genotypes for the CODIS loci is given below.

Table 9.1. Profile of a hypothetical individual set of genotypes for the CODIS loci

Locus	TPOX	D3S1358	FGA	D5S818	CSF1PO	D7S820	D8S1 179
Genotype Frequency	8, 8	15, 15	24, 25	10, 13	11, 11	11, 10	12, 13
Locus	**THO1**	**vWA**	**D13S317**	**D16S539**	**D18S51**	**D21S11**	**AMEL**
Genotype Frequency	9, 9.3	14, 16	10, 11	11, 11	12, 13	29, 31	XY

Step 2

Identify what proportion of the population is at each allele being tested. The population database is created or a pre-existing database identified. The product rule method is based on the assumption that the population shows Hardy-Weinberg equilibrium. This means that the population has random mating and thus the allele selections are statistically independent from a common gene pool, so the results are independent associations. This assumption is based on the Hardy-Weinberg Principle. The Hardy-Weinberg Principle is an elementary formula for population genetics. A chi-squared analysis can be used to determine if the population is in Hardy-Weinberg equilibrium. This test for independence cannot prove independence, but it can find dependence if it exists. Thus, the three possible genotype frequencies in the offspring are:

Table 9.2. Punnett square for Hardy-Weinberg equilibrium for alleles 'A' & 'a' at a given locus

		Female	
	A (p)	a (q)	
Male	*A (p)*	AA (p^2)	Aa (pq)
	a (q)	Aa (pq)	aa (q^2)

$$f(AA) = p2$$
$$f(Aa) = 2pq$$
$$f(aa) = q2$$

Therefore the equation for genotype frequencies is:

$$P2 + 2pq + q^2 = 1$$

There are several DNA databases currently, with the two largest being the UK National DNA Database (>3.4 million profiles) and the US FBI CODIS (Combined DNA Index System) database (>3.5 million profiles). The CODIS system tests for 13 STRs and the amelogenin sex test. Recently a 16-loci multiplex system has been introduced as a possible upgraded system with more loci. The CODIS system includes at least four population substructure reference databases.

Step 3

Calculate the frequency for each locus. For a homozygous genotype:

$$P = p2$$

For the data in Table 9.1, the genotype (15, 15) at locus D3S1358 is calculated as follows. From the population reference database, the genotype 15 frequency is 17.3%, therefore:

$$P = p^2 = 17.3\% \times 17.3\% = 0.173 \times 0.173 = 0.173^2 = 0.030 = 3.0\%$$

For a heterozygous genotype:

$$P = 2pq$$

For the data in Table 9.1, the genotype (14, 16) at locus vWA is calculated as follows. From the population reference database, genotype 14 is estimated to be 15.7% and genotype 16 is 22.7%, therefore:

$$P = 2pq = 2(15.7\%)(22.7\%) = 2(0.157)(0.227) = 0.071 = 7.1\%$$

The two step 3 frequency estimates can be seen in Table 9.3 and the same process would be undertaken for each locus.

Table 9.3. Profile with population frequencies estimated for two loci

Locus	TPOX	D3S1358	FGA	D5S818	CSF1PO	D7S820	D8S1179
Genotype Frequency	8, 8	15, 15 3.0%	24, 25	10, 13	11, 11	11, 10	12, 13
Locus	**THO1**	**vWA**	**D13S317**	**D16S539**	**D18S51**	**D21S11**	**AMEL**
Genotype Frequency	9, 9.3	14, 16 7.1%	10, 11	11, 11	12, 13	29, 31	XY

By calculating all of the loci, a profile such as the one in Table 9.4 is obtained.

Table 9.4. Example of a hypothetical complete 13-loci profile (plus AMEL locus)

Locus	TPOX	D3S1358	FGA	D5S818	CSF1PO	D7S820	D8S1179
Genotype	8, 8	15, 15	24, 25	11, 13	11, 11	10, 10	13, 14
Frequency	3.4%	3.0%	4.2%	12.8%	7.5%	6.9%	8.2%
Locus	**THO1**	**vWA**	**D13S317**	**D16S539**	**D18S51**	**D21S11**	**AMEL**
Genotype	9, 9.3	14, 16	11, 11	11, 12	16, 18	29, 30	XY
Frequency	10.1%	7.1%	1.4%	4.7%	8.4%	12.3%	Male

Step 4

Calculate the DNA profile probability for the multilocus genotype using the product rule. The product rule (multiplication rule) is:

Probability of random match = $P_m = (P_1)(P_2)(P_3)\ .\ .\ .\ (P_n)$

Using the data from Table 9.4 will result in the probability:

$$P_m = (0.034)(0.030)(0.042)(0.128)(0.075)(0.069)(0.082)(0.101)(0.071)(0.014)(0.047)(0.084)\ (0.123) = 9.395^{-19}$$

Thus the probability that two people (other than identical twins) have the profile in Table 9.4 is less than one in a hundred trillion.

Step 5

Calculate confidence limits for each allele. An upper confidence limit should be calculated for each allele frequency in the population. This gives the confidence that the profile is unique, given the population of *N* unrelated people. The upper 95% confidence limit (95% UCL) has the following formula:

$$P + 1.96\sqrt{P(1-P)/N}$$

where *P* is the observed frequency and *N* is the number of chromosomes studied.

The lower 95% confidence limit (95% LCL) has the following formula:

$$P - 1.96\sqrt{P(1-P)/N}$$

Other Issues

'Ceiling' Principle

In cases where the sample and suspect belong to a subpopulation then a 'ceiling' should be placed on the estimate of the profile. This will be a conservative correction of the estimate. It has been used to compensate for any undetected sub- population that may exist in the population database.

The 95% UCL should be used or 0.10, whichever is larger.

The 95% LCL should be used or 0.05, whichever is smaller.

If a subpopulation (population substructure) database is used, instead of the entire population database, then the ceiling principle would not need to be considered.

Prosecutor's Fallacy and Defence Fallacy

An example of the 'prosecutor's fallacy' is given next. Making a statement like 'There is only a one-in-a-trillion chance that the defendant is innocent' is a statement about guilt or innocence, and is not true. The true statement is 'There is a one-in-a-trillion chance that the forensic sample came from an individual other than the defendant'.

An example of the '*defence fallacy*' is as follows. Suppose that a murder occurred in a city with a population of 5 million people. A match was found between the suspect (defendant) and a stain sample from the crime scene. The match probability was calculated to be one in a million. In a city of 5 million, about five people would have a matching profile. Thus the defence argues that the odds are 5 to 1 that the defendant is innocent. This assumes that each of the five people have an equal probability of guilt. This would only be true if the DNA evidence was the only evidence and was used in isolation of any other facts pertaining to the case.

Bayes' Theorem

Bayes' theorem may be utilized in select circumstances, but it is not a commonly accepted statistical method for presenting forensic evidence. This method is based on prior probabilities based on certain facts of a specific case. The major argument against using Bayes' theorem is that the prior probabilities may be subjective.

Likelihood Ratio

A commonly accepted way of expressing the likelihood of matching evidence is by calculating the likelihood ratio (LR). Here is an example of a criminal case utilizing the LR method:

$$\text{LR} = \frac{P(\text{evidence originated from suspect})}{P(\text{evidence originated from an unrelated person in the population})}$$

$$\text{LR} = \frac{\text{Probability that the prosecutor is correct}}{\text{Probability that the defence is correct}}$$

$$= \frac{P(\text{prosecutor's hypothesis})}{P(\text{defence hypothesis})}$$

The likelihood that two people are siblings can be calculated like this:

$$\mathrm{LR} = \frac{P[\text{allele(s) would match if two people were siblings}]}{P[\text{allele(s) would match if two people were unrelated}]}$$

Special Situations

DNA Mixtures

A simple mixture of two individuals may be evaluated by comparing sizes of the fluorescent peaks of the electropherogram. Otherwise, the likelihood ratio can be used, calculations based on the fluorescent peak area or evaluating PCR stutter.

Complex Settings

Special considerations need to be observed in sex-change (sex-reversal) individuals. In this case the AMEL genotype would be in disagreement with the phenotype. Also, in individuals who have had a *bone marrow transplant* (BMT), there would be atypical results, such as a DNA mixture.

10

Single and Multilocus VNTR Analysis

Nonisotopic probes have been widely adopted for DNA fingerprinting and DNA profiling because of their ease and speed of use and obvious safety and environmental advantages. Nonisotopic DNA probes designed to detect *variable number of tandem-repeat* (VNTR) sequences are typically single-stranded oligomers of 200 nucleotides, with sequence complementary to the target tandem-repeat sequence. There are two types of probes used for the analysis of VNTR sequences: *multilocus probes* (MLP) and *single-locus probes* (SLP).

MLPs consist of tandem repeats containing a minisatellite "*core*" sequence that can simultaneously detect a number of highly polymorphic loci to generate individual-specific DNA "*fingerprints*". These probes have found a number of applications in the field of identity analysis, including forensic and paternity testing and cell-line verification. When hybridized to Southern blots under conditions of low stringency, each multilocus probe will detect a family of minisatellites that all share the same "*core*" sequence. This produces the multiband DNA "*fingerprint*" pattern. Several different MLPs have been isolated, and most can be used to detect minisatellites in a wide range of species.

Single Locus VNTR Analysis

Single-locus probes (SLPs), on the other hand, each detect only one minisatellite locus. SLPs are, however, extremely sensitive and tolerant of degraded-target DNA sequence. They are widely used for forensic analysis as well as for paternity testing. Many useful SLPs have been identified, and by using several in series a "*DNA Profile*" can be constructed.

The process of probe design and preparation is not always simple or straightforward if high-quality results are to be guaranteed. A probe used for VNTR analysis should exhibit high sensitivity, high specificity, low backgrounds, reproducibility, and robustness. The cost of setting up probe manufacturing systems that incorporate the process and quality-control steps required to guarantee high performance can be significant. High-quality VNTR probes can be purchased from specialist manufacturers prelabeled and ready to use. Hybridization is more rapid than with traditional radioactive systems; typically, membranes can be hybridized and lumigraphs produced within a normal working day. Hybridized probes can be detected on the membrane by a range of chemiluminescent substrates which are activated by the alkaline phosphatase label on the probe. This enzymatic reaction results in the emission of light that can be recorded on X-ray-sensitive film.

Materials

Autoclaved, purified water must be used in all solutions. The following procedures are optimized for use with NICE probes, but can be successfully applied to alkaline phosphatase-labeled oligonucleotide VNTR probes prepared by alternative methods.

1. 0.5 *M* Disodium hydrogen phosphate buffer, pH 7.2: 71 g/L Na_2HPO_4. Adjust pH with concentrated orthophosphoric acid and autoclave.
2. Standard saline citrate (20X SSC): 88.2 g/L trisodium citrate $Na_3C_6H_5O_7.2H_2O$. 175.3 g/L NaC1.
3. 0.1 *M* magnesium chloride: 20.3 g/L $MgC1_2.6H_2O$. Autoclave.
4. Wash solution 2: 11.6 g/L maleic acid 8.7 g/L NaCl. Adjust pH to 7.5 with concentrated NaOH and autoclave.
5. Membrane blocking reagent. Dissolve 100 g/L casein in wash solution 2 by heating at 50°C for 1 h. Autoclave and store at 0°C.
6. 10% Sodium dodecyl sulfate (SDS): 100 g/L Sodium lauryl sulfate. Prepare the following solutions on the day of use from sterile stock solutions.
7. Prehybridization buffer (1 L): 990 mL 0.5 *M* Na_2HPO_4 pH 7.2, 10 mL 10% SDS. Heat to 50°C before use.
8. Hybridization buffer (1 L): 900 mL prehybridization buffer, 100 mL membrane blocking reagent. Heat to 50°C before use.

9. Wash solution 1: For MLP: 160 mL/L 0.5 *M* Na_2HPO_4 pH 7.2, 10 mL/L 10% SDS. For SLP: 20 mL/L 0.5 *M* Na_2HPO_4, pH 7.2, 10 mL/L 10% SDS. Dilute Na_2HPO_4 before adding SDS. Heat to 50°C before use.
10. Membrane-stripping solution: 10 mL/L 10% (SDS). Heat to 80°C before use.
11. CDP-*Star* assay buffer: 10 mL/L 0.1 *M* $MgC1_2$, 10.5 mL/L diethanolamine (corrosive). Adjust pH to 9.5 with concentrated hydrochloric acid. Store at 4°C.
12. Alkaline phosphatase labeled oligonucleotide VNTR probes (e.g., NICE probes). Store at 0°C.
13. CDP-*Star* concentrate; store at 4°C. Protect from light and heat.
14. Lumi-Phos 530 store at 4°C. Protect from light and heat.
15. Polyester sheets.
16. Spray gun.
17. X-ray film.
18. X-ray film cassette.

Method

1. Prehybridize up to 10 membranes (prepared by Southern blotting) by wetting in IX SSC and placing, DNA side down, in 500 mL of prehybridization buffer at 50°C. Gently agitate for 20 min at 50°C.
2. Add 160 mL of hybridization buffer at 50°C to a hybridization chamber or sandwich box, and add the volume of probe(s) as recommended by the manufacturer.
3. Using forceps, individually transfer the membranes, DNA side down, to the hybridization buffer, ensuring there are no air bubbles. Gently agitate for 20 min at 50°C.
4. Wash the membranes by individually transferring them, DNA side down, to 500 mL of prewarmed wash solution 1. Gently agitate for 10 min at 50°C.
5. Repeat step 4 with fresh wash solution 1.
6. Rinse the membranes by individually transferring them, DNA side down, to 500 mL of Wash solution 2 at room temperature. Gently agitate for 10 min at room temperature.
7. Repeat step 6 with fresh wash solution 2.
8. Using CDP-*Star:*
   (a) Rinse the membranes by individually transferring them, DNA side down, to 500 mL of CDP-*Star* assay buffer at room temperature. Rinse for <10 s.

(b) Dilute an appropriate amount of the CDP-*Star* concentrate with CDP-*Star* assay buffer (1:100 dilution). Add the membranes individually, DNA side down, and incubate at room temperature for 5 min.

(c) Remove the membranes individually from the CDP-*Star* and drain carefully. It is important that treated membranes do not come into direct contact with each other.

or

Using Lumi-Phos 530:

(a) Place each membrane DNA side up on a glass or Perspex plate, transfer to a vented fume cabinet, and support at an angle of approx 80 from horizontal.

(b) Using a spray gun, spray each membrane evenly with 3 mL of Lumin-Phos 530. Spray over the whole membrane but do not oversaturate.

9. Sandwich each membrane between two polyester sheets. Using the straight edge of a ruler (or equivalent), squeeze out any excess substrate. Avoid getting any substrate on the outside of the polyester sheets.
10. Secure the membrane/polyester "*sandwich*" with a piece of tape along each edge, and place in a light-proof cassette against X-ray-sensitive film. Intensifying screens are not required. Incubate at 30°C.
11. Develop the film after 0.5 h (CDP-*Star*) or 2.8 h (Lumi-Phos 530), depending on the quantity of DNA on the membranes. Chemiluminescence continues for several days; therefore, re-exposure is possible, although longer exposure times may then be required.
12. Stripping and Reprobing: Probes can be removed from hybridized membranes by agitating for 15 min in 0.1% SDS at 80°C, thus allowing multiple sequential hybridizations of a panel of probes to the same membrane. Rinse in IX SSC prior to rehybridization or storage.

Notes

1. The quality of the prelabeled probe can affect overall performance characteristics. A poorly designed probe sequence will never produce sensitive or specific results. Ineffective purification of probe conjugate will result in poor detection sensitivity because of competing "unlabeled" probe. Background problems and overall

quality of the autoradiograph can also be affected if probe conjugates used in hybridizations are contaminated with "free" unconjugated alkaline phosphatase and oligonucleotide.

2. Neutral membranes are recommended for use with this protocol. Removal of probes from charged membranes can be difficult, and backgrounds may be high.
3. The short duration of the hybridization and washing steps in this procedure may not allow full temperature equilibration, which can result in an incorrect hybridization stringency. Strict temperature control during the hybridization/washing reactions is essential for high-quality results. Particular problems may be encountered when using dry-air incubators, because heat exchange is poor. The actual temperature attained within the hybridization reaction should be monitored carefully.
4. Contamination with microbial alkaline phosphatase is a common cause of heavy uniform background masking the specific probe signal. Low levels of microbial contamination may produce spots of background. All solutions should be sterilized or prepared immediately before use from sterile stock solutions. Sterile pure water should be used to prepare working solutions and to clean all laboratory apparatus.
5. Insufficient agitation during hybridization may cause membranes to stick together, preventing hybridization solution and/or wash solutions from reaching the entire membrane surface. The resulting autoradiographs are characterized by the presence of uneven areas of background. This problem is particularly common when hybridizing multiple membranes in rotary ovens, where membranes overlap.
6. The formation of bubbles between membranes during the addition of membranes to hybridization solutions may result in unhybridized patches.
7. Uneven application of Lumi-Phos 530 may produce patchy autoradiographs with dark and light areas.
8. DNA fixation by ultraviolet radiation should be standardized to ensure consistent results. It is essential that the ultraviolet output of the irradiation equipment be regularly monitored. Output of 80,000 60,000 $\mu J/cm^2$ is usually sufficient for MagnaGraph membranes (MSI). Each batch of membranes should be optimized for maximum sensitivity.

9. Excess Lumi-Phos 530 remaining on hybridized membranes will cause elevated backgrounds. It is essential to firmly squeeze Lumi-Phos 530-treated membranes to remove any excess. The presence of excess CDP-*Star* substrate is not as problematic. However, excessive removal of either substrate will produce a generalized loss of sensitivity.
10. Photobleaching of chemiluminescent substrates and the exposure of treated membranes to temperatures > 37°C will reduce sensitivity. It is essential that membranes are protected from light following treatment with chemiluminescent substrate.
11. Membranes are prone to surface damage, especially during hybridization, and should be treated with care at all stages (avoid sharp metal forceps).
12. Fungal growth during storage can ruin a membrane. Membranes should be rinsed in IX SSC and completely dried prior to storage at room temperature.
13. Exposure times depend on the quantity and quality of DNA on the membranes, the type of chemiluminescent substrate used, and the length of time since hybridization. Chemiluminescence slowly decreases over several days.
14. Complete digestion of sample DNA with a restriction endonuclease (usually HinfI) is essential for successful multilocus "*DNA finger-printing*". Incomplete or partial digestion can produce anomalous results or prevent the formation of the DNA fingerprint at all.
15. Sample DNA should be highly purified and of high molecular weight (e.g., phenol chloroform extraction). The DNA should be completely resolvated and ideally quantitated prior to digestion with restriction enzyme.
16. Because of the large number of bands, standardization of DNA migration is absolutely necessary for reliable interpretation of multilocus DNA fingerprints. A DNA migration marker such as *HindIII* digest, is recommended. Gels should be run until the 2.3-kb fragment has migrated to a fixed distance from the origin of sample loading (usually approx 20 cm). The portion of the DNA fingerprint pattern below 3.5 kb is not normally analyzed because of poor resolution of the bands.

Multilocus VNTR Analysis

Nucleic acids labeled with the radioisotope phosphorus-32 [^{32}P] are used as probes for various purposes; coupled with autoradiographic detection, they provide a high degree of sensitivity. All forms of nucleic acid can be labeled with isotopes. The majority of labeling techniques are based on enzymatic incorporation of a nucleotide labeled with, e.g., [^{32}P] into the DNA. Labeling techniques can be classified into those that lead to uniformly labeled probes and into those that result in end-labeled ones. Uniformly labeled DNA probes incorporate more dNTP than end-labeled probes. The first category is commonly employed in hybridization analysis, whereas end-labeled DNA is often used in DNA sequencing.

Precautions

Purchase, possession, and use of radioactive isotopes are generally strictly regulated by national law. Many countries have imposed laws that regulate use, storage, and disposal of radioactive materials. Managers and other laboratory staff must possess appropriate training and competence, because radiochemicals require special handling. Even in the most sophisticated laboratory it is inevitable that radioactive aerosols or dusts are generated. Where radiochemicals are not regulated by law, it is strongly recommended to monitor the exposure to isotopes by means of personal dosimetry badges and by health checkups twice a year, which should include the investigation of staff's urine. Shielding material (e.g., Lucite) must be placed between the analysts and the radioactive materials.

Labeling Nucleic Acids for Use as Probes

The choice of the radioactive isotope depends on the desired application. For nucleic acid hybridizations in solution and on filters, ^{32}P is the isotope of choice because of its high energy, which results in short scintillation counting times and short autoradiographic exposures. Each of the four nucleotides is available in an [α ^{32}P] - labeled form suited for incorporation into DNA using one of the polymerase reactions. In addition, [γ ^{32}P] ATP is also available for 5'-end-labeling DNA using polynucleotide kinase. For 3'-end-labeling [α ^{32}P], cordycepin triphosphate can be used. Probes labeled with ^{32}P should be thawed rapidly; they also should be used as soon as possible after preparation because of the isotope's short half-life and also because of its high energy, which can deteriorate the probe's structure.

Theory of Nick-Translation

The method called *nick-translation* was described by Rigby et al. It is well suited to produce uniformly labeled DNA of high specific activity. It utilizes DNase I to create single-strand nicks in double-stranded DNA. (Although double-stranded DNA in any form can be used for nick-translation when recombinant plasmid probes are used, the probe insert is typically cut out, purified, and nick-translated). The 5' → 3' exonuclease and 5' → 3' polymerase actions of *Escherichia coli* DNA polymerase I are then used to remove stretches of single-stranded DNA starting at the nicks and replace them with new strands made by the incorporation of labeled deoxyribonucleotides. As a result, each nick moves along the DNA strand being repaired in a 5' → 3' direction.

Nick-translation can utilize any deoxyribonucleotide labeled with ^{32}P in the α-position ([^{125}J],[^{3}H], and biotinylated nucleotides can also be incorporated). With [α ^{32}P]-labeled nucleotides, final (specific) activities of 5-10^8 dpm/μg DNA can be achieved.

The advantages of "*nick-translation*" as a labeling method are:

1. The simplicity of the reaction,
2. The uniform labeling of the probe, and
3. The high specific activity.

The disadvantage, however, is the nicking itself, because it results in short single-stranded probe molecules in the hybridization reaction. A variation of the protocol was described by Pardue. The standard as well as the modified protocols are given below.

Theory of Radioactive Labeling of Oligonucleotide Probes by Means of T4 DNA Polymerase

Oligonucleotide probes are employed in various disciplines. T4 DNA polymerase reaction is among the strategies available to label Oligonucleotide probes.

The T4 DNA polynucleotidekinase labeling method has some advantages over the nick-translation procedure:

1. T4 DNA technique yields intact double-stranded molecules with no nicks; it can be cut with restriction enzyme;
2. Defined regions of DNA can be labeled by controlling the reaction conditions;
3. DNA can be labeled to extremely high specific activity (10^9 dpm/μg) if high specific-activity nucleotides (2000 Ci/m*M*) are used; and
4. Labeling of one strand of a double-stranded DNA fragment can be achieved.

T4 DNA polymerase has two activities:

1. A 3' → 5' exonuclease activity and
2. A 5' → 3' polymerase.

The exonuclease is active if the exogeneous deoxyribonucleoside triphosphates are absent. Its activity is ≈ 200 higher than the exonuclease of DNA polymerase. Oligonucleotide probes can be labeled by means of ^{32}P-phosphate transfer from the [γ ^{32}P]-ATP to the 5'-OH-end in the presence of T4 polynucleotide kinase (T4 DNA polymerase).

Theory of Labeling DNA by Random Priming (Oligopriming)

This procedure for labeling DNA fragments using oligonucleotide primers and the Klenow fragment of *E. coli* DNA polymerase I was developed by Feinberg and Vogelstein as an alternative to nick-translation to produce uniformly labeled probes. Random priming offers a number of advantages over nick-translation. In this procedure, random-sequence hexanucleotides are hybridized to the heat-denatured double-stranded or single-stranded template at multiple sites along the DNA. The 3'-OH-end of the hexanucleotides serve as primers for the 5' → 3' polymerase activity of the Klenow fragment of DNA polymerase I. If radiolabeled deoxynucleotides are present in the reaction mixture, the hexanucleotide primers are extended to generate double-stranded DNA that is uniformly radiolabeled on both strands. Because the Klenow fragment lacks the 5' → 3' exonuclease activity, its use in primer extension avoids loss of incorporated label. The 3' → 5' exonuclease activity is greatly diminished by the use of a pH 6.6 buffer, permitting synthesis of highly labeled probes. For random priming, [α ^{32}P]-deoxynucleoside triphosphates can be used.

Theory of Filter Hybridization

Filter hybridization is of considerable importance in molecular biology. The technique is derived from the classical experiments conducted by Gillespie and Speigelman. Denatured DNA, for example, is immobilized on a nitrocellulose filter in such a way that self-annealing is prevented. The filters are first prehybridized with hybridization buffer without the probe. Nonspecific DNA binding sites on the filter are thus saturated with carrier DNA, synthetic polymers, or proteins. The bound base sequences are available for specific hybridization with a (single-stranded) DNA probe. The latter is often labeled with ^{32}P. Hybridization is followed by extensive washing of the filter, which is required to remove superfluous probe. Detection of hybridization reactions is usually achieved by means of autoradiography after a preliminary scintillation counting. The procedure is widely applied for various methods (plaque and colony hybridization, Northern- and Southern-blot hybridization, dot blot, and so forth).

Materials

Reagents Required for the "Standard" Nick-Translation

1. 10X nick-translation buffer: 500 m*M* Tris-HCl, pH 7.8, 50 m*M* $MgCL_2$, 100 m*M* 2-mercaptoethanol, 1 mg/mL nuclease-free bovine serum albumin (BSA).
2. 10X dNTP without dATP (depending on the target sequence): 1 m*M* dCTP, 1 m*M* dGTP, 1 m*M* dTTP.
3. [α-^{32}P] dCTP (3000 Ci/m*M*).
4. STOP buffer: 10 m*M* Tris-HCl, pH 7.5, 10 m*M* EDTA, 0.1% (w/v) sodium dodecylsulfate (SDS).
5. DNA polymerase I: follow manufacturer's instructions.
6. DNase I: The enzyme is commercially available at different concentrations. A stock solution can be prepared at a concentration of 1 mg/mL. Aliquots of 10 μL can be stored deep-frozen. For storage at -20°C dissolve DNase I in a solution of 20 m*M* Tris-HCl, pH 7.5, 1 m*M* $MgCL_2$, and 50% glycerol. Enzyme should be dissolved without vortexing and thawed on ice. It cannot be used a second time.

Reagents Required for Modified Nick-Translation

1. 10X nick-translation buffer: 500 m*M* Tris-HCl, pH 7.8,50 m*M* $MgCL_2$, 0.5 mg/mL BSA.
2. 1 μL 0.5 m*M* dGTP.
3. 1 μL 0.5 m*M* dCTP.
4. 1% 2-mercaptoethanol.
5. 1 μL DNase I (commercially available DNase [1 mg/mL stock] is stored in aliquots at-20°C. Before use, the enzyme is diluted by a factor of 10^5 in distilled water).
6. 1 μL DNA polymerase I (10 U/μL).
7. Distilled water.

Reagents Required for Labeling with T4 DNA Polymerase

1. 1 mL solution of oligonucleotide probe (10 pmol/μL).
2. 2.8 μL distilled water.
3. 1 μL 10X kinase buffer: = 500 m*M* Tris-HCl, pH 7.4, 50 m*M* $MgCL_2$, 20 m*M* dithiothreitol (DTT), 1.0 m*M* spermidine.
4. 5 μL [c^{32}P] ATP (370 MBq/mL, 5 m*M*).
5. 0.2 μL T4 polynucleotide kinase (2 U).

Required Reagents for Oligopriming

1. 10X DNA polymerase I (Klenow fragment) buffer: 500 m*M* Tris-HCl, pH 6.6, 100 m*M* $MgCl_2$, 10 m*M* DTT, 0.5 mg/mL nuclease-free BSA, fraction V.
2. 10X dNTP without dCTP: 0.5 m*M* dATP, 0.5 m*M* dGTP, 0.5 m*M* dTTP.
3. Random hexanucleotides, which are commercially available.
4. Large fragment of *E. coli.* DNA polymerase I. Follow supplier's instructions.
5. 0.5 *M* EDTA.
6. 10 mg/mL yeast tRNA.
7. TE buffer: 10 m*M* Tris-HCl, pH 7.6, 1 m*M* EDTA.

Reagents Required for the Prehybridization and Hybridization of Filters

1. Prehybridization solution 1: 10X Denhardt's solution.
2. 100X Denhardt's solution: 10 g Polyvinylpyrrolidone (PVP), 10 g BSA, 10 g Ficoll 400, brought to a total volume of 500 mL with distilled water. The solution can be aliquoted and stored at -20°C.
3. Prehybridization solution 2: 1X SSC, 10X Denhardt's solution, 6% polyethyleneglycol 6000 (PEG 6000), 0.1% SDS, 50 μg/mL sheared herring sperm DNA, 5 μg/mL sheared human-placenta DNA.
4. Sheared herring-sperm DNA; Prepare as follows: Cut 300 mg DNA with scissors and suspend in 40 mL distilled water. After a mechanical shearing in a syringe, dissolve DNA for approx 2 d at 37°C. After two phenol-and one chloroform extractions, precipitate DNA by adding sodium acetate (final concentration 0.2 *M*) and ethanol. Dissolve DNA in 20 mL TE buffer. Confirm degradation of herringsperm DNA on a separate gel. Before use, boil sperm DNA for 5 min and chill on ice.
5. Sheared human-placenta DNA; The placenta DNA is prepared as follows: Dilute 25 mg placenta DNA in 2 mL 0.3 *M* NaOH, 20 m*M* EDTA and boil for 5 min. Follow with neutralization in 2 mL 0.3 *M* HCl, precipitation with ethanol, and centrifugation (3000g). Remaining salts can be removed by washing in 70% ethanol. Dried DNA can be rediluted in 25 mL distilled water and stored aliquoted at -20°C. Prior to adding the placenta DNA to the hybridization solution, boil the DNA for 5 min and cool on ice.

METHODS

"Standard" Nick-Translation

1. Combine 20000 ng DNA probe, 0.4 μL 1 *M* dCTP, dGTP, and dTTP, 1.6 μL 10X nick translation buffer, 2 μL [α ^{32}P]-dATP (5 m*M*, 370 MBq/mL), 0.3 μL polymerase I (5-103 U/mL), and sufficient distilled water to bring the volume to 16 μL.
2. Mix components and incubate at 15°C for 1.5 h.
3. Stop the reaction by adding 34 μL STOP buffer.
4. Separate labeled probe from unlabeled DNA by using a "*Nick-translation column*".

"Modified" Nick-Translation

1. Dry down 150 pmol of [^{3}H] dTTP and 150 pmol of [^{3}H] dATP in a plastic microcentrifuge tube.
2. Add 1 μL 0.5 m*M* dGTP, 1 μL 0.5 m*M* dCTP, 1 μL 10X 0.5 *M* Tris-HCl, pH 7.8, 50 m*M* $MgCl_2$, 0.5 mg/mL BSA, 1 μL 1% 2-mercaptoethanol, 0.1 μg cloned DNA, 1 μg DNase I (commercial DNase I [1 mg/mL stock] is stored in aliquots at -20°C. DNase is to be diluted by a factor of 10^5 in distilled water prior to use), and 1 μg *E. coli* DNA polymerase I(10 U/μL) water to 10 μL final volume.
3. Incubate the mixture at 14°C for 1 h.
4. Add 90 g of carrier DNA (*E. coli* DNA sheared by sonication and denatured by boiling for 10 min) and adjust the total volume to 100 μL with distilled water.
5. Add 3 μL 0.1 *M* spermine. Mix and leave on ice for 15 min.
6. Centrifuge at 10,000g for 10 min. Discard the supernatant.
7. Resuspend the pellet in 75% ethanol containing 0.3 *M* sodium acetate and 10 m*M* magnesium acetate. Vortex. Leave on ice for 1 h, mixing frequently.
8. Centrifuge for 10 min (10,000g) to recover the DNA.
9. Resuspend the labeled double-stranded DNA probe in water.

Labeling with T4 DNA Polymerase

1. Mix reactants 1 are be mixed and incubated at 37°C for 60 min.
2. The reaction is stopped by adding 1 μL 0.5 *M* EDTA, pH 8.0, and 89 μL TE buffer, pH 8.0.
3. The solution is then stored at 0°C.

Oligopriming

1. Keep all components on ice.

2. DNA probes (e.g., single-locus probes YNH24, MS 1) are denatured (to single-stranded DNAs) at 95°C and mixed with random hexanucleotides after cooling to 0°C.
3. The reaction tube is centrifuged (microfuge) for a few seconds to collect the DNA solution as a single drop in the bottom of the tube. Place the tube on ice.
4. Combine: 2.5 μL 10X dNTP minus dCTP, 2.5 μL 10X Klenow buffer, 5 μL α^{32}P-dCTP (3000 Ci/m*M*) = 50 μCi, and 1 μL Klenow fragment (3 U).
5. Add the reaction mix to the denatured DNA; adjust the reaction volume to 25 μL with distilled water and mix briefly.
6. Incubate the mixture at room temperature for 1 h.
7. Stop the reaction by adding 1 μL of 0.5 *M* EDTA and dilute the reaction mixture to 100 μL with TE buffer.
8. Separate the labeled DNA from unincorporated radioactive precursors by column chromatography.
9. Ethanol-precipitate the labeled DNA-probe fragments if desired, and estimate the activity as described above.

Separation by Means of Column Chromatography

1. Unincorporated [γ^{32}P]-ATP has to be separated by means of column chromatography with DE-52 cellulose. Cellulose must be washed in TE buffer, pH 8.0, several times until the fresh TE buffer remains at this pH value.
2. Preparation of columns: Polypropylene Econo Columns are filled to the 0.3 mL mark with washed DE-52 cellulose.
3. The labeling solution is poured onto the surface of the cellulose and allowed to entirely soak. Thereafter, unincorporated [^{32}P]-ATP is eluted by means of 4 mL TE buffer and 4 mL 0.2 *M* NaCl in TE buffer. The labeled probe is then eluted by adding 2X 500 μL 0.5 *M* NaCl in TE buffer.

Control of Incorporation

By means of ^{32}P-solutions of known activities, a reference curve can be established. The success of labeling reactions can be estimated using a scintillation counter at a constant distance.

Hybridization Procedures Using ^{32}P-Labeled Single-Locus Probes

Prehybridization is carried out in as follows:

1. Incubate nylon filters for 1 h (at 53°C) in prehybridization solution 1 and thereafter for 2 h in solution 2 (at 62°C) by adding 50 μL/mL herring-sperm DNA plus 5 μg/mL placenta DNA.

2. The radiolabeled DNA probe is denatured by boiling for 5 min and cooled on ice for 10 min.
3. At least 10^6 counts per minute (cpm) of ^{32}P-labeled probe per milliliter of prehybridization solution 2 is introduced to produce the hybridization solution. The probe should have a specific activity of at least 10^8 cpm/tg. An incorporation rate of 4-10^9 cpm/μg DNA is recommended.
4. Hybridization is carried out overnight at 62°C. All hybridizations are preferably carried out in tubes with 4 cm diameter and a length of 28 cm that are rotated in a hybridization oven. Up to 12 filters can be hybridized simultaneously. *Caution:* Air pressure within the heated tubes is raised during hybridization. Great care should be taken when opening.
5. After hybridization, carry out the following washes:
   (a) 2 10 min in 2X SSC, 1.5% SDS at room temperature.
   (b) 1 15 min in 1X SSC, 1.0% SDS at 62°C.
   (c) 2 10 min in 0.1X SSC, 0.1% SDS at 62°C.
6. After the last washing, the solution is drained carefully, and excess moisture is blotted from the filter. The filters are then wrapped in clear plastic wrap. Wrinkles are smoothed out.

Autoradiography Procedure

^{32}P emits X-and β-rays, which are able to blacken films. Intensity of blackening depends on the rate of isotope decomposition.

1. In a dark room, the filter is placed against a sensitive X-ray film in a film cassette. Employment of two selected intensifying screens is recommended, because this allows working at -20 instead of -70°C without any loss of information. Filter and film are sandwiched between the intensifying screens.
2. Expose the film either at -20 or -70°C for the chosen amount of time.
3. Remove the cassette from the freezer and allow equilibration to room temperature. Remove the film in the dark.
4. Process the film by using standard X-ray development techniques.

Reprobing of Filters

After hybridization and autoradiography, the filters can be stripped of the first probe by means of a high-stringency wash and hybridized again with a second probe. How often filters can be stripped and reprobed depends on the membrane material. Nitrocellulose membranes are quite fragile. It is essential that filters do not dry out completely after hybridization, because this may bind the initially used probe to the filter. Stripped filters must be prehybridized again in order to block nonspecific DNA-binding sites. Short-term storage of filters is possible if they are stored moist in sealed bags at 4g until reprobed. Longterm storage is recommended at -20°C.

1. After autoradiography the filter is immersed in 500 mL high-stringency-wash buffer and incubated at 95°C for 20 min under gentle shaking.
2. The buffer is poured off and replaced with a second 500-mL preheated buffer; incubation at 95°C for 20 min is continued.
3. The filter is placed in a hybridization tube that contains 20 mL prehybridization solution 2 and incubated at 62°C overnight.
4. The filter is removed from the prehybridization solution. Excess fluid is blotted off. The filter is ready for second hybridization.

Notes

Factors affecting the rate of filter hybridization

Anderson and Young have compiled variously important factors that affect the rate of filter hybridization. For gaining detailed information, it is recommended to read their article. The following list is a rough compilation of factors:

1. Concentration of the probe: When single-stranded probes are used, no reassociation of single-stranded nucleic acids in solution is to be expected unless regions of extensive self-complementarity exist. Probe concentration must not be increased without limit, because if more than approx 100 mg ^{32}P-labeled probe/mL is used, nonspecific and irreversible binding to the filters will be observed.
2. Molecular weight of the probe: Two situations exist: When the concentration of filter-bound nucleic acid sequence $[=C_f]$ is low compared to the concentration in solution $[=C_s]$, the rate of hybridization is independent of the molecular weight. However, when $[C_f]$ is high compared with $[C_s]$, the rate of hybridization is roughly inversely proportional to the molecular weight of the probe.
3. Base composition: Increased percentage of G + C increases the rate of hybridization.
4. Temperature affects the rate of any hybridization reaction. Typically, a Gaussian curve is observed: At 0°C hybridization proceeds extremely slowly. The rate increases to a maximum, which is 20-50°C below T_m. At higher temperatures, the duplex

molecules tend to dissociate, and at T_m-50°C, the rate is extremely low.

5. Formamide has several practical advantages, because it decreases the T_m of duplex molecules. By introducing 30% formamide to the hybridization solution, the incubation temperature can be reduced to 30-20°C. Usually, a probe is more stable at lower temperatures. However, we always try to avoid formamide, because it is considered to be hazardous. Hybridization can be carried out in trays, plastic bags, or tubes in hybridization ovens. Working with tubes in an oven is highly advantageous, because of easier handling and reduction of contamination.

Some background information concerning DNA reassociation

The rate at which complementary strands of nucleic acid form stable basepaired duplexes depends on a variety of factors.

6. Length of nucleic acids: Wetmur and Davidson theoretically predicted that the rate of reannealing would be proportional to the length *(L)* of the fragments involved. Appropriate experiments, however, revealed that the reannealing rate is proportional to the square root of *L*.
7. Composition of bases: It has been demonstrated by Hutton and Wetmur that the base composition of nucleic acids has a negligible effect on the rate of either DNA-DNA annealing or RNA-DNA hybridization. This was also demonstrated by Bishop by means of hybridization experiments.
8. Ionic strength: It has been shown by Wetmur and Davidson that the DNA reannealing rate depends strongly on the salt concentration. At concentrations up to 0.2 *M*, the rate has been shown to be proportional to the cube of ionic strength. Britten et al. have compiled experimental data on the variation of DNA reassociation rates with ionic strength.
9. Viscosity: If considering the effect of viscosity, one has to distinguish between "*microscopic*" and "*macroscopic*" viscosity. The first refers to the microenvironment around the DNA bases, which can be altered by the addition of, e.g., sucrose and glycerol. The "*macroscopic*" viscosity depends on the presence of polymers, which will have no effect on the microenvironment. A detailed study by Chang et al. revealed, e.g., that in a 5.7% Ficoll solution, the rate of phage T4 DNA renaturation was increased by 50%. Dextran sulfate is now widely used to accelerate reactions.

10. Denaturing agents: The optimal temperature for nucleic-acid reassociations (in aqueous salt solutions) lies between 60 and 75°C. However, the extended incubation at optimal temperatures can cause thermal strand scissions. Therefore, it is desirable to reduce the temperature while maintaining the stringency of nucleicacid reorganization. This can be achieved by introducing a reagent (e.g., formamide), which destabilizes double-stranded nucleic acid. In other words, a 1% increase in formamide concentration lowers the melting temperature (T_m) of double-stranded DNA by 0.72°C. Reagents other than formamide that can reduce the T_m are sodium perchlorate, tetramethylammonium chloride, tetraethylammonium chloride, and urea.
11. Mismatching: It is common knowledge that the presence of mismatched base pairs reduces the thermal stability of DNA duplex molecules. Thus, it was expected that imperfect base complementarity will influence the rate of reassociation. From several studies it is clear that mismatching of DNA that results in a decrease in the T_m of 15°C will reduce the reannealing rate by a factor of 2.
12. Temperature: Marmur and Doty observed that, as the temperature was reduced from the T_m, the rate of reassociation increased until a maximum is reached, which lies about 25°C below the T_m.

11

ANALYSIS, ASSESSMENT AND INTERPRETATION OF STR

Short tandem repeats were first used in forensic casework in the early 1990s. By the end of the decade they had become the standard tool for just about every forensic laboratory in the world. Today the vast majority of forensic genetic casework involves the analysis of STR polymorphisms and this situation is unlikely to change in the near future.

ANALYSIS OF STR

Structure of STR loci

Short tandem repeats contain a core repeat region between 1 and 6 bp long and have alleles that are generally less than 350 bp long. A large number of STR loci have been characterized but only around 20 are commonly analysed in forensic casework.

The STRs that are widely used in forensic genetics have either a four or five base-pair core-repeat motif and can be classified as a simple repeat, simple repeat with non-consensus repeats, compound repeat or complex repeat.

Development of STR Multiplexes

The forensic community has selected STR loci to incorporate into multiplex reactions based on several features including:

1. Discrete and distinguishable alleles;
2. Amplification of the locus should be robust;
3. A high power of discrimination;

4. An absence of genetic linkage with other loci being analysed;
5. Low levels of artefact formation during the amplification;
6. The ability to be amplified as part of a multiplex PCR.

Table 11.1. The development of STR systems.

QUAD	*SGM*	*SGM Plus*	*Identifiler*	*PowerPlex 16*
vWA	Amelogenin	Amelogenin	Amelogenin	Amelogenin
THO1	vWA	D2S1338	D2S1338	D2S1338
F13A1	D8S1179	vWA	vWA	vWA
FES	D21S11	D16S359	D16S359	D16S359
	D18S51	D8S1179	D8S1179	D8S1179
	THO1	D21S11	D21S11	D21S11
	FGA	D18S51	D18S51	D18S51
		THO1	THO1	THO1
		FGA	FGA	FGA
			D13S317	D13S317
			CSF1PO	CSF1PO
			D7S820	D7S820
			TPOX	TPOX
			D5S818	D5S818
		D2S1338	D2S1338	Penta D
		D19S433	D19S433	Penta E

An essential feature of any STR used in forensic analysis is that biological material should give an identical profile regardless of the individual or laboratory that carries out the analysis. Without this standardization it would not be possible to compare results between laboratories and developments like national DNA databases would not be possible. All new multiplexes have to be vigorously validated before they are used for the analysis of casework.

In the UK the Forensic Science Service (FSS) developed the first STR-based typing system that was designed for forensic analysis. Four STR loci were amplified in the same reaction. This was replaced by the SGM (second generation multiplex) that was also developed by the FSS. Two commercial companies, Applied Biosystems and Promega Corporation, have developed a series of multiplexes that are now used by most laboratories. The AmpF*l*STR SGM Plus that is produced by Applied Biosystems replaced the SGM in the UK and has been adopted by many other countries around the world as one of their standard multiplex kits. In the USA, STR technology was adopted into forensic casework following a survey of 17 previously characterized STR loci and in 1997 13 loci were selected as the CODIS (*Combined DNA Index System*) loci. These loci can be analysed in one PCR using one of two commercially available kits; the AmpF*l*STR Identifiler produced by Applied Biosystems and the PowerPlex 16 produced by Promega Corporation.

In addition to STR loci, the amelogenin locus which is present on the X and Y chromosomes has been incorporated into all commonly used STR multiplex kits. The amelogenin gene encodes for a protein that is a major component of tooth enamel matrix; there are two versions of the gene, the copy on the X chromosome has a 6 bp deletion and this length polymorphism allows the versions of the gene on the X and Y chromosomes to be differentiated.

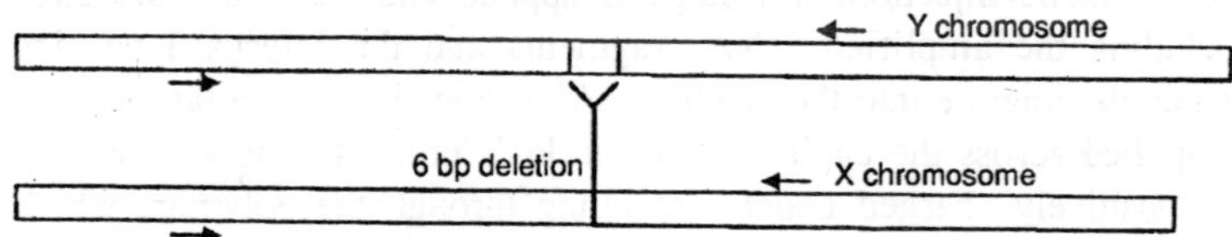

Fig. 11.1. The amelogenin locus is present on both the X and Y chromosomes.

Detection of STR Polymorphisms

After STR polymorphisms have been amplified using PCR, the length of the products must be measured precisely – some STR alleles differ by only one base pair. Gel electrophoresis of the PCR products through denaturing polyacrylamide gels can be used to separate DNA molecules between 20 and 500 nucleotides long with single base pair resolution. Early systems detected the PCR products after electrophoresis on polyacrylamide slab-gels using silver staining but this limited the number of loci that could be incorporated into the multiplexes because the allelic size ranges of the different loci could not overlap. To overcome this limitation, fluorescence labelling of PCR products followed by multicolour detection has been adopted by the forensic community. A series of fluorescent dyes has been developed that can be covalently attached to the 5' end of one of the PCR primers in each primer pair and detected real-time during electrophoresis. Up to five different dyes can be used in a single analysis which allows for considerable overlap of loci. The electrophoresis platforms have evolved from systems based on slab-gels to *capillary electrophoresis* (CE) that use a narrow glass tube filled with an entangled polymer solution to separate the DNA molecules. Applied Biosystems provide the most commonly used capillary electrophoresis systems and all these have multicolour detection capacity. The ABI PRISM 310 Genetic Analyzer that has a single capillary and analyses up to 48 samples per day, the ABI PRISM 3100 and Applied Biosystems 3130*xl* Genetic Analyzers, which have 16 capillaries and can analyse over 1000 samples per day, and the ABI PRISM 3700 and Applied Biosystems 3730*xl* Genetic Analyzers, which can have up to 96 capillaries that can analyse over 4000 samples per day.

Before electrophoresis, the PCR sample is prepared by mixing approximately 1 μl of the reaction with 10–20 μl of deionized formamide. The internal-lane size standard is also added at this point. The deionized formamide denatures the DNA, heating the samples to 95°C is routinely done to ensure that the PCR products are single stranded. The samples are transferred into the capillary using electrokinetic injection, a voltage is applied and charged molecules, including the amplified DNA fragments and the internal-lane size standards, migrate into the capillary. After injection, a constant voltage is applied across the capillary and the PCR products migrate towards the positively charged anode, travelling through the polymer, which fills the capillary and acts as the sieving matrix. Urea and 2-pyrrolidinone in the gel polymer and a temperature of 60°C help to prevent the formation of any secondary structure during electrophoresis. Through-out the period of electrophoresis, an argon ion laser is shone through a small glass window in the capillary and as PCR products labelled with fluorescent dyes travel past the window they are excited by the laser, emit fluorescence that is detected by a *charged coupled device* camera (CCD), and then are recorded by collection software. The electrophoresis of a sample takes up to 30 minutes after which the polymer in the capillary is replaced with fresh polymer and the next sample can be analysed.

Interpretation of STR Profiles

The spectra of the dyes used to label the PCR products overlap and the raw data contains peaks that are composed of more than one dye colour. After data collection the GeneScan or GeneMapper *ID* software removes spectral overlap in the profile and calculates the sizes of the amplified DNA fragments. The software calculates how much spectral overlap there is between each dye and subtracts this from the peaks within the profile. A good matrix file, which contains information on the amount of overlap in the spectra, will produce peaks within the profile that are composed of only one colour. The height of the peaks is measured in relative fluorescent units (rfu) –

the height is proportional to the amount of PCR product that is detected. To be able to size the PCR products an internal-lane size standard is used. The internal-lane size standards contain fragments of DNA of known lengths that are labelled with a fluorescent dye, and the fragments are detected along with the amplified PCR products during capillary electrophoresis. Commonly used commercial internal-lane size standards are the GeneScan-500 standards that can be labelled with either ROX or LIZ dyes and the ILS600.

Because the internal-lane size standard is analysed along with each PCR any differences between runs that could affect the migration rates during electrophoresis, such as temperature, do not impact significantly on the analysis. The software generates a size calling curve from the internal-lane size standards - the data point of the unknown fragments are compared to the size calling curve. Different algorithms have been developed to measure the size of DNA molecules, the most common one is the local Southern method.

After analysing the raw data with the software, the end result is an electropherogram with a series of peaks that represent different alleles: the size, peak height and peak area is also measured by the software. The final stage of generating a STR profile is to assign specific alleles to the amplified PCR products. Each peak in the profile is given a number that is a description of the structure of that allele - this is straightforward when naming simple repeats but is more problematic with complex repeat sequences.

The loci used in forensic casework have been well characterized and multiple alleles have been sequenced to determine the allelic structure and verify that the size of the peaks is a good indicator of the alleles they represent. However, because the migration of PCR products and internal-lane size standard varies slightly with factors such as temperature and the electrophoretic conditions, and because some STR alleles differ by only one base pair, the use of allelic ladders that contain all the common alleles at each locus has been adopted by the forensic community to ensure accurate profiling. Unlike the internal-lane size standards the allelic ladders cannot be analysed in the same injection as the samples but are run periodically during the analysis of a batch of samples.

When assigning the alleles, the unknown peaks are compared to the allelic ladder and should fall within a one base-pair window that is +/- 0.5 bp of the allelic ladder size - if the unknown alleles differ by more than this then they are classified as *off-ladder* (OL) and require further analysis. This comparison of unknown peaks to the allelic ladder can be done manually or by using the Genotyper or GeneMapper *ID* software, which will compare all the unknown alleles in the profile to the allelic ladder.

The STR profiles should be identical regardless of the laboratory where the analysis took place or the variations in the methodology that may have been used to generate the profile, such as different DNA extraction and quantification techniques and capillary electrophoresis platforms. Loci that are included in different commercial kits should also produce identical results.

Assessment of STR Profiles

DNA profiles generated from casework samples require some experience to interpret. Guidelines have evolved to assist with the interpretation of STR profiles, ensuring that the results are robust and consistent; this is especially important when dealing with samples that contain very small amounts of DNA, degraded DNA or mixtures of profiles that come from two or more individuals – all situations that complicate interpretation. This section explores a number of artefacts that can occur in DNA profile. Some casework scenarios that can lead to complex profiles are also considered.

Stutter Peaks

During the amplification of an STR allele it is normal to generate a stutter peak, that is one repeat unit smaller or larger that the true allele; smaller alleles are formed in the majority of cases. Stutter peaks are formed by strand slippage during the extension of the nascent DNA strand during PCR amplification.

Even in good quality profiles there will be some stutter peaks; these are recognizable and do not interfere with the interpretation of the profile. Threshold limits are normally used to aid in the identification and interpretation of stutter peaks, so, for example, while

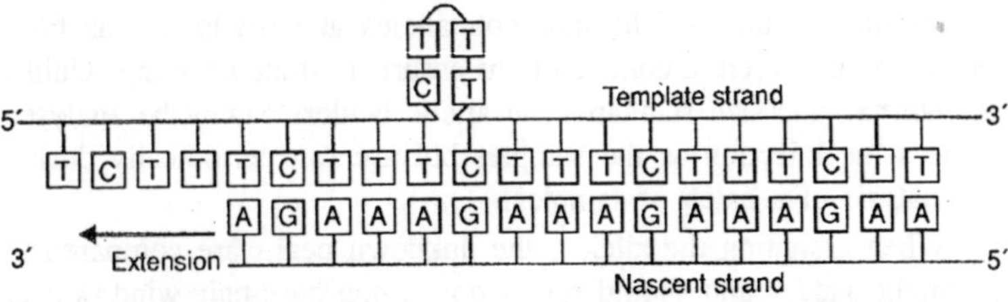

Fig. 11.2. During PCR, slippage between the template and the nascent DNA strands leads to the copied strand containing one repeat less than the template strand.

the degree of stutter varies between loci, they are typically less than 15% of the main peak – understanding stutter peaks is especially important when interpreting mixtures.

Different STR loci have varying tendencies to stutter. This is dependent on the structure of the core repeats: shorter di- and trinucleotide repeats are more prone to stutter than are tetra- and pentanucleotide repeats and this is one of the reasons that all the autosomal STRs that have been adopted by the forensic community have tetra and pentanucleotide core repeats. STRs with simple core repeats tend to have higher stutter rates than compound and complex repeats.

Split Peaks (+/– A)

The *Taq* polymerase that is used to drive the polymerase chain reaction adds nucleotides to the newly synthesized DNA molecule in a template-dependent manner. However, it also has an activity, called *terminal transferase*, whereby it adds a nucleotide to the end of the amplified molecule which is non-template-dependent. Approximately 85% of the time an adenine residue is added.

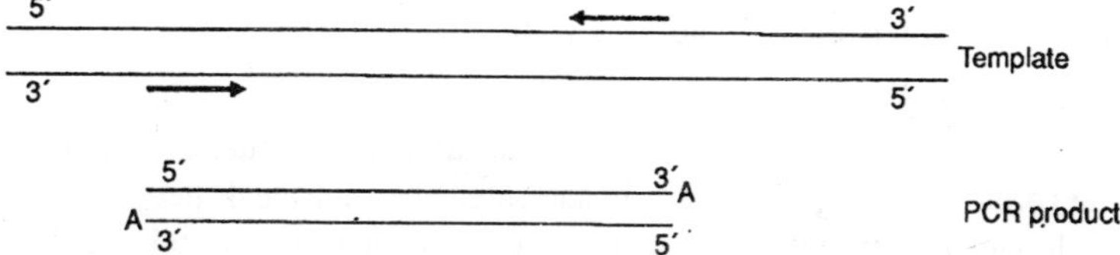

Fig. 11.3. The Taq polymerase adds a nucleotide to the 3' end of the newly synthesized strand.

It is important that the vast majority of PCR products have the non-template nucleotide added, otherwise a split peak is observed in the DNA profile. Split peaks are usually caused either by the sub-optimal activity of the *Taq* polymerase or by too much template DNA in the PCR.

In order to minimize the formation of split peaks in a profile, at the end of the cycling stage of the PCR, the reaction is incubated at 65–72°C for between 45–60 minutes, allowing the *Taq* polymerase to complete the non-template addition of all the PCR products.

The interpretation of profiles with split peaks is possible because the peak with the nucleotide added is taken as being the correct peak. Problems can occur when alleles are present that differ by only one base pair; the THO1 9.3 allele for example could be confused with the THO1 allele 10. In most cases a profile with a high degree of split peaks would have to be re-analysed to minimize the possibility of incorrect interpretation.

Pull-up

The matrix file contains information about the levels of spectral overlap that exist with the dyes that have been used to label the PCR products. This information is used by the Genescan and GeneMapper *ID* software to produce peaks that are made up of one colour. If the matrix file is not of good quality then this correction is not perfect and the peaks in the resulting profile are composed of more than one colour; this phenomenon is called *pull-up*. Pull-ups are easy to recognize as a smaller sized product will appear at exactly the same size as the real STR allele. Pull-up can also occur when there has been over amplification, even if the matrix file is of good quality.

Template DNA

Commercial STR kits have been optimized to amplify small amounts of template DNA, commonly between 0.5 and 2.5 ng, which represents approximately 166 and 833 copies of the haploid human genome. It is not always possible to add the optimum amount of DNA to a PCR when the sample size is limited.

Overloaded Profiles

Overloading the PCR can also lead to a profile that is difficult to interpret. If the CCD camera is saturated then the peak height/area is no longer a good indicator of the amount of product and this can lead to problems in assessing peak balance and can make the interpretation of mixtures difficult. Overloaded profiles also tend to have a noisy baseline, increased levels of stuttering, split peaks and pull-ups.

Low Copy Number DNA

At many crime scenes it may be possible to infer surfaces with which the perpetrator has had physical contact, for example the handle of a gun, a knife, a ligature, a door handle or a steering wheel. These areas can be swabbed to collect any epithelial cells that have been shed during the contact. The amounts of DNA extracted can be extremely low but in some circumstances it is possible to get a full DNA profile from less than 100 pg of template DNA: the normal range of template DNA is between 500 and 2500 pg (2.5 ng). To analyse such small quantities of DNA the number of amplification cycles is increased to 34. The standard number of cycles in the amplification using commercial kits is between 28 – 32 cycles. Empirical studies have shown that above 34 cycles the amount of artefacts that are detected outweigh the benefit of higher levels of artefact.

Extreme care has to be taken when interpreting the LCN profiles. A number of features can be seen when amplifying low amounts of template DNA. These are: allele drop-out, and drop-in; severe peak imbalance; locus drop-out; and increased stutter. Allele drop-out occurs when through chance events one allele in a heterozygous locus is preferentially amplified; this can give the false impression that the profile at a particular locus is homozygous. To minimize the possibility of this occurring the PCR must be repeated at least two times and only alleles that appear consistently can be called.

This phenomenon also leads to a peak imbalance that is much higher than when using higher amounts of template DNA. Allele drop-in is also a common phenomenon when amplifying low amounts of template DNA. The drop-in alleles are spurious amplification products and are not amplified in the duplicate or triplicate reactions but can still confuse the interpretation of the profile. Locus drop-out, particularly of the larger STR loci, can also occur; this reduces the amount of information from the profile but does not confuse the interpretation. At present, there is no clear consensus in the scientific community about the use of LCN PCR.

Peak Balance

STR loci that are used in forensic analysis are commonly heterozygous, producing two peaks in the profile. In a perfect profile the two peaks that are produced are balanced 1:1 in terms of peak height and area but in reality this is very rare and one peak will be larger than the other. The variations in peak height can be due to chance events, where one allele is more efficiently amplified than another. In good quality DNA extracts, the smaller peak is, on average, approximately 90% the size of the larger peak.

Laboratories will use different values that are based on their own validation studies but commonly require the smaller peak of a locus to be within 60% of the larger peak. Peak imbalance can be more extreme when profiling degraded DNA and when amplifying low amounts of template DNA. On rare occasions the mutation of a primer binding site will reduce the efficiency of the PCR for one allele, which can result in high levels of peak imbalance and even allele drop-out. The frequency of these mutations is low, ranging between frequencies of 0.01 and 0.001 per locus.

Mixtures

Many biological samples that are recovered from a scene of crime will contain a mixture of cellular material from more than one person. Clothing will often contain cellular material from the wearer and may also contain material from an assailant after an assault; the handle of a door or a steering wheel may have been handled by several people – there are many circumstances when mixtures of material can be collected. A mixture in a DNA profile can be recognized by the presence of more than two alleles at any locus within the profile, normally there will be several loci that have three or four alleles present and a loss of peak balance.

Having determined that the profile is mixed, the first task is to assess how many contributors are represented in the profile. Two person mixtures are most commonly seen in forensic casework; with a two person mixture a maximum of four alleles will be present at any locus whereas three person mixtures will contain up to six alleles at a locus. When four alleles are present at a given locus and there is a major and minor component, the interpretation is relatively simple. The ratio of peak areas within a locus generally corresponds with the ratio of template molecules, peak areas that consider the morphology of the peak as well as the height, are commonly used as a guide to interpret mixed profiles. Even in a two-person mixture when there are shared alleles between the major and minor profiles, the interpretation becomes more difficult – especially in mixtures where the minor profile is less than one-third of the level of the major profile.

In mixtures where the major component is in large excess, it is often possible to deduce the major profile; however, in such cases it is difficult to get much information from the minor component where the interpretation is complicated by artefacts in the profile such as stutter peaks, and also by the major profile masking the minor profile. Software has been developed that helps with the interpretation of complex mixtures.

Degraded DNA

Many samples that are collected from a crime scene may have been exposed to the environment for hours, days, or even longer if the crime scene has gone undetected. When DNA analysis is being used to identify human remains, the remains may be several years old before they are analysed or may have been exposed to severe environmental insult such as high temperatures. In all these circumstances the DNA in the cellular material will not be in pristine condition and will have degraded. This leads to a characteristic DNA profile with over amplification of the smaller loci and the successful amplification declines with the size of the alleles. There are two examples of degraded DNA sample; the first one is from a bone sample that had been in water for 30 years. The small loci have over amplified whereas the larger loci are barely detectable - the decrease in amplification is gradual as the length of the alleles increases.

In the second example an example of locus drop out can be seen, the first two blue loci, D3S 1358 and vWA have amplified successfully but there is no FGA allele. This profile is from human muscle tissue that had been exposed to high temperatures and has degraded to the extent that there is very little or no DNA that is 200 bp or longer. The interpretation of degraded profiles can be difficult and particular attention has to be taken when homozygous loci are detected - are they really homozygous and not heterozygous with one of the alleles having dropped out? When the levels are very low, if there is enough material the PCR is carried out in duplicate, as with LCN PCR, to minimize the possibility of generating an incorrect profile.

To assist with the analysis of degraded DNA, a series of multiplexes have been developed with the primers positioned close to the core repeats of the STRs, thereby minimizing the lengths of the amplicons.

Statistical Interpretation of STR Profiles

Once it has been established that two DNA profiles are the same, the significance of the match has to be estimated. This requires some knowledge of population genetics and some statistical analysis of the data. This section will briefly cover the fundamental concepts involved with estimating the frequency of an STR profile in a given population.

Population Genetics

It is necessary from the outset to define what is meant by a population. In the context of forensic genetics a population can be described as a group of people sharing common ancestry. In forensic terms the classification of a population within a country is usually quite broad and many subgroups that can differ in language, culture and religion are placed together and classified as, for example, Caucasian, sub-Saharan African and East Asian.

Hardy–Weinberg law

Population genetics can be defined as the study of factors affecting the allele and genotype frequencies of different genetic loci in a population. The *Hardy–Weinberg Law* (HW law), also called the *Hardy–Weinberg principle*, provides a simple mathematical representation of the relationship of genotype and allele frequencies within an ideal population and is central to forensic genetics. The HW law states that within a randomly mating population the genotype frequencies at any single genetic locus remain constant. When a population is obeying the HW law it is said to be in *Hardy–Weinberg equilibrium* (HWE). Importantly, when a population is in HWE, the genotype frequencies can be predicted from the allele frequencies. This relationship can be represented in a Punnett square.

The polymorphic STR loci used in forensic genetics have multiple alleles; however, the genotype frequency of a homozygote can be calculated using p^2 and that of heterozygotes can be calculated using $2pq$, removing the need to construct elaborate Punnet squares.

Deviation from the Hardy–Weinberg Equilibrium

The HW law states that certain conditions must be met. These are:

1. The population is infinitely large;
2. Random mating occurs within the population;
3. The population is free from the effects of migration;
4. There is no natural selection;
5. No mutations occur.

Clearly no human population will meet these criteria and they will deviate from HWE to a greater or lesser extent.

Infinitely large population

A consequence of finite population size is that the frequency of alleles will change through a process known as *random genetic drift*, where the frequency of any given allele will increase or decrease through chance events. The effect of genetic drift is more pronounced in smaller populations. However, most populations are sufficiently large for allele frequencies not to be significantly affected by genetic drift. Even in relatively small isolated human populations, it has been shown that alleles that are present at a frequency of more than 1% are rarely lost in recently diverged populations.

Random mating

Humans clearly do not mate completely randomly. However, because STR genotypes do not have any impact on a person's phenotype, such as height, strength or intelligence, selection of an STR through sexual selection is unlikely and has not been demonstrated.

No migration

Human history is full of migrations and this obviously can lead to changes in the gene pools of populations. If two distinct populations are living in the same geographical area and they have different allele frequencies, each population can be in HWE. If the two different populations are not recognized within the larger population and are not treated as separate populations, there can appear to be deviation from the HWE; this is known as the Wahlund effect. If random admixture occurs between the two populations, the admixed population would be in HWE after one generation. In reality, where two populations have differences in language, culture or religion, admixture is normally a much longer process.

Natural selection

At some loci in the human genome the effect of selective pressures can be detected, for example lactase persistence that is present in populations where milk has been a sustained part of the diet. Mutations that can confer disease resistance can also exhibit strong selection effects. The mutation CCR5-*A*32 allele, that is thought to offer protection against the haemorrhagic plague that led to vast numbers of Europeans dying between 1347 to 1670 AD, occurs at a frequency of almost zero in Asian, African and American Indian populations, whereas it is present at a frequency of 0.16 (16%) in European populations. However, the loci that are used for forensic testing are not located within functionally important regions of the genome and there is no evidence that they are under selective pressure.

Mutation

Mutation at STR loci is relatively rapid and it is the instability at these loci that leads to their high levels of polymorphisms - a trait that makes them valuable genetic markers. However, the mutation rates of STRs are still relatively low at less than 0.2 % per generation and do not have a significant effect on the allelic frequencies within a gene pool.

Statistical Tests to Determine Deviation from the Hardy–Weinberg Equilibrium

Given that no human population can meet the requirements of the HW law can we then use it to calculate genotype proportions based on allele frequencies? The answer from most forensic scientists is yes - because we can empirically measure the predicted genotype frequencies under HWE and detect if there is a significant amount of deviation.

Many statistical tests have been developed to calculate the deviation of the allelic frequencies from HWE. These include the goodness-of-fit test (also called the *chi square* test), homozygosity test, likelihood ratio test and the exact tests. However, when analysing polymorphic STR loci these tests do not have the required sensitivity because there are many undetected genotypes, and numerous genotypes, that are detected at very low frequencies at each locus. The multi-locus exact test was developed and can detect deviation from HWE when a large dataset is tested. Significant deviations from HWE have not been detected in the vast majority of populations. An exact test will not detect variations from HWE in small datasets, unless the deviation is extreme, and therefore conclusions from performing the exact test should not be over interpreted.

Estimating the Frequencies of SIR Profiles

In forensic DNA analysis the HWE is used along with an allele frequency database to calculate genotype frequencies. An allelic frequency database is constructed by measuring the occurrence of alleles within the defined population. It has been recommended that a database of at least 200 alleles per locus (or 100 individuals) be used for a particular population when using the database for generating the statistical estimates of the strength of DNA evidence. The larger the database, the more representative of the population it will be, and current practice dictates that several hundred individuals should be sampled when creating an allelic frequency database. These people should not be direct relations, therefore siblings or mother and child, etc., combinations should not be incorporated into an allele frequency database.

Using the HWE, the expected genotype frequency at each locus is calculated using the observed allele frequencies. Using these frequencies along with the above HWE equations we can calculate the frequency of a STR profile. If we take the profile that was analysed previously, the genotype proportions for each locus are calculated using p^2 for the homozygote and $2pq$ for the heterozygote loci. The overall profile frequency is calculated by multiplying the genotype frequency at each locus. This multiplication is termed the product rule – it is possible because the inheritance of alleles at each locus is independent of the other loci.

There have been some challenges to the approach presented above, namely that the inaccurate estimation of allelic frequencies can lead to inaccurate profile frequency estimates. To overcome this problem

Table 11.2. The profile frequency is estimated using the principles of the Hardy–Weinberg law and an allele frequency database that was constructed using 400 alleles.

Locus	*Allele*	*Allelefrequency*	*HWE*	*Genotype frequency*
D3S1358	15	0.2825	*2pq*	0.1257
	17	0.2225		
vWA	14	0.0850	*2pq*	0.0425
	17	0.2500		
D16S539	11	0.2975	*2pq*	0.1041
	13	0.1750		
D2S1338	24	0.1000	*2pq*	0.0240
	25	0.1200		
D8S1179	11	0.0625	*2pq*	0.0434
	13	0.3475		
D21S11	30	0.2625	*2pq*	0.0551
	31.2	0.1050		
D18S51	14	0.1675	*2pq*	0.0477
	15	0.1425		
D19S433	14	0.3275	*2pq*	0.0164
	15.2	0.0250		
THO1	9	0.1375	*2pq*	0.0963
	9.3	0.3500		
FGA	21	0.1775	p^2	0.0315
	21	0.1775		
			Profile frequency	$7.579\ 10^{-14}$

several methods have been employed that take into consideration the limitations in allele frequency estimates.

Corrections to Allele Frequency Databases

Allelic frequencies are calculated by measuring a number of alleles in the target population. The more alleles that are measured as a part of the allelic frequency database the more accurate it will be. However, it is impractical to measure all of the alleles in a large population and the frequencies are only estimates, prone to inaccuracies due to the limited size of the database. For common alleles the impact is small but with rare alleles, which can easily be under represented in a frequency database, the impact of limited sampling can have a large effect. It should be noted that the deficiencies in the frequency databases can also lead to over representation of allele frequencies but, as a general principle, when we are estimating the significance of forensic evidence the emphasis is not to over state the strength of the evidence. Different approaches have been taken to overcome the limitations of allele frequency databases. These include the allele frequency ceiling principle, the Balding size bias correction, allowing for the effects of subpopulations and using a maximum profile frequency.

Allele ceiling principle

Very rare alleles may not appear at all in the frequency database. If a rare allele not previously represented on the frequency database is detected in a crime scene sample then the frequency of the allele would be 0– which cannot be the case! A mechanism must be put in place to deal with this situation. One approach is to set a minimal allele frequency. The minimum frequency values that are used vary from country to country but are typically around 0.01 (1%). Any allele occuring with a frequency of less than 0.01 will be adjusted to this figure. An alternative approach is to use a minimal allele count, for example five alleles being the smallest number of alleles that is considered: the allele frequency is simply calculated using the formula $5/2N$, where N is the number of individuals in the database.

Simple correction for sampling bias

Allele frequency databases are relatively small when compared with the populations from which they are drawn and therefore there remain sampling uncertainties. A simple method for addressing such uncertainties, which are inherent in allele frequency databases, is suggested by Balding. The allelic information in the evidential material is incorporated into the database to adjust for the potential under-representation of alleles. When there are matching DNA profiles there must be two DNA profiles: one from the crime scene and one from the reference sample. The alleles from these profiles are added to the allelic frequency database. By adding both profiles we are making the assumption that the material found at the crime scene did not come from the suspect. If we look at the profile in Table 11.2, at the vWA locus is a heterozygous locus with alleles 14 and 17; these have frequencies of 0.0850 and 0.2500 respectively. By multiplying the allele frequency with the total number of alleles in the database, we can calculate that the numbers of observed alleles in the database are 34/400 for allele 14 and 100/400 for allele 17. We now have two profiles to add to the database; we have seen a total of four new alleles: 14, 17 in the crime scene sample and also 14, 17 in the suspect's sample. These can be added to the database and the frequency recalculated. The database now has 36 observations of allele 14 out of a total of

404 observed alleles, which leads to an allele frequency of 0.090. Similarly, for allele 17 we now have 102/404, which gives us an allele frequency of 0.2525. This procedure is repeated for each heterozygous locus.

In Table 11.2 the FGA locus is homozygous and in the original database we have 71/400 observations but now need to add four more observations (21, 21 and 21, 21) to both the frequency of allele 21 and the total number of alleles, so the new frequency is 75/404 = 0.1856.

The Balding correction for size bias has the greatest impact when the database is made from a small number of alleles or when the allele is rare. If the allele is common and the database is large, the effect is negligible.

The above methods both compensate for the limitations of allele frequency databases that are caused by sampling effects. Other more complex methods, such as calculating the confidence 95% interval, can be employed but are not widely used.

Subpopulations

In addition to correcting for sampling effect, it may also be necessary to allow for the presence of subpopulations when calculating profile frequencies. Even within populations of the same broad ethnic group, the population is not homogeneous but comprises related subpopulations. The subpopulations form because people do not mate randomly, but tend, for example, to have children with people from the same geographical area or same social group. Allelic databases are normally composed of samples that have been drawn from the general population, and not from one subpopulation, and therefore provide us with an average estimate of the allele frequencies in the whole population. The effect of subpopulations has been demonstrated as leading to errors in the estimation of profile frequencies. In a subpopulation there is a higher degree of relatedness between individuals than there is to the whole population, i.e. a higher probability that two individuals would have some genetic markers in common through descent from a common ancestor (identical by descent) than by a random match (identical by state). To incorporate this substructure factor into the profile frequency calculations, a theta value (θ) is used to describe the degree of differentiation between subpopulations (the amount of inbreeding). The level of population substructure, and therefore the theta values at the STR loci, have been demonstrated to be low. In general a theta value of 0.01 is used for seemingly homogeneous populations, while for more isolated/differentiated populations a theta value of 0.03 has been recommended. To calculate the profile frequencies that allow for subpopulations the following equations are used commonly used:

For homozygotes:

$$\text{Profile frequency} = \frac{[2\theta + (1-\theta)p_i][3\theta + (1-\theta)p_i]}{(1+\theta)(1+2\theta)}$$

For heterozygotes:

$$\text{Profile frequency} = \frac{[2\theta + (1-\theta)p_i][\theta + (1-\theta)p_j]}{(1+\theta)(1+2\theta)}$$

We can use this to recalculate the profile frequency presented in Table 11.2: the calculations for the vWA and FGA locus are shown below with a theta value of 0.01.

vWA:

$$\frac{2[0.01 + (1-0.01)0.0850][0.01 + (1-0.01)0.2500]}{(1+0.01)(1+(2\times 0.01)}$$

$$\frac{2[0.0942][0.2575]}{(1.01)(2.02)}$$

$$\frac{0.0485}{1.0302} = 0.0471$$

FGA:

$$\frac{[2\times 0.01) + (1-0.01)0.1775][3\times 0.01 + (1-0.01)0.1775]}{(1+0.01)(1+(2\times 0.01)}$$

$$\frac{[0.1975][0.2057]}{(1.01)(2.02)}$$

$$\frac{0.0403}{1.0302} = 0.0391$$

The impact of a theta value of 0.01 on this particular profile is a modest three fold increase in the profile frequency, whereas a theta value of 0.03 leads to a frequency that is over 20 times more common – but still exceedingly rare. It should be noted that the impact of applying theta to a profile frequency calculation differs between profiles.

The current practice in most legal systems is to use a theta value of between 0.01 and 0.03, apart from in exceptional circumstances where very high levels of inbreeding may have occurred.

Profile ceiling principle

In some countries, such as the UK, the approach has been to use a match probability of 1 in a billion (1 000 000 000). This approach is highly conservative. It does have the advantage that individual profile frequencies do not have to be calculated because the value used is much lower than the most common profile frequency, even if conservative corrections are incorporated.

Which Population Frequency Database should be Used?

In some cases, the ethnic origins of material recovered from the crime scene are known: for example, if a woman has been sexually assaulted she can normally describe the assailant as white, black, Asian, etc. In such a case, for example, if the assailant was described as white, then it would be logical to use a white Caucasian allele frequency database to calculate the profile frequency. In other contexts, there may be no information about who could have left the material at the crime scene. In countries or regions having substantial populations with different ethnic backgrounds, a common practice is for the profile frequency to be calculated using an allele database for each major population group, and to use the most conservative profile frequency. If we take the example, the allele frequency data used is from a white Caucasian database (USA); if we recalculate with allele frequency data representing an African American population we get a profile frequency of 3.36×10^{-16}, which is over 200-times less frequent than when we use the Caucasian frequency data. In this case it is clear that the Caucasian data provides a frequency estimate that is more conservative.

The methods that are employed for the correction of profile frequencies vary widely between different judicial systems and even different laboratories within the same judicial system. The allele ceiling principle, Balding correction, 95% confidence interval to correct for sampling error, accounting for population sub-division using theta, and the profile ceiling principle have all been used in forensic casework to calculate profile frequencies.

It should be noted that the impact of the different correction methods will vary depending on the individual profile and the size of the allele frequency database. The end result of analysing a profile is to produce a profile frequency, which is an estimate. Incorporating one or more of the correction factors into the profile frequency estimates reduces the chances of overstating the DNA evidence.

12

Screening Significance

Since the introduction of *capillary electrophoresis* (CE) in 1981, there has been a marked increase in the number of applications of CE to the analysis of drugs in various situations. For example, the pharmaceutical industry has made extensive use of CE in analysis of main drug components, of drug-related impurities, of trace impurities in the process stream, and of the isomeric composition of numerous drugs. At the same time, Lurie, and others have reported on the analysis of drugs of abuse in street preparations. Several workers, notably Thormann, Eap et al., and Penalvo et al., have applied CE in one or another of its configurations to the problems of analysis of drugs in urine or plasma. These efforts have mainly been directed toward the goals of *therapeutic drug monitoring* (TDM), but Caslavska et al. have also addressed the application to emergency toxicology. This chapter will focus on CE as a tool for screening biological specimens for drugs of forensic significance. Naturally, information derived from pharmaceuticals, street drugs, and from TDM analysis can be exploited in the development of a comprehensive screening procedure. In forensic analysis a screening procedure, as discussed in detail later, must be comprehensive, fast, inexpensive, and easy to use.

Initially, the screen must be comprehensive. It must detect as many forensically significant drugs as possible in a single analytical pass. In this case, "*forensically significant*" means, in a broad sense, all drugs that might reasonably be involved in fatal poisonings or in the impairment of human functions such as driving a motor vehicle. With the notable exception of the barbiturates, the vast majority of drugs fitting this description are basic (nitrogenous) compounds. Examples are, amphetamines, antihistamines, narcotic analgesics and tricyclic antidepressants. Until recently, comprehensive screens have utilized *gas chromatography with nitrogen-phosphorus detectors* (GC-NPD) to screen extracts from biological specimens. Often extracts must be derivatized to make the compounds more volatile. Our focus and the focus of this chapter has been to consider the question: "Can CE replace GC/NPD in a comprehensive drug screen?"

Forensic analysis poses a number of potential problems for any such screening procedure but possibly the most pressing is the type of sample analyzed. For a forensic toxicologist the specimen that must most often be accommodated is whole blood in variable stages of hemolysis and in varying degrees of putrefaction. Simpler specimens such as urine may be available in any given case but any screening procedure must first and foremost be able to handle hemolysed whole blood.

Oda and coworkers, note that "in forensic toxicology, the analysis is required to be only qualitative, but without false positive or false negative results." While generally agreeing with this observation most operations confirm all positive screen results by another analysis, usually mass spectrometry. Toxicologists can, therefore, tolerate a few false-positive results at the screening stage. However, a negative screening result may well end analysis in the case. Thus, it is more important that false negative results be minimized. For example, in a GC screen the more precise the retention behavior, the greater the confidence with which potentially positive results can be ruled out. In essence this means that the screening procedure must be reliable and consistent day after day. If CE were to be seriously considered as replacement for GC-NPD, then migration behavior must be comparably precise.

Sensitivity of the screen must be high enough to detect drugs found in forensic specimens at low concentrations. Many of the drugs of forensic interest are used in relatively low dosages which, naturally, give rise to correspondingly low blood concentrations. Therapeutic levels of basic drugs typically range from a few nanograms per milliliter of blood up to a few hundred nanograms per milliliter. Since such levels are well within the sensitivity limits of GC-NPD, it is critical that CE has at least comparable sensitivity.

Ideally, any forensic screening procedure must be robust, fast, inexpensive, and simple to use. The screen should be available with a minimum of fine-tuning, minimal instrument down-time, and low maintenance and operating costs. These conditions also imply that no extensive sample cleanup or preparation should be needed. In addition, no derivatization of the analyte should be required. Such desirable properties are not specific to forensic drug screening. However, since GC-NPD is considered the "*gold standard*," these are inevitable points of comparison with any potential replacement.

Capillary Electrophoresis (CE) System

Most commercially available instruments offer similar capabilities. The main differences appear to be in the degree of automation, sample capacity, flexibility of injection techniques, and detector options. Our early work was done on a Beckman P/ACE 5500 equipped with both a single-wavelength UV and *diode array detectors* (DAD). More recently, we have used a Beckman System MDQ with a DAD.

For us, the decision to use CE for drug screening was dictated primarily by the need for simplicity. Lurie reported separation and detection of drugs of forensic interest in a *micellar electrokinetic capillary chromatography* (MECC) system. Thormann et al., Renou-Gonnord and David, and Hyotylainen et al. have also used MECC successfully for drug detection. Gonzales and Laserna, used *capillary zone electrophoresis* (CZE) to screen for banned drugs in sport. Chee and Wan also showed the feasibility of using CZE to screen for 17 basic drugs in urine and plasma. Since our major interest initially was on basic drugs, it seemed reasonable to evaluate CZE, the simplest possible CE configuration. Using the procedure of Chee and Wan, 60 cm (to detector) × 50 μm id at 25 kV or 50 cm (to detector) × 75 μm at 18 kV id uncoated fused silica capillaries were used. The run buffer was 100 mmol/L sodium phosphate at pH 2.38 along with electrokinetic injection, typically 10 kV for 8 s, although the injection time may be varied. Pressure injections have been used but experience suggests that electrokinetic injection is more selective for cations. Considering the rather straightforward extraction methods chosen, such selectivity is beneficial. Typically, separation voltages of 18–25 kV with normal polarity have been used giving a total run times of about 25 min.

This approach to a screen for basic drugs clearly excludes those that are not protonated at pH 2.38. Some of the benzodiazepines (very weak bases) are not detected in this screen. Tomita and Okuyama have reported, however, a MECC system (phosphate/borate/SDS/methanol) that can potentially detect and separate benzodiazepines, and presumably other neutral compounds, at concentrations applicable in the forensic toxicology situation.

Detector sensitivity is a matter of great concern in a forensic drug screen because, as noted earlier, the drugs of major forensic interest tend to be present at low concentrations. This places special demands on any analytical system used to analyze samples without any pre-treatment. CZE, with the common UV detectors or DAD, monitoring at wavelengths in the range 200–220 nm, are known to be rather insensitive. From experience we have found that drug concentrations must be on the order of 0.3 μg/mL of the injected solution to ensure consistent detection while avoiding expensive detector modifications. This is in agreement with reports in which urine, and plasma or serum, were injected directly onto a capillary. Limits of detection in such direct-injection methods have typically been reported to be approx 1 μg/mL. While this is adequate for most acidic drugs, in order to be useful in the analysis of basic drugs of forensic interest, the sensitivity has to be increased 10–100 times. As attractive as direct sample injection is, it cannot work for most basic drugs in our simple instrumental configuration. Thus, sample preparation that provides a pre-concentration step appears to be inevitable.

Sample Preparation

A useful overview of sample pretreatment has been provided by Lloyd. Although pre-concentration of the analyte is an important reason for considering extraction as a preliminary step to CE analysis, it is not the only one. Extraction also eliminates protein, which is important to prevent fouling of the capillary in CZE, and helps to eliminate interferences in MECC. Further, it is noted that liquid-liquid extraction practically eliminates the inorganic salts present in the original sample, which can interfere with CE analysis.

The first choice for sample preparation is *direct solvent extraction* (DSE) of whole blood with a solvent such as 1-chlorobutane/NH_4OH for basic and neutral drugs. This is a simple, relatively quick extraction that has long been used to prepare samples for chromatographic screening. For GC-NPD this simple extraction method has been shown to require no additional steps to separate the complex mixture of neutral compounds from basic drugs. Thus, it seemed reasonable that sample preparation for CE analysis also be as simple and easy.

Using 1-chlorobutane/NH_4OH, a direct solvent extraction of 1.0 mL whole blood was performed. The solvent, containing traces of NH_4OH, must be evaporated to about 1 mL before the addition of 10 μL of 1% HCl in MeOH. The resulting HCl salt of the basic drug is less volatile and more water-soluble. The remaining solvent was evaporated to dryness. The residue was redissolved in 30 μL of water, with warming. Our experience indicates that 30 μL is the smallest volume that can be conveniently and consistently handled. The resulting solution is centrifuged at 12,000 rpm for 20 min in 0.2 mL PCR vials to remove any insoluble material, reducing the risk of plugging the CE capillary during injection. The centrifugation step also eliminates filtration that would inevitably results in sample loss. The solution in the PCR vials can be used directly for electrokinetic injection without further processing. This procedure provides a simple but effective cleanup, concentrating the analyte approx 30-fold.

That such a procedure is effective in bringing most basic drugs within the reach of simple CE detection can be illustrated as follows. In practice, we analyze a solution of 20 basic drugs (1 μg/mL) dissolved in water as an instrument performance standard. The same drug mixture is also spiked into whole blood at a concentration of 10 ng/mL for each drug. This is the whole blood QC standard analyzed with each batch of cases. All drugs are consistently detected in both instances.

Liquid–liquid extraction is not the only way to prepare samples for CE analysis, and it may not be the best. *Solid-phase extraction* (SPE) has been successfully used to replace DSE in the preparation of samples. It is also important to note that SPE is more amenable to automation than is DSE. This must be taken into consideration when setting up mass screening methods. In addition to SPE, Palmarsdottir and coworkers, have demonstrated use of supported liquid membranes to extract basic drugs from plasma, an approach that may offer its own unique advantages.

In keeping with the goal of maximizing sensitivity, a number of special methods of sample injection have been devised. These are techniques by which a larger fraction of the analyte is transferred onto the capillary than is generally possible with simple electrokinetic or pressure injections. Such "*preconcentration*" methods result in increased sensitivity. Perhaps the simplest of these methods is called stacking, in which sample components are injected from a matrix of lower ionic strength than the run buffer. The example procedure described above in which the sample, dissolved in water, is injected into the run buffer comprising 100 mmol/L sodium phosphate, pH 2.38, is an example of a stacking procedure. A more powerful method has been reported by Palmarsdottir et al., in the analysis of bambuterol where sensitivity was increased about 400 times by a double-stacking procedure after preconcentration using a *supported liquid membrane*

(SLM). The reported limit of detection in this assay was <1 ng/mL of plasma. In addition, Eap et al. reported a method for determining mianserin in plasma that uses both liquid–liquid extraction and on-capillary preconcentration to obtain a limit of quantitation of 5 ng/mL. If such methods can be generally applied, they may offer a simple way to further increase sensitivity of a general drug screen for basic drugs.

Sample Quality

Sample quality (i.e., putrid samples), although of little consequence in most other fields is of considerable concern in forensic toxicology. It is important to know whether the screening method, including sample preparation, functions satisfactorily with fresh specimens and putrid samples. To test the ruggedness of our own sample treatment method, we left spiked whole blood samples at room temperature and compared the results obtained by CZE and GC-NPD. The process of putrefaction can generate artefacts that may mask basic drugs that might be present in the sample. GC-NPD detects these artefacts which soon renders the chromatogram uninterpretable. However, corresponding electropherograms are much less affected. This could be due to the fact that most of the artifacts are neutral or weakly basic compounds that are not electrokinetically injected or are practically transparent to UV detectors.

Identity of Peaks

In most toxicology laboratories, final identification of a peak will not be made from observed retention or migration behavior. But the decision whether or not to pursue identification will be made solely on the basis of this behavior in either the GC or CE analytical systems. Thus, it is imperative that retention or migration behavior be as reproducible as possible. The more precise the retention behavior, the narrower the window that can be used to decide whether a given peak is a potential positive result. When using a simple UV detector, interpretation of electropherograms and tentative identification of peaks is limited to migration behavior. Use of the DAD adds UV spectral data to migration data and greatly improves the discriminating power of the screen.

Migration behavior

It has been often noted that raw migration time is not highly reproducible. Yang et al., note that this is especially true of micellar systems because the *electroosmotic flow* (EOF) is a powerful influence on migration in such systems. EOF, in turn, is affected by variables, such as the condition of the interior surface of the capillary, that are difficult to control. Even at pH 2.38 when EOF is reduced almost to zero, raw migration times are less reproducible than is desirable. Migration times have been found to drift with time, presumably as a result of changes occurring to the inside surface of the capillary. In order to have a good screening procedure, it was clear that it would be necessary to have an expression of migration behavior that was more reproducible than raw migration time. This could be considered analogous to the retention index when using GC.

The analogy with GC (and *thin-layer chromatography* [TLC]) suggests the expression of *relative migration time* (RM) as a way to obtain more reproducible results. That is, the migration time of the analyte in question is divided by the migration time of a reference compound analyzed simultaneously. Yang et al., examined the effect of the "*migration time ratio*", in which they chose a neutral marker as the reference compound. With their test mixture of amino acids, the *relative standard deviation* (RSD) for simple migration times was 2–5%, whereas the RSD for the migration time ratio in the same system was 1% or less.

Williams and Vigh, took the expression of migration behavior a step further, discussing effective mobility (μeff). This quantity may be described as the mobility of the analyte (with dimensions of $cm^2/v.s$) corrected for the mobility of EOF. For us this appeared to offer the most precise expression of migration behavior. For example, we have observed RSD for raw migration time to be about $\pm$ 6%, relative migration about $\pm$ 2%, and for μeff $< \pm 0.3\%$. We have not observed that the RSD for relative migration and μeff are the same. In all our studies, relative migrations have shown more variation. We have also observed that mobility is independent of capillary diameter and can be reproduced from laboratory to laboratory. Also it should be noted that Ahuja and Foley suggested calculation of a migration index for MECC, an index quite analogous to a chromatographic retention index.

In order for a screening procedure based on migration behavior to be useful a list of potential analytes along with their migration data must be available. In this regard we have reported on some 650 drugs and metabolites, giving relative migration and μeff for each.

UV spectra and searchable libraries

It is inevitable that a CE screen for basic drugs will show numerous instances of comigration. Even the best precision noted aforementioned yields, in any statistically sound window, several possibilities of drugs that could be present. With detection by single-wavelength UV detector, such migration information is all that the analyst has to interpret screen results. This does not present an obstacle to confirmation by MS. However more information on individual peaks is always useful and it is easily obtained with the DAD.

Kobayashi et al. reported early use of a diode array as a detector for CE, showing the potential of collecting UV spectra on all emerging peaks. Caslavska et al. compared three CE methods for rapid determination of drugs in cases of intoxication. They were able to collect UV spectra on peaks and provide rapid results of drug screens by CE. UV spectra were not considered rigorous identification but were sufficient to meet the needs of emergency toxicology. Quick turnaround in such analyses was shown to be possible by CE "provided that instrumentation with a database for peak identification is available". Lilley and Wheat have reported use of DAD data and CE, with emphasis on specialized software that allows sophisticated spectral analysis of emerging peaks. This was shown to be particularly effective in eliminating false-positive amphetamine results without the need for MS. In our laboratory, the compounds we have listed by μeff and relative migration also have their UV spectra stored in a spectral database. A CE system, such as Beckman's MDQ, has software that allows the spectrum from an unknown sample to be searched against stored spectra. This makes drug screening by CE even more powerful and discriminating. However, a detection limit of 10 ng/ mL whole blood, referred to earlier, does not apply to searches of UV spectra generated by DAD. Generally, analyte peaks from samples spiked at 40–50 ng/ mL are required for meaningful library searches. Also the best matches are obtained, not surprisingly, when the spectra for the unknown and the standard are collected at approximately the same concentration.

It is now appropriate to return to the question posed at the beginning of this chapter: "Can CE replace GC-NPD in a comprehensive drug screen?" It has been shown that CZE is capable of analyzing whole blood specimens, whether hemolysed or putrid, by use of a simple liquid–liquid extraction. Detection of basic drugs using a simple UV detector or DAD has been shown to be on the order of 10 ng/mL of whole blood. More powerful sample stacking methods have been shown to increase the detection limit to about 1 ng/mL. Additional improvement in sensitivity is possible but requires a new detector or detector cell and more complicated sample preparation. For a forensic drug screen, however, the ability to detect most basic drugs at 10 ng/mL of blood meets most needs.

The cost of screening basic drug by CE compares favorably to GC-NPD. Initial instrument costs are roughly similar. However, replacement GC columns cost 20–30 times as much as replacement capillaries (i.e., untreated fused silica). Operating costs are roughly similar. For example, both CE and GC-NPD can use the same sample extraction procedure. Total run time of the two methods is, however, significantly different with the CZE screen taking approx 25% less than the run time in a parallel GC-NPD screen. This is primarily because of the shorter time needed by the CZE system to return to initial conditions after an analytical run. Hyotylainen et al. describe an approach to CE that may permit even shorter analysis times. Using MEKC, they were able to perform their separations in a short capillary (23 cm). This led to run times of 2 min, an interesting development for those engaged in mass drug screening.

The CZE system can be highly robust, as might be hoped with such a simple system. Aside from physical breakage, which occurs occasionally, capillaries appear to be all but immune to hazards common in GC. In our laboratory, CZE capillaries have been exposed to gross overloading with very complex samples. Adsorption of analyte or contaminant molecules to the capillary appears to be reversible, such that with judicious rinsing between samples with sodium hydroxide, sodium dodecylsulfate, and run buffers or water, complete regeneration of the capillary surface is possible. Such rinses that are part of routine screens, take up about 15% of the analysis cycle for each sample. In our hands, one capillary was subjected to over 10,000 injections of pure solutions of drug standards and of whole blood extracts before it needed to be replaced. The capillary performance remained unchanged except for a decrease in the analysis time by about 5 min.

Finally, analyte decomposition, whether due to thermal or other causes, or irreversible absorption of the analyte to the columns, common observations in GC systems, are rarely, if ever, observed in the CZE screen. From the evidence presented here it would appear that CZE, is capable of providing a comprehensive screen of basic drugs in whole blood and, in some analytical situations, may be the method of choice.

Use of the AmpliType PM + HLA DQA1 PCR Amplification and Typing Kits for Identity Testing

Direct analysis of the composition of DNA has been used for forensic and paternity analysis since 1985. Since each person, except for identical twins, has a unique DNA composition, methods that allow the detection of differences in the DNA are useful to resolve identification issues involving the origin of forensic biological samples or to resolve paternity disputes. Methods that detect insertions, deletions, or sequence changes are used for identity testing. In forensics, because all cells from a specific person have the same DNA, comparisons between a known reference sample (i.e., from a victim or suspect) and an evidentiary sample of unknown origin can provide evidence to help to identify the origin of the evidentiary sample. If the DNA profiles of the evidentiary sample and the known sample differ, then the evidentiary sample did not originate from the known individual. If the DNA profiles are the same, the known individual is not excluded as the source of the evidentiary sample and a likelihood of finding the DNA profile can be calculated based on population-genetics principles and an appropriate database. In cases of questioned parentage, since we obtain half of our DNA from each of our biological parents, comparisons between the DNA of a child and an alleged parent can help to resolve questions of paternity or maternity. For example, in a paternity test, if the child's paternal allele is not present in the alleged father, he is excluded as the biological father (barring mutation or recombination). If the child's paternal allele is present in the alleged father, he is not excluded as the biological father and a *paternity index* (PI) can be calculated as the genetic odds in favor of paternity.

The first methodology used to answer questions about DNA-based identification was RFLP analysis, a technique first published in 1975. This approach relies on the separation and identification of DNA fragments generated by restriction endonuclease digestion of the DNA. Analysis of the human genome led to the discovery of a number of highly polymorphic loci that were composed of insertions and deletions of DNA known as variable number tandem repeats (VNTRs). Such loci were very powerful in resolving identification issues. However, RFLP analysis requires relatively large amounts (0.5 μg) of high-mol-wt DNA in order to obtain results. The amount and quality of DNA isolated from forensic evidentiary samples often did not contain a sufficient quantity of DNA for analysis. A new testing method was required to obtain results from such samples.

The second method used to analyze DNA for identification was *polymerase chain reaction* (PCR), first published in 1985. This method allows the amplification of small quantities of DNA, amounts insufficient for RFLP analysis. The first locus examined extensively for identification was the HLA DQA1 locus, originally called HLA

DQalpha. This locus was made commercially available as a kit in a reverse-dot-format by Perkin-Elmer. This kit was followed by a second reverse dot blot format kit known as Polymarker, which allowed the simultaneous amplification and analysis of five loci. The most recent kit, AmpliType PM+DQA1, allows the simultaneous amplification of all six loci. Using the AmpliType PM + DQA1 PCR Amplification and Typing Kit, it is possible to amplify six loci simultaneously: HLA DQA1, *low-density lipoprotein receptor* (LDLR), glycophorin A (GYPA), hemoglobin G gammaglobin (HBGG), D7S8, and group-specific component (Gc).

All six of these loci are typed using the reverse-dot-blot approach where an allele-specific oligonucleotide probe is immobilized to a nylon strip. The reverse dot blot allows the determination of alleles without separation by electrophoresis. During the amplification process, a biotin molecule is incorporated into the synthesized DNA. Strips are prepared that contain the specific alleles to be detected as oligonucleotide sequences attached to a poly dT tail used to bind the oligonucleotide sequence to the membrane. During the hybridization reaction, sequences complementary from the sample bind to the immobilized oligonucleotide on the membrane. The biotin molecule is subsequently recognized by streptavidin, which is in turn attached to an enzyme (alkaline phosphatase) that can produce a color reaction in the presence of a substrate-like horseradish peroxidase. Thus, when an amplified DNA binds to the membrane, a sandwich is formed that ultimately produces a color change to form a blue dot. The intensity of the blue dot is determined by the amount of starting DNA and the time allowed to produce a color reaction. Controls are built into the strip to provide a threshold of intensity for interpretation.

Materials

Reagents supplied the AmpliType PM+DQA1 PCR amplification and typing kit

1. AmpliType PM+DQA1 PCR Reaction Mix (2.4 mL). This contains the enzyme AmpliTaq DNA polymerase, $MgCl_2$, dATP, dGTP, dCTP, dTTP, and 0.08% sodium azide in a buffer and salt. This should be stored at 2°C.
2. AmpliType PM+DQA1 Primer Set (1.2 mL). This contains 12 biotinylated primers and 0.05% sodium azide in buffer and salt. This should be stored at 2°C.
3. Control DNA (0.2 mL). This contains 100 ng/mL of human genomic DNA in 0.05% sodium azide and buffer. The genotype of this

control DNA is as follows: LDLR, BB; GYPA, AB; HBGG, AA, D7S8, AB; GC, BB; DQA1, 1.1, 4.1. This should be stored at 2°C.

4. Mineral oil (5 mL). This is supplied in a dropper bottle and should be stored at 2°C. Do not expose to strong ultraviolet light.
5. AmpliType PM and HLA DQA1 DNA probe strips (50 strips each). These strips are provided in a screw-top tube with a packet of desiccant. Store the strips at 2°C in the screw-top tube with the desiccant and protect from light.
6. Enzyme conjugate: HRP-SA (2.0 mL). This contains horseradish peroxidase and streptavidin (HRP-SA) enzyme conjugate in a buffer with preservative. Store at 2°C.
7. Chromogen: TMB (60 mg). This contains powdered 3,3',5,5'-tetramethlybenzidine (TMB). Dissolve before use as indicated earlier. Store at 2°C.

Reagents not supplied with kit

The following reagents are not included in the kit but are required for PCR amplification; PCR product-gel analysis, hybridization, and color development. This list does not include reagents required for DNA isolation.

1. Agarose. For example, NuSieve GTG and SeaKem GTG from FMC.
2. Alcohol. 95% ethanol and 70% isopropanol.
3. 0.5X TBE running buffer: 44.5 m*M* Tris-borate, 1 m*M* EDTA, pH 8.0.
4. Gel loading buffer: 0.2% bromophenol blue, 50% glycerol, 20 m*M* Tris-HCl, pH 8.0, 2.5 m*M* EDTA.
5. Ethidium bromide, 10 mg/mL.
6. Citrate buffer: 0.1 *M* sodium citrate, pH 5.0.
7. Glycerol.
8. Tris base.

DNA analysis

1. AmpliType DNA Typing Tray.
2. Aspirator apparatus.
3. Electrophoresis equipment including gel trays, boxes, and power supplies.
4. Forceps with nonpointed tips.
5. Wratten 22, orange filter for use with a Polaroid camera.

6. Microcentrifuge.
7. Pipetters to deliver 20, 1000, and 5000 μL. These should be positive displacement pipetters, and there should be one set each for use pre-PCR and post-PCR amplifications.
8. Shaker, variable speed with orbital platform.
9. Thermocycler and equipment including thin-walled reaction tubes and temperature-verification system.

In addition, standard laboratory supplies like gloves, lab coats, and protective eyewear are required during the analysis.

Method

Amplification

The following protocol describes the PCR amplification procedures required using a Perkin-lmer 480 thermal Cycler and the typing procedures specific for the AmpliType PM+DQA1 Amplification and Typing Kit. An area should be dedicated for preparation of the PCR reactions. Ideally, this should be in a separate room inside a biological, laminar-flow hood. All equipment and supplies used to set up the amplification reactions should be kept in this dedicated facility. Pipet tips plugged with hydrophobic filters should be used to prevent contamination. Use of disposable gloves and dedicated lab coats is required.

1. Prepare the DNA samples for PCR amplification. The quantity of each sample should be determined so the final DNA concentration is in the range of 0.1-0.5 ng/μL to allow addition of 20 ng in 20 μL to the PCR reaction. If the DNA in a sample is degraded, which is especially true in forensic samples, it may be necessary to add more than 10 ng of DNA.
2. Determine the number of samples to be amplified including positive and negative controls. The positive control can be the Control DNA included in the kit or can be another DNA sample, well-characterized for the loci in question. One of the negative controls consists of 20 μL of DI H_2O in place of the DNA sample. Other negative controls can be included that check the integrity of the solutions used for DNA isolation.
3. The required number of reaction tubes containing 40 μL of aliquoted AmpliType PM+DQA1 PCR Reaction Mix (contains AmpliType *Taq* enzyme, $MgCl_2$, and dNTPs) are labeled on the sides and placed in a rack.
4. Add 40 μL of AmpliType PM+DQA1 Primer Set to each tube. It is important to begin the PCR amplification within 20 min after

the addition of the primer set to minimize the formation of primer dimers and other nonspecific PCR products.

5. Carefully add two drops of mineral oil to each tube from the dropper supplied with the kit. Be careful not to touch the reaction tubes with the dropper. Cap tubes loosely, and do not vortex, mix, or spin.
6. Add 20 μL of sample DNA or DI H_2O for negative control to the appropriate tubes by carefully inserting the pipet tip through the mineral oil. Discard the pipet tip, and recap the tube before proceeding to the next sample so that no more than one tube is open at any time to prevent contamination. This results in a final reaction volume of 100 μL.
7. Place all tubes into the thermal cycler block and start the 32-cycle amplification. Using the DNA Thermal Cycler 480, the following parameters are required for each of the 32 cycles: denature at 94°C for 60 s, anneal at 60°C for 30 s, and extend at 72°C for 30 s.
8. Verify the cycling parameters by monitoring the first cycle, and check the tubes after the first cycle to ensure they are all seated tightly in the block.
9. After the PCR amplification is completed, remove the tubes from the thermal cycler. Add 5 μL of 200 m*M* disodium EDTA to each tube. The samples are now ready for analysis by gel electrophoresis, DNA hybridization, and color development. Amplified samples containing 9.5 m*M* EDTA may be stored at 2°C for 2 mo or -20°C for 6 mo. Store amplified DNA samples separate from all PCR amplification reagents, extracted DNA samples, and casework samples.

Product-gel loading and electrophoresis

The presence and size of PCR products generated post-amplification can be determined by agarose-gel electrophoresis. This should be performed prior to denaturing the samples for DNA hybridization to ensure sharp product bands on the gel.

1. Prepare a 3% NuSieve/1% SeaKem agarose solution in 0.5X TBE gel running buffer. Melt the agarose and add 5 μL of a 10 mg/mL stock of ethidium bromide to each 100 mL of agarose. (Ethidium bromide is a mutagen. Avoid contact with skin.) Cast the agarose gel (i.e., 5.5 × 9.0 × 0.45 mm), and insert a gel comb at one end. After the gel has solidified at room temperature, remove the

comb, place in a gel box, and add sufficient 0.5X TBE gel running buffer to cover the gel.

2. Add 2 μL of gel loading buffer to an 0.5 mL microcentrifuge tubes. Add 5 μL of each amplified DNA sample to each of the tubes containing gel loading buffer. Mix and add the entire 7 μL to the appropriate well in the gel. Include a sizing standard like the 123 bp ladder.
3. Connect the power supply so that the DNA travels toward the positive electrode. Run the gel at 115 V (7.5 V/cm) for about 1 h or until the bromophenol blue dye from the loading buffer has run 7.5 cm down the gel to allow adequate resolution of the six amplified product bands.
4. After the gel has run, disconnect the power supply and remove the gel. Wearing UV protective eyewear and gloves, photograph the gel by placing it on a UV transilluminator box under a fixed Polaroid camera with a Kodak 22 or 23A Wratten filter. Photograph the gel in the dark under UV illumination with type 55, 57, or 667 black and white Polaroid film.
5. The following six bands should be present in samples in which the DNA amplified: 242/239 bp (HLA DQA1), 214 bp (LDLR), 190 bp (GYPA), 172 bp (HBGG), 151 bp (D7S8), and 138 bp (Gc). Primer-dimer bands and unincorporated primers may appear as broad bands near the bottom of the gel in the region of lower molecular weight.

DNA hybridization

The AmpliType DNA Hybridization process involves three steps performed sequentially: hybridization of amplified DNA probe strips; binding of HRPSA enzyme conjugate to hybridized PCR products; and stringent wash to remove nonspecifically bound PCR products. Color development is performed after the stringent wash step.

1. Heat a shaking water bath to 55°C and maintain the temperature between 54°C and 56°C.
2. Warm the hybridization solution and the wash solution provided in the kit to 55°C to dissolve all solids. Allow the tube with the AmpliType DNA Probe Strips to equilibrate to ambient temperature to prevent condensation inside the tube, and remove the required number of strips from the tube. Label each strip on the right edge using the pen provided with the kit. (Some inks may effect the typing results.)

3. Place one strip each in the same orientation into each well of the AmpliType DNA Typing Tray. Tilt the typing tray towards the labeled end of the strips and add 3 mL ofprewarmed hybridization solution to each well.
4. Denature the amplified DNAs by incubating at 95°C for 30 min.
5. Withdraw 20 μL of amplified DNA and immediately add it below the surface of the hybridization solution in the well of the appropriate DNA PM probe strip. Cap tube and return to the 95°C heat block 30 min.
6. Withdraw another 20 μL of amplified DNA from the tube and immediately add it below the surface of the hybridization solution in the well of the appropriate DNA HLA DQA1 probe strip.
7. The remaining amplified DNA can be stored at 2°C for 2 mo or at 0°C for 6 mo. Store amplified DNA samples separate from all PCR amplified reagents, extracted DNA samples, and casework samples.
8. Place a lid on the tray and mix by carefully rocking the tray. Ensure that each strip is completely wet. Once wet, strips should remain wet through the conclusion of the color development and photography steps.
9. Place the tray with the typing strips into a 55°C rotating water bath and place a weight on the cover to ensure that the tray does not float. Resume the rotation of the water bath at 500 rpm. Be sure that water does not splash into the wells of the tray. Incubate at 55°C for 15 min.
10. About 5 min before the end of the hybridization reaction, prepare the enzyme conjugate solution in a glass flask using the following formula to determine the volume of each component required: number of strips times 3.3 mL equals the volume of hybridization solution; number of strips times 27 μL equals the volume of enzyme conjugate: HRP-SA. Mix the solutions thoroughly to ensure that solids are in solution and leave at room temperature until ready to use.
11. After hybridization is completed, remove the tray from the water bath and aspirate the contents of each well from the labeled end of the strip while tilting the tray slightly. Remove condensation from the tray lid with a clean lab wipe.
12. Add 5 mL of prewarmed 55°C wash solution to each well. Rinse by gently rocking the tray for several seconds. Aspirate off this solution from each well.

13. Add 3 mL of the enzyme conjugate solution to each well and cover with the lid. Transfer to the rotating 55°C water bath. Place a weight on the tray and adjust the rotation of the water bath to 500 rpm. Incubate the enzyme conjugate solution with the DNA probe strips at 55°C for 5 min.
14. After incubation, remove the tray and aspirate the contents of each well from the labeled end of the strips while tilting the tray slightly. Remove condensation from the tray lid with a clean lab wipe. Add 5 mL of prewarmed wash solution into each well. Rinse by gently rocking the tray for several seconds. Aspirate the solution from the wells.
15. Add another 5 mL of prewarmed wash solution, cover the tray, and incubate at 55°C in shaking water bath as before. Incubate the strips for 12 min. The temperature and timing of this stringent wash step are critical.
16. After incubation, remove the tray from the water bath and aspirate the contents from the labeled end of the strips. Add 5 mL of wash solution to each well. Gently rock for several seconds then aspirate.

Color development

1. Add 5 mL of citrate buffer to each well. Cover the tray with lid and place on an orbital shaker set at 50 rpm at room temperature for 5 min.
2. Prepare the color development solution during this wash step and use within 10 min. Add the following reagents in the order listed to a glass flask and mix thoroughly be swirling. Protect from light and do not vortex. Use the following formulas to determine the volumes required: number of strips times 5 for the volume of citrate buffer; number of strips times 5 μL of 3% hydrogen peroxide; number of strips times 0.25 mL of Chromogen TMB Solution.
3. Remove the tray from the orbital shaker. Remove the lid and aspirate off the contents from each well. Add 5 mL of freshly prepared color development solution to each well. Replace the lid and cover the lid with aluminum foil. Develop the strips at room temperature by rotating on an orbital shaker set at approx 50 rpm for 20 min. Develop until the S and C dots are visible.
4. Stop the color development by removing the solution from the well. Immediately dispense 5 mL of D1 H_2O into each well. Place tray on an orbital shaker set at approx 50 rpm for 50 min.

Remove the D1 H_2O from the wells and repeat the wash steps three times.

Photography and storage of strips

1. Photographs should be taken for a permanent record of the typing results. Photographs must be taken while the DNA probe strips are still wet. Place wet strips on a flat nonabsorbent surface (i.e., a black surface like an exposed X-ray film). Use a Polaroid camera with type 55, 57, or 667 black and white film or Type 59 or 559 color film. An orange filter will enhance contrast. Follow the film exposure and development instructions.
2. After photography, the strips may be air-dried and stored. The dot intensities fade upon drying.

Reuse of typing trays

The AmpliType DNA Typing Trays are designed to be disposable, but may be reused.

1. To reuse, immediately wash the trays and lids as follows. Add approx 50 mL of 95% ethanol or 70% isopropanol to each well. Do not use detergent or bleach. Cover the tray and gently agitate 15 s to dissolve any residual Chromogen: TMB. Remove the lid and visually inspect each well for the presence of a blue or yellow color that indicates the presence of Chromogen: TMB.
2. Repeat the ethanol wash if necessary until no color is present and then rinse each well and the tray lid with DI H_2O and dry before reuse.

Interpretation of PM typing results

Results are interpreted by observing the pattern and relative intensities of blue dots on the wet AmpliType PM and AmpliType HLA DQA1 DNA Probe Strips to determine which alleles are present in the DNA sample.

The AmpliType PM DNA Probe Strips have been spotted with a total of 14 sequence-specific oligonucleotide probes to distinguish the alleles of five genetic loci (a mixture of two probes is spotted at the GYPA A allele position).

1. To read the developed AmpliType PM DNA Probe Strip, the S dot is examined first and then each locus is examined separately. The S dot is designed to be the lightest typing dot on the PM DNA Probe Strip and acts as a minimum dot-intensity control for the remaining probes. It is recommended that a DNA probe strip with no visible S dot not be typed for any locus.

2. When an S dot is visible on the AmpliType PM DNA Probe Strip, the intensities of the dots at the remaining twelve positions are compared to the intensity of the S dot. Those dots that appear either darker than or equivalent to the S dot are considered positive. Each positive dot indicates the presence of the corresponding allele. Dots that are lighter than the S dot should be interpreted with care.
3. The dots on the AmpliType PM DNA Probe Strip correspond to the following alleles:
   (a) The A dot for each locus is positive in the presence of the A allele. (*Note:* The A dot for the GYPA locus is positive in the presence of both the A allele and the A prime allele. Both the GYPA AB and GYPA A prime B heterozygotes have balanced intensities, but additional GYPA A and B variant alleles, observed in <8% of African-American populations, may produce a slightly imbalanced heterozygous signal.)
   (b) The B dot for each locus is positive for the B allele.
   (c) The C dot for HBGG and Gc loci is positive for the C allele.

Interpretation of HLA DQA1 results

The AmpliType HLA DQA1 DNA Probe Strips have been spotted with a total of eleven sequence-specific oligonucleotide probes to detect eight alleles of the HLA DQA1 locus.

1. To read the developed AmpliType HLA DQA1 Probe Strip, the C dot is examined first. The control probe C on the AmpliType HLA DQA1 Probe Strip detects all of the HLA DQA1 alleles and is identical to the standard probe S on the AmpliType PM DNA Probe Strip. The C dot is designed to be the lightest typing dot on the strip, and it indicates that adequate amplification and typing of the HLA DQA1 in the sample has occurred. If the C dot is absent, an accurate determination of the type cannot be made.

   An accurate interpretation of the HLA DQA1 results depends on the presence and intensity of the C dot. The intensities of the dots at the remaining ten positions are compared to the intensity of the C dot. Those dots that appear either darker than or equivalent to the C dot are considered positive. Each positive dot indicates the presence of the corresponding HLA DQA1 allele. Dots with signals less than the C dot should be interpreted with care.
2. Dots on the AmpliType HLA DQA1 Probe Strip correspond to the following alleles: the 1 dot is positive in the presence of the

HLA DQA1 1.1, 1.2, and 1.3 alleles; the 2 dot is positive only in the presence of the HLA DQA1 2 allele; the 3 dot is positive only in the presence of the HLA DQA1 3 allele; the 4 dot is positive in the presence of the HLA DQA1 4.1, 4.2, and 4.3 alleles.

3. Four HLA DQA1 subtyping probes differentiate the HLA DQA1 1.1, 1.2, and 1.3 alleles as follows: The 1.1 dot is positive only in the presence of the HLA DQA1 1.1 allele (*Note*: A faint 1.1 dot will appear with some HLA DQA2 pseudogene alleles.); the 1.3 dot is positive only in the presence of the HLA DQA1 1.3 allele (*Note*: There is no probe that detects only the HLA DQA1 1.2 allele.); the 1.2, 1.3, 4 dot is positive in the presence of HLA DQA1 1.2, 1.3, 4.1, 4.2, and 4.3 alleles (*Note*: The 1.2, 1.3, 4 dot can be lighter than the C dot when the genotype has an HLA DQA1 4.2 or 4.3 allele because the HLA DQA1 4.2 and 4.3 alleles each have single partially destabilizing mismatch in the 1.2, 1.3, 4 probe. The partially destabilizing mismatch allows these two alleles to bind to this probe weakly relative to the HLA DQA 1 1.2, 1.3, and 4.1 alleles). The All but 1.3 dot is positive in the presence of all HLA DQA1 alleles except 1.3. This probe is necessary to differentiate the 1.2, 1.3 genotype from the 1.3, 1.3 genotype (*Note*: The All but 1.3 dot can be equal or lighter than the C dot when the genotype has an HLA DQA1 1.3 allele paired with an HLA DQA1 4.1,4.2, and 4.3 allele because the HLA DQA1 4.1, 4.2, and 4.3 alleles have a single partially destabilizing mismatch to the All but 1.3 probe. The partially destabilizing mismatch allows these three alleles to weakly bind to this probe relative to the HLA DQA1 1.1, 1.2, 2, and 3 allcles.)
4. Two additional HLA DQA1 subtyping probes differentiate the HLA DQA1 4.1 allele from the HLA DQA1 4.2 and 4.3 alleles. The 4.1 dot is positive only in the presence of the HLA DQA1 4.1 allele; the 4.2/4.3 dot is positive in the presence of HLA DQA1 4.2 and 4.3 alleles.

Frequency of occurrence calculations

1. The number of alleles detected by the PM portion of the kit is two of three at each locus. Two alleles designated A and B are detected at the LDLR, GYPA, and D7S8 loci while three alleles designated A, B, and C are detected at the HBGG and GC loci. The number of genotypes at these loci is either three for LDLR, GYPA, and D7S8 (AA, AB, and BB) and six for HBGG and GC

(AA, AB, AC, BB, BC, and CC). The frequency of each genotype is calculated using the Hardy-Weinberg Equation. The number of genotypes is a function of the number of alleles detected and is calculated as n(n+1)/2 where *n* is the number of alleles. The total number of possible genotype combinations at the five loci detected by the Polymarker kit is 972.

Table 12.1. The allele frequency distribution and two hispanic populations for the polymarker loci

Allele	*African-American*	*Caucasian*	*SE Hispanic*	*SW Hispanic*
LDLR A	0.224	0.453	0.415	0.563
LDLR B	0.776	0.547	0.585	0.438
GYPA A	0.479	0.584	0.532	0.656
GYPA B	0.521	0.416	0.468	0.344
HBGG A	0.507	0.470	0.426	0.344
HBGG B	0.197	0.524	0.548	0.609
HBGG C	0.297	0.007	0.027	0.047
D7S8 A	0.614	0.615	0.585	0.682
D7S8 B	0.386	0.385	0.415	0.318
Gc A	0.103	0.257	0.277	0.271
Gc B	0.707	0.172	0.223	0.208
Gc C	0.190	0.571	0.500	0.521

2. The number of alleles detected by the HLA DQA1 portion of the kit is seven. The frequency of occurrence is calculated using the Hardy-Weinberg Equation. The number of genotypes at this locus is 28. The total number of genotypes for the PM+DQA1 kit is 27,216.

3. Generally, the allele dot intensities across the Polymarker typing strip are balanced. Thus, the dot intensities of each allele of a heterozygote at one locus (i.e., LDLR) are equivalent to the dot intensities of each allele of a heterozygote at another locus (i.e., Gc). The dot intensity of the allele of a homozygote is more intense (generally twofold) than the alleles of a heterozygote. Unbalanced dots do occur in the analysis of forensic samples. This may be because of the presence of more than one DNA in different amounts. If more than two alleles are detected at the HBGG of Gc loci, this is consistent with the presence of more

than one DNA. Mixtures are often difficult to resolve using the reverse-dot-blot approach and may require additional analysis. The intensity of dots should be used as a guide for resolving such mixtures.

Table 12.2. The allele frequency distribution and hispanic populations for the HLA DQA1 locus

Allele	*African-American*	*Caucasian*	*Hispanic*
1.1	0.125	0.158	0.105
1.2	0.329	0.190	0.130
1.3	0.058	0.073	0.053
2	0.130	0.145	0.115
3	0.090	0.192	0.218
4.1	0.185	0.214	0.269
4.2/4.3	0.083	0.028	0.110

4. The frequencies of the alleles detected at the Polymarker loci and HLA DQA1 locus have been determined. There is no detectable deviation from Hardy Weinberg Equilibrium for these loci in the four population groups based on the homozygosity test, likelihood ratio test, or the exact test.

Notes

The following section deals with troubleshooting the AmpliType PM+DQA1 Amplification and Typing Kit.

1. No signal or faint signal: If no signal or a faint signal is detected from both the control DNA as well as the sample DNAs at all loci, there may be no or insufficient PCR amplification. Running a portion of the amplification reaction on a product gel should reveal whether there is any PCR product. If PCR product is observed, the hybridization conditions may be improper. Repeat the hybridization reaction with PCR product.

   If no amplified product is observed after agarose-gel electrophoresis on the product gel, there may have been an insufficient amount of DNA added to the PCR reaction mix. The DNA sample should be quantitated and 20 ng of DNA used in a repeat test. No amplified product may also be a result of not adding the AmpliType PM+DQA1 primers to the reaction mix. Add the primers and repeat the reaction. A lack of amplified product might also be because of a failure of the thermocycler or the reaction tubes not seated tightly in the thermocycler.

If an amplification product is observed on the product gel, but no signal or faint signal is detected on the typing strips, the hybridization and/or wash conditions may be too stringent. This results from too high temperature (>55°C), too low salt concentration, or too long wash. Check temperatures and prepare new solutions and repeat the analysis. This could also be caused by inadequate agitation of the typing strips during the hybridization. No signal or a faint signal could result from the amplified DNA not being added or the amplified DNA not being denatured. Repeat of the analysis and checking that the heating block used to denature the DNA is at 95°C, and the samples remain 3 min is advised. Also, lack of signal or faint signal could result from inadequate enzyme conjugate, development solution, or Chromogen:TMB. Preparation of new solutions and a repeat of the analysis is advised.

If the positive control produces signal, but no signal is detected from the test samples, either an inhibitor may be present in the sample(s) or the test sample DNA is degraded. If an inhibitor is suspected, washing the sample in a Centricon 100 column might remove it. Also, the addition of 16 μg BSA to the reaction might stabilize the enzyme. If the DNA is degraded, reanalysis with more DNA might yield results.

2. High DNA probe strip background color: High-DNA probe-strip background may be caused by low or lack of SDS in the hybridization and/or wash solution or inadequate agitation. Prepare new solutions, check equipment, and repeat analysis. This may also be caused by too much HRP-SA being added to the enzyme conjugate solution. Prepare new solution and repeat analysis. Also, exposure to light during color development can cause increased background. Be sure that water used for the water rinses is deionized or glass-distilled. Stored strips can have increased background if exposed to strong light and oxidizing agents.
3. Presence of additional dots in control: Additional or unexpected dots can appear because of cross-hybridization caused by the hybridization and/or wash temperatures being too low, the salt concentrations too high, or the time too short. Preparation of new solutions and monitoring of the equipment is advised. This could also be a result of contamination of the control DNA sample.
4. Signals weaker than the S or C dots: Signals weaker than the S or C dots may be a result of hybridization and/or stringent-wash temperatures being too high or too low, hybridization and/or wash

solution salt concentrations too high or too low, stringent wash time too long or too short, or a mixed sample (i.e., contaminant). Repeat testing with new solutions and monitoring of equipment is advised. Weak signals may also result from failure to add EDTA to the reaction prior to the heatdenaturation step. If this is the case, add EDTA and repeat test. A faint 1.1 allele can be caused by the amplification of an HLA DQA2 pseudogene.

5. More than two alleles present: More than two alleles may be detected at the HLA DQA1, HBGG, and GC loci. This may be a result of cross-hybridization caused by hybridization and/or stringent-wash temperatures being too low, hybridization and/or wash-solution salt concentration too high, or stringent-wash time too short. Repeat testing with new solutions and monitoring of equipment is advised. The presence of more than two alleles may be because of a mixed sample. Also the amplification of an HLA DQA2 pseudogene may result in a faint 1.1 dot.
6. Some, not all, loci observed on product gel: The lack of detection of some PCR products by agarose gel electrophoresis may be a result of the test sample DNA being degraded. Evaluate the amplified product by agarose-gel electrophoresis to determine whether all six product bands are present. If degraded, repeat the amplification with more DNA. The lack of detection of some PCR products may be caused by the presence of an inhibitor (i.e., heme or dyes). Repeat testing with less DNA sample, Centricon 100 washed DNA, or with the addition of 16 μg BSA is advised. Alternatively, if the thermocycler did not sufficiently denature the input DNA and/or PCR product during amplification, some PCR products may not appear on the agarose gel. Repeat the testing and check the equipment.
7. Some, but not all, loci produce dots: The lack of some alleles on the typing strips may indicate that not all loci amplified. Check the PCR amplification product by agarose-gel electrophoresis for the presence of all six product bands. Lack of some alleles may be a result of the amplified DNA not being denatured. Monitor the equipment and repeat the analysis.
8. Imbalanced dot intensity: An imbalanced dot intensity may be because of the hybridization and/or stringent-wash temperature being too high or too low, the hybridization wash-solution salt concentration too high or too low, the stringentwash time too long or too short, or EDTA was not added to the reaction prior to the

heat-denaturation step of the DNA hybridization. Repeat analysis with new solutions and monitor the equipment. A mixed sample could also result with an imbalanced dot intensity proportional to the starting DNAs.

9. Weak or absent 4.1 dot on control DNA: A weak or absent 4.1 allele can result from EDTA not being added to the reaction prior to the heat-denaturation step of the DNA hybridization. Add EDTA and repeat the analysis.
10. 1.2, 1.3, and 4 dots weaker than C: A weak 1.2, 1.3, 4 dot on the HLA DQA1 typing strip can result from a sample that has an HLA DQA1 4.2 or 4.3 allele paired with an HLA DQA1 1.1, 2, 3, 4.2, or 4.3 allele.
11. 1.1 Dot weaker than C, but not signal for 1 dot: A weak 1.1 dot can result from the amplification of an HLA DQA2 pseudogene.
12. All but 1.3 signal weaker than C: A weak all but 1.3 dot can result from a sample that has an HLA DQA1 1.3 allele paired with an HLA DQA1 4.1, 4.2, or 4.3 allele.

Mitochondrial Analysis

Mammalian mitochondrial DNA (mtDNA) is a small 16.5 kbp circular genome. Human mtDNA was found to contain two adjacent, highly polymorphic regions, which are designated hypervariable regions I and II (HV-I and HV-II). The most common polymorphisms are nucleotide substitutions (transitions and transversions) followed by deletions and insertions. Polymerase chain reaction (PCR)-amplification and subsequent sequencing of these two polymorphic regions is currently referred to as '*mtDNA typing*' and the sequences obtained by this technique as '*mtDNA types*'.

Short tandem repeat (STR) typing, an established forensic typing method based upon *nuclear DNA* (nDNA) polymorphisms, is highly effective when DNA is of sufficient amount and quality. Frequently, due to inadequate quantity or degradation of the sample into small fragments, DNA extracted from forensic samples is of limited use. Samples notorious for unsuccessful STR typing include old bones, teeth and hair, particularly hair that has been shed, as these samples generally lack detectable nDNA. Even blood and body fluid samples, which are frequently used for STR typing, occasionally give unsuccessful results due to sample aging or decomposition. For these types of samples, mtDNA typing has proven to be more successful than STR typing, though the individual discrimination power of mtDNA typing is in general lower than with STR typing.

Mitochondrial DNA (mtDNA) Biology

Origins of mitochondria and mtDNA

The production of ATP by the process of oxidative phosphorylation is the principal function of the mitochondrion, which is an organelle of eukaryotes (fungi, plants and animals). Endosymbiosis may explain how mitochondria came to be incorporated within eukaryotic cells. While not the only endosymbiotic theory describing the evolution of mitochondria, the hydrogen hypothesis postulates that small ancient bacteria capable of producing hydrogen (H_2) were integrated into and survived within larger H_2-consuming bacteria. Through this symbiotic relationship, primordial mitochondria evolved from the small H_2-producing bacteria and acquired the ability to conduct oxidative phosphorylation. Eventually, the eukaryotic (enveloped) nucleus was derived from genes of the larger bacteria. Over evolutionary time, most of the initial mitochondrial genes (genes from the small bacteria) were transferred into the eukaryotic nucleus. Genes escaping transfer eventually developed into the present-day mtDNA genome.

High copy number per cell

Most mammalian cells contain a dozen to hundreds of mitochondria, though it was found that mitochondria are not static units. They are capable of dynamically fusing with and separating from each other to form a single functionally complex network structure. Each mitochondrial unit (mitochondrion) contains a few to a dozen copies of mtDNA genomes. One somatic cell may contain hundreds to more than a thousand copies of identical mtDNA genomes, with larger numbers being found in tissues that demand a greater amount of oxygen, such as the brain and skeletal muscles. This is in contrast with the two copies of nDNA genomes per somatic diploid cell. The relative abundance of mtDNA imparts a correspondingly higher degree of recovery from forensic samples, and is one of the principal reasons why mtDNA typing achieves a higher degree of sensitivity than those obtained by STR typing.

Maternal inheritance and recombination rate

In mammals, each somatic diploid cell has two copies of the nDNA genomes, with one inherited from each parent. On the other hand, the progeny inherits its mtDNA directly from the mother. Mechanisms behind the maternal inheritance of mtDNA include the reduction of paternal (*spermatic*) mtDNA during spermatogenesis, the simple dilution of spermatic mtDNA at fertilization (an overwhelming copy number of oocyte mtDNA relative to spermatic mtDNA) and ubiquitin-mediated proteolysis of spermatic mitochondria and the active digestion of spermatic mtDNA within a fertilized ovum. Due to these numerous safeguards, the paternal mtDNA that enters an oocyte becomes undetectable after the fertilized egg undergoes its first mitotic division.

Whether mammalian mtDNA undergoes recombination or not is a longstanding question. In recent experiments using human somatic hybrid cells and mice carrying two different mtDNA, only three of 318 clones of mtDNA purified from mouse tissues corresponded to recombinant mtDNA, whereas no recombinants were found in human somatic hybrid cells. These results strongly suggest that recombination can occur within mammalian cells but at a very low frequency or at an operationally undetectable level. This implies that recombinant mtDNA observed in mice might be gene conversion products resulting from the repair of damaged mtDNA molecules.

Maternal inheritance and a very low recombination rate means that mtDNA genomes are essentially clonal copies of the mother's mtDNA genomes (provided that the sequence of all mtDNA molecules within an oocyte are the same, the recombinant mtDNA structure will also be the same). From a forensic viewpoint, maternal inheritance can be a helpful tool in the identification of a body or the remains of a missing person. The missing person's biological mother, siblings and maternal relatives all have the same mtDNA sequence, with few exceptions resulting from heteroplasmy as described later. Therefore, biological samples (e.g. blood, buccal swabs) taken from these individuals can provide reference samples for the identification of the missing individual. On the other hand, since a progeny's mtDNA contains no paternal information, mtDNA typing cannot be used for paternity tests.

High mutation rates

In addition to maternal inheritance, mtDNA and nDNA mutation rates differ. The low fidelity of mtDNA polymerase, the lack of protective histone proteins and a less effective repair system lead to a higher base substitution rate in mtDNA. Within mtDNA, HV-I and HV-II appear to evolve quickly, with their mutation rates being about 5–10 times higher than that of nDNA. Together with maternal inheritance, higher mutation rates have made mtDNA typing an interesting tool for human population genetics and evolutionary studies. Additionally, the somatic accumulation of mtDNA mutations has been proposed to play a role in human aging.

Structure of mtDNA

The complete sequence of human mtDNA was first determined in the laboratory of Frederick Sanger in Cambridge, England. This human mtDNA sequence, also called Anderson reference, is designated as the Cambridge Reference Sequence (CRS). Following the sequencing of human mtDNA, mtDNA sequences of animals were determined. A comparison of sequences revealed that the gross structure and genetic arrangements are remarkably conserved among mammalian species. Human mtDNA is a double-stranded circular molecule 16,569 bp in length. Based upon differences in buoyant density, the strands are termed the heavy strand (H-strand) and the light strand (L-strand). The H-strand is rich in purines (A, G), whereas within the L-strand, pyrimidines (T, C) dominate. When metabolically active cells are observed by electron microscopy, a large population of mtDNA appears to contain a short three-strand structure. This structure represents an initial stage of replication and is called a *displacement loop* (*D-loop*).

According to the numbering system offered by the CRS, the initial position '1' was arbitrarily assigned near the middle of the control region. The base number then increases in the (5' → 3') direction on the L-strand, and, because of its circular nature, the final position '16,569' is located next to '1'. The CRS was revised and termed the 'rCRS'. By this revision, the original CRS, which had been determined from a single individual, was found to contain several rare polymorphisms. This discovery emphasized that the CRS (rCRS) cannot be regarded as the 'authentic' sequence but should be used as a 'reference' sequence to facilitate the comparison among sequences cited in the literature and those determined from samples. It is also noted that, because of the same gross structure and genetic arrangements among mammalians, animal mtDNAs can be numbered using CRS (rCRS).

Functionally, mammalian and hence human mtDNA is divided into coding and control regions. The coding region contains 37 intronless genes encoding 2 ribosomal RNAs (12S and 16S rRNAs), 22 *transfer RNAs* (*tRNAs*) and 13 protein enzymes. The 22 tRNAs are the minimum set required for the translation of mtDNA, and all of the 13 proteins are involved in the process of oxidative phosphorylation.

The control region, which corresponds to the D-loop, is bound by the genes for $tRNA^{phe}$ and $tRNA^{pro}$. The length is 1122 bp (CRS) and may vary by one or more bases owing to deletions, insertions or repetition. The control region contains the binding sites for the major promoters of transcription and the origin of H-strand replication. This region also contains the HV-I and HV-II polymorphic regions. The HV-I ranges from position 16,024 to 16,365, and HV-II ranges from position 73 to 340. These hypervariable regions represent ongoing mutational hotspots rather than the remnant of previously incorporated or fixed mutations.

Heteroplasmy

Reflecting the clonal replication of maternal mtDNA, all copies of mtDNA genomes are identical (*homoplasmic*) as a rule. Due to the high copy number of mtDNA, however, a mutation in some of the mtDNA results in a mixture of variant mtDNA genomes, a condition known as heteroplasmy. Heteroplasmy is operationally defined as the presence of two or more subpopulations (types) of mtDNA genomes within a mitochondrion, cell, tissue, organ or individual, and may be observed in several ways, such as two or more mtDNA types in one tissue sample, and one mtDNA type in one tissue sample and a different mtDNA type in another sample. On occasion, children of a heteroplasmic mother may be homoplasmic. This occurs through the inheritance of the mother's predominant mtDNA type (or one of the predominant types) due to a '*bottleneck*' mechanism that segregates minor mtDNA types.

Heteroplasmy is most often observed in hair samples because genetic drift is allowed to operate and bottlenecks are created due to a hair follicle's semiclonal nature. One disadvantage of using mtDNA for forensic individual identification is the possibility that the occurrence of heteroplasmy will confuse the interpretation of the results and potentially lead to an erroneous exclusion rather than a match. However, the presence of heteroplasmy can also increase the power of the match when it is present in both the unknown and reference samples.

Identification of Individuals (mtDNA Typing)

Procedures and interpretation of results

Due to maternal inheritance and the very low rate of recombination, all copies of mtDNA are generally identical (*homoplasmic*). In other words, the mtDNA genome is haploid and its sequence is treated as a single locus (*haplotype*). Thus, two hypervariable regions (HV-I and HV-II) of mtDNA can be determined by direct sequencing after PCR-amplification of the regions. Even for heteroplasmic mtDNA containing two mtDNA types, the sequences can often be determined by direct sequencing because there are usually only one or at most two base differences between the two types.

Mitochondrial DNA typing starts with the extraction of total genomic DNA from samples, and then PCR-amplification is performed on HV-I and HV-II. Forensic investigators thought that the size of each region (~400 bp) was too large to amplify simply by using one primer that targets the entire HV- 1 region and another primer that targets the entire HV-II region. As it is difficult to amplify large fragment sizes in aged or decomposed samples, they reasoned that reducing fragment sizes in such samples could allow for PCR-amplification to be performed. They therefore targeted amplicons ~250 bp in length, including the primer binding sites, with a total of four overlapping primer sets for HV-I and HV-II. The PCR-amplified products were then sequenced using a fluorescent automated sequencing system, and the sequencing information was confirmed by analysis of both forward and reverse DNA strands. The sequence of the unknown (evidence) sample was displayed as the L-strand sequence, and nucleotide differences between the evidence sample and CRS (rCRS) were noted. For example, an mtDNA type of '263G, 315.1C' indicates that an adenine (A) at position 263 in the CRS was substituted by a guanine residue (G), that there was an insertion of cytosine (C) between position 315 and 316 and that the remaining sequence of this mtDNA type was the same as that of the CRS.

In order to evaluate the sequencing results from evidence and reference samples, useful interpretation guidelines have been provided by the DNA Commission of the International Society for Forensic Genetics as follows: If the sequences are unequivocally different, then the samples can be excluded as having originated from the same source. If the sequences are the same, then the reference and evidence samples cannot be excluded as potentially being from the same source. In cases where the same heteroplasmy is observed in both the known and unknown samples, its presence may increase the strength of the evidence. If heteroplasmy is observed in the questioned sample but not in the known sample, a common maternal lineage cannot be excluded. If the two samples differ by a single nucleotide, and there is no indication of heteroplasmy, the interpretation may be that the results are inconclusive. However, a one-nucleotide difference between two samples, on occasions, may provide evidence against the samples either originating from the same source or having the same maternal lineage; in particular, where both samples are a tissue such as blood, a single nucleotide difference points towards exclusion of a common maternal origin. The source of the tissue being investigated should be taken into consideration, because differences in mtDNA sequences due to mutations seem to be more likely between e.g. hair and blood than between two blood samples taken from the same individual.

Technical difficulty due to C-stretch

Both HV-I and HV-II of the human mtDNA contain homopolymeric tract of cytosines (C) (i.e., C-stretch). In HV-I, the most common sequence between positions 16,184 and 16,193 is ••CCCCCTCCCC•• (the position of thymine 'T' is at 16,189). When the T undergoes mutational transition to C, length heteroplasmy (polymorphism of the number of repeated cytosine residues) supervenes. A similar homopolymeric region resides in HV-II at positions 303–315. These length heteroplasmies are believed to be supervened by an additional increase or decrease of cytosine residues through the replication slippage mechanism, which has been observed in poly G: C tracts. In general, direct sequencing of DNA from these samples exhibits reading frame shifts and thereby both the exact number of cytosine residues of the C-stretch and sequences beyond the C-stretch cannot be determined. The additional reactions using primers that sit on the C-stretch provide sequence information from both strands following the C-stretch but the exact number of cytosine residues in the C-stretch still cannot be accurately determined.

Topics of Forensic Interest

Species identifications

Samples subjected to mtDNA typing are not necessarily derived from humans, but usually this does not impose much trouble because the sequencing of HV-I and HV-II not only provides individual identification but also confirms whether the sample is of human origin. However, when amplification of HV-I and HV-II fails, species identification of DNA extracted from a sample may be useful in order to ascertain whether failure in amplification is due to the sample being non-human in origin (e.g. plants and animals) or whether it resulted from other causes (e.g. an insufficient amount of DNA and/or decomposition).

Cytochrome *b* (cyt *b*) is one component of the electron transport (respiratory chain) enzyme complexes involved in oxidative phosphorylation. In many types of species, including plants and animals, the cyt *b* gene exists in mtDNA. In view of the endosymbiosis hypothesis, the cyt *b* gene escaped incorporation by the nucleus and accumulated mutations over evolutionary time, leading to the present cyt *b* gene sequence differences among species. In other words, cyt *b* genes are species-specific and have been used for species determination in phylogenetic and forensic investigations. In these investigations, a portion of the cyt *b* gene is amplified using 'universal' primers and then sequenced. The universal primers were carefully designed to hybridize to highly conserved sites in order to allow the amplification of mtDNA across a broad range of species, yet sequence differentiation in a region sandwiched between the hybridization sites is sufficiently large to allow the discrimination of species.

The sequencing approach is very efficient because DNA samples from different species can be positively identified. However, confirmation of human samples is likely to be useful in routine forensic cases. Matsuda *et al.*, (2005) developed a PCR-based method in which DNA extracted from samples was amplified using '*human-specific*' primers and then subjected to gel electrophoresis. The human-specific primers were designed to hybridize to human cyt *b* gene sites, which differed from those of the chimpanzee by 26%. The results of this method were determined simply by the presence (positive results) or the absence of a visible band (negative results), with no bands observed in DNA of animals, including non-human primates (chimpanzee, gorilla, Japanese monkey, crab-eating monkey). Thus, samples producing a single band can be reasonably interpreted as being of human origin. Samples producing no visible bands, however, are inconclusive. In such cases, the employment of other cyt *b* gene primers as a positive control, and if necessary, the subsequent sequence analysis may achieve conclusive results.

Single nucleotide polymorphism (SNP) typing

A random match probability of mtDNA types (HV-I/HV-II types) is estimated to be about 0.5–1%. However, this value is an average of all mtDNA types, and for a particular mtDNA type the chance that a random individual will share the same type depends greatly upon the relative rarity of that particular mtDNA type. Indeed, the overall distribution of mtDNA types in many populations studied to date is highly skewed towards very rare types. For example, of 1175 different mtDNA types in the US Caucasian populations, 982 types are unique. When these very rare types are observed in both evidence and reference samples, it increases the likelihood that the two samples are from the same source. The increased likelihood of a positive match may often be sufficient to make a definite identification, especially if taken in conjunction with additional physical and/or circumstantial evidence. However, there are some relatively common mtDNA types. In the same population, the frequency of the most common mtDNA type, '263G, 315.1C' is 7%, and there are 13 additional mtDNA types with frequencies of 0.5% or larger. If both the evidence and reference samples contain the same relatively common type of mtDNA, it does not increase the likelihood of the two samples having come from the same source. Thus, we must seek further biological evidence that will allow us to make a more definite conclusion regarding whether the two samples match. While the probabilities at individual STRs can be multiplied to obtain the total likelihood of a match, the HV-I and HV-II loci must be treated as a single locus, thereby reducing the power of obtaining a highly significant match.

To increase individual discrimination power, polymorphisms residing outside two hypervariable regions (HV-I and HV-II) have been increasingly explored. One approach, which has been promoted by SWGAM (the Scientific Working Group on DNA Analysis Methods) and by Carracedo and his colleagues, is to expand targeting regions from the 600 bp HV-I and HV-II region to the entire 1100 bp control region. Using this approach, over 200 SNP sites were found, and, based upon the SNP profiles, phylogenically related mtDNA were grouped into haplo-groups. The term 'SNP' was initially introduced to indicate a single DNA base substitution that is observed with a frequency of at least 1% in a given population. Currently, however, this term refers to any SNP, including insertions and deletions, and the 1% frequency prerequisite has been eliminated. It is noted that, with the exception of length polymorphisms (C-stretch), HV-I and HV-II polymorphisms are regarded as a collection of densely clustered SNPs.

Another attempt to increase individual discrimination power is to profile SNPs across the entire mtDNA. Even though the density of SNPs in the coding region is low due to functional restraints, the coding region is 14 times larger than the control region, therefore the number of SNPs in the coding region is comparable to the number of SNPs found in the control region. However, it is impossible to sequence the entire mtDNA, therefore the accumulation of data regarding SNP positions over the entire mtDNA and the selection of an efficient method to spot the targeted SNPs will increase individual discrimination power considerably. Among various methods applicable to such a task, the authors feel that microarray is the most promising in that it allows fast simultaneous detection of a large number of SNPs.

INDEX

A

Acquired immune deficiency syndrome, 40

Adrenogenital syndrome, 177

Amplification-created restriction sites, 178

Amplified fragment length polymorphisms, 85

Autosomes, 106

B

Background electrolyte, 13

Biomarker, 29

Blueprint, 43

Blueprint of life, 43

Boiling, 59

Bone lysis buffer, 69

Bone marrow transplant, 191

Bottleneck, 256

Bovine serum albumin, 91

C

Capillary electrophoresis, 10, 94, 144, 161, 180, 211, 228

Capillary gel electrophoresis, 37

Capillary isoelectric focusing, 10, 40

Capillary isotachophoresis, 37

Capillary zone electrophoresis, 10, 11, 155, 230

Chain-termination, 138

Charged coupled device, 212

Checkerboard, 68

Chi square, 222

Coefficient of variation, 163

Combined DNA index system, 211

Core, 192

Cortisol binding globulin, 174

Counting method, 185

Criminal justice system, 1

Cytosine stretch, 185

D

D-loop, 185, 255

Deactivation, 62

Defence fallacy, 190

Deficiency paternity test, 116

Dendroaspis jamesoni kaimosae, 25

Deoxyribonucleic acid, 71

Diode array detectors, 230

Direct solvent extraction, 231

Discrimination loop, 185

Displacement loop, 255

DNA fingerprinting, 197

DNA Profile, 193

Dodecyl trimethylammonium bromide, 181

E

E. coli, 26, 86, 200, 203
Electroosmotic flow, 10, 12, 37, 153, 161, 233
Electropherogram, 183
Electrospray ionization, 11
Escherichia coli, 25, 199
Ethnic group, 130
Ethnic identification, 130

F

Fingerprint, 85, 192
Fluorescein isothiocynate, 149
Forensic stain, 62
Forensically significant, 228

G

Gas chromatography, 32, 179
Gas chromatography mass spectrometry, 179
Gas chromatography with nitrogen-phosphorus detect, 229
Gas chromatography-mass spectrometry, 161
Gas chromatography-mass spectroscopy, 160
Glomerular filtration rate, 176
Gold standard, 230
Guanidinium thiocyanate, 63

H

Haplotype, 256
Haplotype surveying method, 127
Hardy–Weinberg equilibrium, 220
Hardy–Weinberg Law, 220
Hardy–Weinberg principle, 220
High-performance liquid chromatography, 10, 145, 179
Homoplasmic, 256
Hot start, 87
Human-specific, 259

I

In situ, 110
In vitro, 86
Indigo, 90
Integrated systems, 66
Isoelectric focusing, 11
Isotachophoresis, 16

J

Junk, 183

L

Laser-induced fluorescence, 34, 94, 146, 163
Limit of detection, 34, 164
Linkage disequilibrium, 112, 116, 119
Long interspersed elements, 46
Long terminal repeats, 46
Low copy number, 2, 89, 126
Low-density lipoprotein receptor, 238
Lysis, 59

M

Macroscopic, 207
Mammalian mitochondrial DNA, 252
Mass spectrometry, 11
Mass spectroscopy, 147
Mean exclusion chance, 109
Membrane pre-concentration, 14
Messenger RNA, 186
Metapopulations, 132
Micellar electrokinetic capillary chromatography, 151, 180, 230
Micellar electrokinetic chromatography, 146
Microscopic, 207
Mierurus fulvius, 25
Migration time ratio, 234
Mini-sequencing reaction, 139
Minimal haplotype, 123
mtDNA types, 252
mtDNA typing, 252
Multilocus probes, 192

N

Naja naja sputatrix, 25
Nick-translation, 198, 199

Nick-translation column, 203
Non-random, 116
Nuclear DNA, 252
Nuclear magnetic resonance, 147

O

Off-ladder, 213

P

Paramagnetic particles, 67
Paternity index, 101, 237
Plasmodium, 131
Polymerase chain reaction, 38, 59, 72, 78, 93, 109, 122, 183, 237
Power of discrimination, 111
Preconcentration, 232
Product rule, 187
Profile chart, 56
Pseudo-epiphyses, 55
Pseudoautosomal regions, 106
Pull-up, 216
Putative father, 117
Putative grandmother, 117

R

Radioimmunoassay, 179
Random genetic drift, 220
Relative migration time, 234
Relative standard deviation, 234
Restriction fragment length polymorphisms, 77, 109, 183
Reverse-phase, 33
Royal disease, 109

S

Sandwich, 195
Sex chromatin, 107
Sex determining region Y, 121
Short interspersed elements, 46
Short tandem repeat, 2, 48, 64, 86, 109, 110, 183, 252
Single nucleotide polymorphisms, 4, 109, 137, 184
Single-locus probes, 192
SNaPshot, 140
Sodium dodecyl sulfate, 59, 180
Solid-phase extraction, 14, 232
Spermatic, 253
Spinal and bulbar muscular atrophy, 120
Supported liquid membrane, 232

T

Terminal transferase, 215
Therapeutic drug monitoring, 228
Thermus aquaticus, 87
Thin-layer chromatography, 234
Transfer RNAs, 255
tRNAs, 255

U

Ultraviolet, 144
Urinary free cortisol, 181

V

Variable number of tandem-repeat, 48, 71, 192